The Peopl

A Multicultural Legacy

Louis Mendola · Jacqueline Alio

Trinacria Editions
New York • Palermo

Photographs, maps, illustrations and cover design by Louis Mendola.

Printed in the United States of America on acid-free paper.

10 9 8 7 6 5 4 3 2

Electronic editions of this book are available in several formats.

ISBN 9780615796949

Library of Congress Control Number 2013951702

A CIP catalogue record for this book is available from the British Library.

IN MEMORIAM

Richard Knox
Artist • Teacher • Humanist
1961 - 2013

"A man lives as long as he is remembered."

ABOUT THE AUTHORS

This book is the first "generalist" history of Sicily written in English in the original by Sicilian authors based in Sicily. Both are popularizers as well as scholars. Read by millions, their work has appeared in everything from books to academic journals to in-flight magazines to the internet. *Sicilian Genealogy and Heraldry,* a guide and reference written by Louis Mendola with a chapter by Jacqueline Alio, was original enough for the British Library to assign it the first Dewey classification number of its subject category: 929.10720458.

Louis Mendola is one of Sicily's foremost historians, and one of the very few whose work is known beyond Italian borders. The focus of his most significant scholarly papers is the comparative history of the medieval Normans in Sicily and England. Having researched in Britain, Italy, Germany, France and the Vatican, he has been consulted by The History Channel, the BBC and The New York Times, and lectured at New York University. His writing draws on three decades of experience.

Jacqueline Alio has written numerous articles for a general readership, and published original research on the erstwhile Jewish community of Palermo. A popular lecturer, she has worked with The Discovery Channel and other media, earning an international reputation as an expert in her field. Her extraordinary breadth of knowledge allows her to write about Sicily's ancient and medieval societies with exceptional insight. She is the author of *Women of Sicily: Saints, Queens and Rebels.*

PREFACE

"If we cannot end our differences, at least we can help make the world safe for diversity."

— John Fitzgerald Kennedy

Monochrome is boring. Our world is much more than a single color.

At Palermo's Zisa, a royal palace built during the twelfth century in the eclectic Norman-Arab style, is displayed a tombstone created in Byzantine polychrome inlay (shown on this book's back cover) commemorating a certain Anna, a Norman wife and mother who died in 1148. Bearing inscriptions in Latin, Hebrew, Greek and Arabic, it survives as a tangible legacy of what, in its time, was the world's only truly multicultural society, a convergence not only of peoples but of ideas.

Here, on this island variously claimed by Europeans, Africans and Asians, are the foundations of a lesson for our times. For all time. In Sicily, for two centuries, from around 1060 to 1260, people of diverse cultures, faiths and lifestyles lived together in something approaching harmony. Theirs was a polyglot society virtually untainted by the bigotries of religion, devoid of oppression based on gender or ethnicity. Sadly, it was not to survive the thirteenth century.

Not that it was ever perfect, or even very novel. Ancient Rome, to cite but a single prior example, was a center of immigration from a sprawling empire and its far-flung provinces, with Roman citizenship acquired on an equal basis by people from places as diverse as what are now Scotland, Germany,

England, Turkey, France, Iraq, Egypt, Libya, Tunisia, Lebanon, Syria, Romania, Spain, Greece, Albania and Italy. All could become Romans and many did.

But if only for the diversitudes of their faiths, the medieval Sicilians represented something far more sophisticated, embodied in synagogues, churches and mosques. Sicily reached its cosmopolitan apogee in the first half of the twelfth century. It was not Camelot, but Sicily came closer to that legendary ideal than any other European kingdom of the Middle Ages.

In certain quarters "multicultural," a word whose appearance in the popular lexicon is rather recent, has become a meaningless mantra, a subjective idea that signifies something different in the mind of each person who expresses it.

For all the talk of multiculturalism, the concept itself is widely misunderstood, the word too often burdened by a modern political weight it was never meant to bear, dividing us when it should unite us. The term *multicultural* describes the presence of several distinct cultures in the same society at the same time, with social equality guaranteed to persons of each culture. Sicily's language, traditions and even its cuisine have been shaped by its multicultural heritage. Call it a grand experiment, and call all who share its ideals "Sicilians."

Culture is broadly defined: the beliefs, customs, arts, social practices and other manifestations or intellectual achievements of a particular society, group, place or time, regarded collectively.

Understandably, that encompassing definition — and there are others still more encompassing — educes more questions than answers. To Thomas Carlyle, culture was very simply "the process by which a person becomes all that they were created capable of being."

When we speak of culture, what do we really mean?

Is culture a way of expressing ourselves, a way of doing things, a mode of thinking or believing? Is it simply art, or cuisine? Is it the music we make or the stories we tell? How many cultures are there? Is there one, or perhaps more than one, for each of us? Is culture identity? Are all cultures equal, and equally worthy of preservation? How do we arrive at culture? Who creates culture, and who propagates it? Who are its keepers, its shapers, its custodians, its defenders? Is culture destiny? Do we define culture, or does it define us? Is culture something to live with, or is it something to be lived? Should culture be loud and arrogant, or silent and humble? Does it shout, or does it whisper? Who "owns" culture? Can there be many cultures within a greater one? How many cultures can exist together peacefully in one place? How does a monoculture divide into subcultures? Who decides what *is* culture?

Culture, with its nuances and idiosyncrasies, is what makes each of us, and each group of us, different from every other. Were it not for our distinguishing cultures, we would all be the same. Culture is personality. It is humanizing. It touches every one of us. A celebration of cultural diversity is a celebration of ourselves, for to appreciate the culture of others is to enrich our own.

What follows is not an *apologia* for a specific world view, but a guide to a voyage whose precise course can be charted only by you, the explorer. Perhaps it needs no course. Whatever route you take, yours will be a journey across time, traversing a sea of complexity to reach a crossroads of humanity. The journey is about knowledge and discovery. The points along the way will be at least as meaningful as the destination you arrive at.

Twelfth-century Sicily is a timeless metaphor, for our Arabs, Normans, Byzantines, Jews, Lombards and Germans could just as easily be the peoples of any part of the world. The lessons would be the same. Like so many lessons rooted in human nature and experience, these transcend any single place, defying facile generalities.

Any lessons to be found in these pages will be left to your

interpretation. They will be served with only a few morsels of dogmatism — the dogmatism of tolerance. We'll try to avoid rigid conclusions. Pontification has no place in historical narrative, but neither does indifference.

Would that the more elusive lessons had survived the Middle Ages. These pages are part of an effort to revive a few of them as something more than shadows.

Sicily's was a diverse population seeded by successive waves of conquerors, spawning a complex genetic patrimony of diverse haplogroups and a plethora of brown-eyed blondes and blue-eyed brunettes in a place where redheads are still called *Normanne* (Normans) and raven-haired women *More* (Moors).

Be it agreed that golden ages are ephemeral by definition, two hundred years is a long time by any measure. Yet our Normans, Fatimids, Swabians and Byzantines would barely be remembered at all were it not for their accomplishments. Normandy today is but a region of France, its dynasties in England and Sicily little more than a faint race memory of heroic conqueror kings. The Fatimid Empire, like that of the Romans, is now a cacophony of disunited nations. Swabia, the cradle of a great dynasty that ruled a Holy Roman Empire, is today an anonymous piece of Germany, while the Byzantines' capital is now a city in Turkey, where the basilica dedicated to Saint Sophia is a museum and the Patriarchate of Constantinople is relegated to a tiny presence.

Like a desert's shifting sands, ethnic identity evolves, its shape ever changing to accommodate continuous influences from within and without. We see only what is left to us, a vestigial trace of something different and perhaps better. But to neglect it altogether is to ignore something of the present.

"Study the past," said Confucius, "if you wish to define the future."

History, like science, sometimes teaches us something even when the experiment fails. But Sicily's multicultural experiment was a success for some twenty decades. To describe it requires no hyperbole, no soaring prose, for its barest facts are sufficient to impress the modern mind.

Alas, today's *Sicilia* is but a shadow of her former incarnation, the Sicilians themselves slightly downtrodden, their island governed from afar for the last five or six centuries, administered since 1946 via a tenuous regional autonomy. There is uncomfortable evidence to suggest that their ancestors were more literate, and perhaps more free, in 1100 than in 1900. By 1300, a radical shift had occurred. For better or worse, the confluence of cultures described in these pages had given way to the largely homogeneous monoculture we see today. But history can be cyclic, and in the present century Sicily has welcomed an influx of new immigrants from around the world.

The annals of medieval history tended to overlook half the population. Sicily bequeaths to us the stories of a few women courageous enough to negotiate treaties, enhearten followers, shelter refugees and run a government while raising families. Their mellifluous names color the chronicles of the Middle Ages: Judith of Evreux, Constance of Hauteville, Elvira of Castile, Margaret of Navarre, Constance of Hohenstaufen.

Their modern heirs are the little Tunisian girl who splashes her face with cool water from the Arab fountain in Monreale's cloister, and her German sister who places a floppy flower at the tomb of Frederick II in Palermo's cathedral. The spirit of the sisterhood traverses the miles, the languages, the centuries.

Rarely does synergy come easily. Sicily is the world's most conquered island, but only on occasion have the conquests been bloodless. The Byzantine Greeks defeated the Vandals and Goths. The Arabs, in turn, defeated the Byzantines, only to be challenged by the Normans. Later, in an age of pilgrimages and crusades, Messina became a springboard for Europeans *en route* to their Holy Land, where contested Jerusalem — briefly ruled by a Sicilian king — could boast nearly as much cultural diversity as Palermo.

But for all that, there is much in Sicily for today's visitors to appreciate, and here the flame of the island's past flickers to life. Millions of tourists, students and culture vultures descend upon Sicily each year. For the Greeks, Arabs, Germans, English, French, Albanians, Jews and Spaniards among them, the discovery evokes a feeling of shared affinity with a common heritage. To Germans and Austrians, Frederick was "their" emperor, while the Arabs claim Abdullah al Idrisi as one of their own and the Jews revel in the story of Benjamin of Tudela.

It was here that Swabians befriended Fatimids, and it was here that history witnessed the rare triumph of commonalities over differences.

We should not be surprised. We should be inspired.

ACKNOWLEDGEMENTS

"No man was ever wise by chance."
— Lucius Annaeus Seneca

Every historian is a link in a chain. To achieve any continuum or cohesion in their efforts, all historians worth their salt must stand on the shoulders of giants, for history cannot be written — or even much appreciated — without a solid foundation. It cannot thrive in a vacuum. It *perforce* builds upon what has come before us, recorded through the ages by perceptive predecessors. What would we know of the ancient Germans if not for the *Germania* of Tacitus, or the medieval Byzantines without the *Alexiad* of Anna Comnena?

It was my uncommon privilege to benefit from the tutelage of a number of seasoned sages while still in my twenties. Some are no longer among us. The world is immeasurably the lesser for their passing, and here I shall posthumously acknowledge three distinguished multiculturalists who had much to say about history and historiography.

Sir Steven Runciman (1903-2000) wrote defining works on the Crusades, the Byzantine Empire and the Sicilian Vespers, unbiased histories presented from two or three perspectives rather than just one as was customary since Gibbon's time. Trustee of the British Museum and sometime professor, he was a gentleman scholar in the best Oxbridge tradition. His gracious advice was worth far more than its weight in platinum.

Prince Cyril Toumanoff (1913-1997) was High Historical Consultant of the Sovereign Military Order of Malta and longtime professor of history at Georgetown University, where his students included many budding leaders and at least one future American president. An inveterate Mediterraneanist, he offered invaluable counsel and granted me access to the archive of his knightly order in Rome.

Jacques Cardinal Martin (1908-1992) served as Prefect of the Pontifical Household under three Popes. Fluent in half a dozen languages, he administered Vatican diplomatic protocol for decades, and he is credited with developing the international face of the Roman Curia that we see today. He made possible my unrestricted access to the Vatican Archives.

Among the living, co-author **Jacqueline Alio** contributed extensively throughout and wrote the chapters on Margaret of Navarre, Joan Plantagenet, Thomas Becket, and the Sicilian Jews, as well as the sections on Elvira of Castile, Judith of Evreux, and the Genoard Park, introducing some details drawn from her original research in medieval records.

In the age of the internet and the ready availability of information, the traditional keepers of knowledge are too often overlooked. Thanks are due the staffs at archives and libraries in Italy, Britain and France, especially the British Library, the state archives of Palermo and Naples, and the Vatican Secret Archives.

For their suggestions and input, special thanks to **Professor Beniamino Inserra**, a fine historian, **Bishop Lorenzo Casati**, an exceptional theologian, and the erudite **Philippa Leslie.**

Any shortcomings which might present themselves in the pages that follow are, of course, solely my responsibility as *redactoris* of this work.

— L. Mendola

Palermo, November 2013

TABLE OF CONTENTS

INTRODUCTION

"If you wish to understand anything, observe its beginning and its development."

— Aristotle

Aristotle's "beginning and development" are what many of us call *history*. This book is not just about Sicily, but neither is it a sweeping "comparative history" in the Toynbee mold or a monumental tome in the style of Barbara Tuchman. It is about the varied cultural heritage of the Western World expressed in a single place at one moment in time.

It shall be an extended moment. Here you will meet all of the ancient and medieval peoples of Sicily under one roof, without the need to consult separate books to read about the Elymians and the Normans, or the Sicanians and the Goths. It is an approach as pragmatic as it is unorthodox.

Conventional study does little to prepare you for the complicated history that confronts you in a place like Sicily. Those who visit the island, either physically or via the written word, encounter a complex cultural patrimony. But the visitor is rarely rewarded with information sufficient to explain the complexity. Fatimids, Normans and Swabians are mentioned, of course, yet very few histories or guidebooks explain who, exactly, these peoples were. It's as if the visitor were presumed to be an ethnographer. It is still more annoying that, beyond their names, little information is set forth about the contributions of each civilization to the society of Sicily and indeed the world.

In the worst case, one might be led to believe that Arabs,

Germans, Normans and Jews shared Sicily at the same moment purely by happenstance. The visitor's bewilderment stems from nothing more sinister than the mediocre, perhaps superficial, explanation of history provided by the vast majority of travel books and websites. For all but the avid history aficionado, encyclopedic works stuffed with events and dates are tedious, even intimidating. In some books one must muddle through a swamp of platitudes and clichés to find a few facts.

We hope to address that situation to the reader's satisfaction in the following pages, where we shall scratch into the crusty patina of Sicily's multilayered history. With luck, something of interest will be revealed. Let us stand apart from those who have made the study of history dull and prosaic. And monochromatic.

"Everything that built Western civilization emanated from the Mediterranean," historian Cyril Toumanoff was fond of saying, observing *en passant* that the cultures of Georgia and Armenia, where his father's family was rooted before ending up in Saint Petersburg, are essentially Mediterranean. Those lands eventually became part of the Russian Empire.

This book is not about empires. It is about the people who lived in them. We'll occasionally cite original, medieval sources, people like al Idrisi, bin Jubayr, Godfrey Malaterra, Benjamin of Tudela and nasty, pseudonymous Hugh Falcandas. Our format is the simple narrative, arranged for the most part by topic.

History is about people and their stories. It is a canvas dripping with color that doesn't leave a single millimeter unobserved or unconsidered. After viewing the painting, the expert turns the picture around to examine the integrity of the canvas and how it was stretched and mounted into the frame. And how well it has withstood the test of time. But the frame, the presentation of history, is not history itself. It is something that was added later, an enhancement. Accurate history prompts a sober reckoning with the past, serving us the bad with the good. Grasping history takes equal parts of courage and curiosity. There are no shortcuts.

Too many histories published nowadays are officious and condescending, presented in simplistic language that presupposes the reader's total ignorance. But anybody reading *this* one is presumed *ipso facto* to be intellectually curious. This *entrée* may even serve as a gateway to further reading about Sicily or — better yet — the world's other multicultural societies, especially those of Asia and Africa.

We agree with Sir Harold Acton that the footnote can be "a tedious form of exhibitionism." Original sources, an essential element in any book of history, are given after the Reading List.

Here we shall not consider at length either the *philosophy* or *political theory* behind the concept of multiethnic societies in the modern world, their framework or evolution. Medieval Sicilian society never accommodated more than a half-dozen distinct cultures and three (Western) religions simultaneously, so it would be misleading to suggest that its complexities could be compared *directly* or *precisely* to the pluralism which characterizes certain nations today.

A prevailing school of thought posits that there are now two principal approaches to the study of history — the "political" dealing with great events and the "social" concerning society at large. At work in these pages are elements of each. There also exist the related concepts of "macro" and "micro" history.

Although it presents a succinct historical synopsis (the outline) and a clear timeline (the chronology) sufficient to the needs of those just discovering our island, this is a concise survey rather than an exhaustive history filled with *minutiae,* which in the case of Sicily's three or four millennia would require many volumes. This is a book for the general reader. It strives for accuracy without pedantry.

For the most part, this book does not reflect its authors' original, scholarly research, which would have resulted in an esoteric publication of little interest to most readers. The few revelatory exceptions germane to this work are mentioned in the Sources.

That said, you will find woven into this tapestry a certain degree of original commentary on art, architecture, literature and social practices. This book is not an exercise in ethnography or anthropology, but it caresses those fields and others. It is not about history for its own sake. Most of us study history to learn more than a few names, dates and fugacious facts.

The Reading List suggests accurate, reliable works by Siculophile intellectuals; while it is not a bibliography, it is a good starting point for those seeking more information on the subjects presented here. Karla Mallette's insightful literary history is a good example. For this volume, we have drawn upon many sources, including obscure monographs and journals heretofore published only in Italian, Arabic, German or French, as well as the occasional academic symposium.

How we study history is at least as important as why we study it. A word about epistemology is in order. While the best historians bring a special passion to their work, the study of history should be approached scientifically. History is not religion. It has experts but no authorities. Scientists should be as consistent and impartial as possible; so too historians. Prosopography, for instance, is an important element in historical analysis, and it relies on logical thinking, as does "contextual analysis." What in the burgeoning common parlance is referred to as the "historical method" is not too different from the scientific method, but here we shall not digress to a discussion of hermeneutics, semiotics and other tools of the historian. What is important, nay essential, is that the methodology be solid, leading to an *accurate* rendering of history. Not every "accepted" historical detail is beyond cavil. Sometimes insufficient evidence is available to reach a definitive conclusion. "Absence of evidence," declared Carl Sagan, "is not evidence of absence."

By no means is establishing historicity a challenge of recent vintage. In histories written by Romans, the Carthaginians, Vandals and Goths were maligned, but in retrospect their greatest "shortcoming" was nothing more than the fact of their being outsiders, easily painted as interlopers, who contested Rome's zealous hegemony.

The approach to historiography continually evolves, and with it the modern view of history — generally for the better. There was a time, not long ago, when American school children were taught that Christopher Columbus "discovered" their continent in 1492. In 1960, it was revealed that Norsemen arrived some five centuries before him. It was belatedly acknowledged that the Americas were discovered by Asiatic peoples, ancestors of the Paleo-Indians, many millennia ago, and this fact is now taught in schools. But it was *always* a fact.

A few curmudgeons may disparage this kind of perspective as "revisionist" or "politically correct," as if your authors were part of an army of iconoclasts — or perhaps a swarm of locusts — intent on shredding the last leaf of Eurocentrism. We recognize it as the dispassionate view that should be embraced by *every* historian.

Detractors should heed the words of Cicero: "The first law of historical writing is that the author dare not state anything but the truth." The great orator went on to add impartiality to his list of *dicta*.

The truth is not European, Asian, African or American. It is Human. Is that not what history should be?

Unlike most "Italian" histories, this one is not ethnocentric, judging earlier societies *in toto* as if they were mere stepping stones to something greater. Like Bavaria, Scotland and Catalonia, Sicily had a distinct heritage long before its annexation to a larger, unitary state. In Sicily this occurred during the modern era, coeval with the reign of Queen Victoria and the presidency of Abraham Lincoln. The perspectives reflected here are neither Italocentric or, for that matter, Siculocentric. Rather, they seek to place medieval Sicily in a wider social context, from a *global* point of view.

Without wishing to place undue emphasis on subjective labels or broad definitions, let us bear in mind that the chapters dedicated to the Arabs, Jews and Byzantine Greeks describe what are usually regarded as *entire* civilizations, while those on the Goths, Normans and Swabians pertain to specific cultures *within* a greater European society. By way of analogy, the Fatimids were a single subgroup within the wider Muslim-Arab world, and in that respect their position was similar to that of the Normans in Christian Europe.

Our focus, of course, is Sicily during the Middle Ages. The *literati* invariably concentrate on a handful of figures and events from this era. Having no political or social "agenda," we have attempted to mention a few personages who are lesser known to a general readership.

To contrast the *status* of medieval Sicily to what came later, we'll make a few comparisons between society then and now, including two or three examples rarely — if ever — published elsewhere.

Exempli gratia: In considering medieval law, it is hard to overlook the fact that divorce existed in Sicily when the Normans arrived in 1061 but was illegal throughout Italy in 1961.

Beyond considerations in that vein, one or two of the social phenomena we report may strike some readers as slightly disquieting.

Videlicet: A comparison between estimated literacy rates in 1061 and those of eight centuries later.

This nugget is original if only for the mode of its presentation here. If anything, its exclusion from the "traditional" Italian historical narrative results from Italians' mundane embarrassment or denial rather than deliberate expurgation. The facts supporting the medieval statistic relative to Sicily's Muslim and Jewish populations are cited in these pages. As regards the modern one, general literacy throughout Italy at the time of unification in 1861 was at best twenty percent. That figure is accepted by Italian historians, but over the years we have confirmed it ourselves through extensive research in contemporaneous vital statistics records, which often include the annotation that "the declarant cannot read." Only in 1877 did primary education, the completion of three scholastic years, become compulsory in the unified Italy.

While such observations are useful in establishing perspective regarding social evolution over time, a general comparative analysis of that kind lies beyond the scope of this book.

The words you are reading were written *ex novo* for this publication. Essential content of some chapters was previously published, in one form or another, on the internet beginning around 2002 — the exposition on the Maliki School and English common law aired on the BBC in 2008 — with elements finding their way into various hardcopy books and magazines written by other authors over the last decade, sometimes verbatim and usually without attribution. This is a frequent occurrence. In some cases the information was corrupted in the process, so it's just as well that our authorship was not cited.

For example, we had suggested that Saint Mary of the Germans, in Messina, was the only church standing in Sicily, albeit in ruins, constructed in the "pure" Gothic style. True, it was built by the Teutonic Knights around 1200, but upon closer inspection it is clear that its Gothic lines are perhaps more tenuous than the impression one has initially when viewing its graceful arches. We might better characterize its style, shared with other churches in Sicily, as an evolving, transitional Romanesque with early Gothic elements, and we coined the oxymoronic phrase *Romanesque Gothic* to describe it.

Proto Sicanian is another term we introduced. Here we shall simply recognize that imitation is, after all, the sincerest form of flattery, and that no author need be credited for every published thought. Nevertheless, it is unfortunate when errors are propagated, and we must lay at least a modicum of blame with the internet and the misguided souls who misuse it.

We will begin with an overview of Sicily's ancient and medieval history, its geography, peoples, faiths, cuisine, flora and fauna. What follows these introductory chapters will be presented more-or-less chronologically. For this reason, the geographer Abdullah al Idrisi finds himself placed after the introduction to the Normans and Roger II rather than somewhere immediately following the chapter on the Arabs. But that is not unlike what visitors found in Sicily during the twelfth century, namely people of diverse backgrounds in the same place.

Malta and Gozo were part of Sicily's world, first as the site of impressive temples built by a civilization native to southeastern Sicily, then as the domain of the Phoenicians, Arabs, Normans and others who ruled Sicily, and finally (from 1530 until 1798) as a fief of the Sicilian Crown held by the Knights of Saint John. Yet many authors of Sicilian histories ignore Malta.

Should you actually visit Sicily — something your authors enthusiastically encourage — a good guidebook would complement this volume, although "Places to Visit" offers insightful suggestions. Here we present chapters dedicated to just a few historic sites that reflect Sicily's rich, multicultural heritage with exceptional eloquence: the opulent Norman Palace in Palermo, hilltop Monreale Abbey a few miles away, the austere mikveh in the Ortygia district of Siracusa. The splendid Genoard Park is described, though few of its architectural jewels, and none of its gardens, exist today. To these could have been added dozens of other sites at Palermo and Siracusa as well as Erice, Taormina, Agrigento, Cefalù, Segesta, Selinunte, Mozia...

The historical legacy is ubiquitous, firmly rooted in ground as solid as the golden limestone of Sicily's temples and castles. In Siracusa, Erice, Taormina and Palermo the architecture speaks for itself. In just one anonymous building along Palermo's narrow Via Protonotaro are window openings carved from stone by Arabs, Normans and Swabians, while the medieval cathedral nearby bears the marks of these civilizations and others.

Were you alive when those structures were erected, you might have read of the marriage of Roger de Hauteville in the *lingua franca* of the day as *comes Rogerius uxorem ducit.*

Few are the Italy-based historians whose work is published in today's international language, English. We draw attention to this not out of *schadenfreude* or *protagonismo,* but to explain why the only books in the Reading List written by Italians are ours.

The benighted Sicilian academy is of little concern here except to note that it did not always grope in the darkness. Archimedes stands out, of course, but we need not look to antiquity for inspiration. The multilingual Michele Amari published the first edition of his defining ethnography of Sicily's medieval Arabs in 1854. For many decades, a creeping Italianism, fostered by nationalist movements like the *Risorgimento* and then Fascism, discouraged the study of "foreign" cultures, legal systems and languages — the Fascist regime actually prohibited the study of English in most public schools — and in officialdom the lasting effects of this xenophobic mentality are still felt. But here we need not wade too deeply into the murky waters of Italian politics. Let us turn to religion.

Why is a dispassionate consideration of religion, or in any

case philosophy, essential to our study of history? Quite simply, it is because ethos and religion condition motives and actions, influencing everything from law, economics and social mores to politics, conquest and war. On too many occasions have continents, regions and islands — including Sicily — been invaded in the name of religion, even when this was merely a flimsy pretext to justify expansionism.

One of the glaring defects in most general histories of Sicily is that their presentation of religion is bereft of clear explanations of the differences between the denominations which existed within Islam and Christianity by 1100. In Sicily this concerns the legal traditions (Maliki law, Canon law, Halakha law) that influenced jurisprudence and government during that period. Keeping to generalities, without engaging in a theological treatise or a comparative analysis of religions, we have made an effort to define the essential differences that existed during this period between Sunnis and Shiites, Roman Catholics and Greek Orthodox. A precise characterization of Sicily's Judaic tradition proves more elusive; clearly it was Maghrebi in the twelfth century and essentially Sephardi by the fifteenth.

It is our conviction that those who eschew the topic of religion implicitly ignore its correlation to ethnicity and culture. In the Kingdom of Sicily most Arabs were Shia Muslim, most Byzantines were Greek Orthodox, and most Normans and Germans were Roman Catholic.

Strikingly, Sicily's Shiites ended up with certain Sunni traditions, while her Catholics retained some Orthodox ones. Syncretism of this kind touches the very soul of multiculturalism.

At best, each chapter *introduces* its subject. Neither Chapter 4 (religion) nor Chapter 25 (law) are intended as exhaustive treatments. The relative brevity of some biographical chapters is obvious; it would be impossible to present a complete biography of Roger II or Frederick II in a book of this length. The

28

lengthier treatment of certain personages reflects no bias on our part. It so happens that more is known about some figures than others, and at all events an effort was made to focus on the connection of each to Sicily rather than generally, an emphasis evident in the biographical sketches of Thomas Becket and Benjamin of Tudela.

Considering the significant discoveries made during the last decade — not least in the field of population genetics and in research on Sicily's Jews — what is presented in the following chapters is in some ways far more "complete" than it might have been if it were written just ten years ago.

The topical structure of this book lends itself to a certain redundancy, though we have attempted to minimize this. Our apologies for any annoyance this creates for anybody reading the entire text, where we mention the invention of spaghetti in the cuisine section as well as Abdullah al Idrisi's chapter. The intent was to make it easy to read about a topic in a single section or chapter, without the need for consulting the entire book for additional information. Admittedly, such a format may be better suited to a digital environment, with its searches and links, than a traditional (paper) one.

We make use of the designations BCE and CE in each chapter's initial citations, and sometimes subsequently, alongside BC and AD. An attempt has been made to give credit where it is due: *Arabic* numerals are now *Hindu-Arabic* numerals.

In this paper edition, the text in the appendices is slightly smaller than in the numbered chapters. For some readers that may be an incentive to download the ebook. In our publisher's defense, we can only say that failure to resort to such measures as reducing the point size would have resulted in a much bulkier, 600-page volume.

The Chronology is the most complete, most accurate timeline of Sicily's ancient and medieval history ever to see print.

In keeping with the convention established by the best traditional histories, maps are presented in a specific section following this one, not within chapters or appendices. No printed photograph in the dimensions permitted by this book's size could do justice to any place described here, but the internet offers quite a few, many in fairly high resolution showing good detail from every possible angle, and most are easily searchable in English.

Following the maps, the first chapter is an introduction to the Sicilians and their antecedents. Let's meet them.

MAPS

© 2013

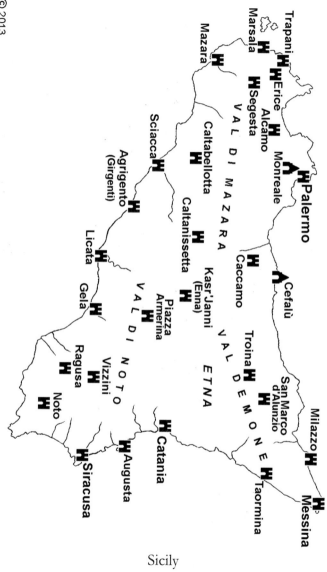

Sicily

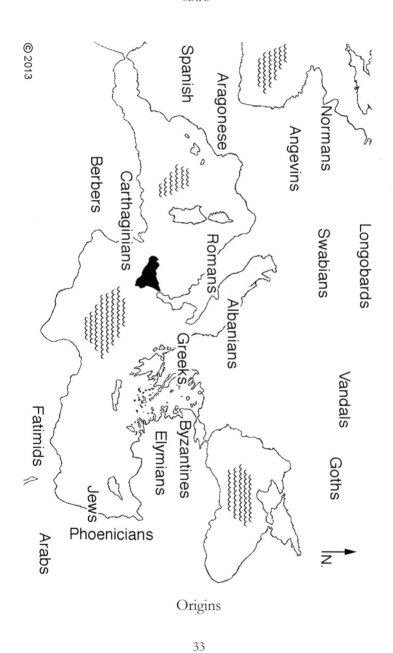

Origins

Emirate of Sicily under Kalbids - 948

Norman Kingdom of Sicily - 1160

Greatest extent of Hohenstaufen dominion under Frederick II - 1230

Kingdoms & Emirates

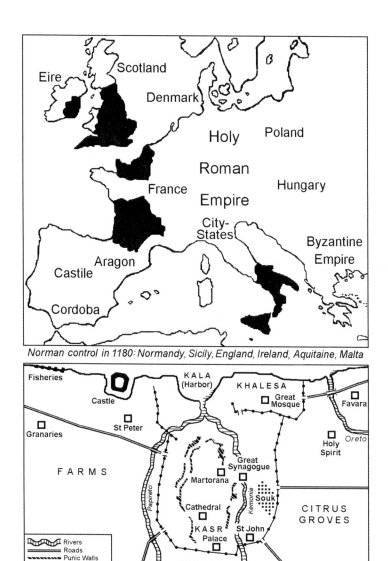

Norman control in 1180: Normandy, Sicily, England, Ireland, Aquitaine, Malta

City of Palermo in 1180

Normans & Palermo 1180

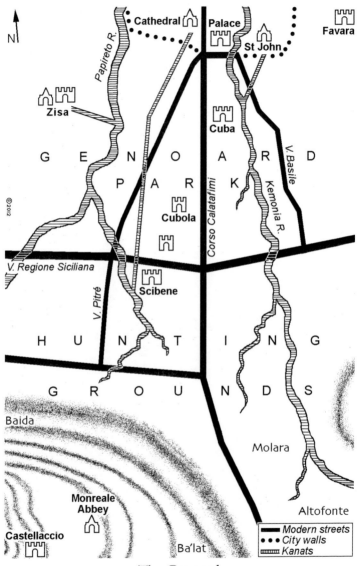

The Genoard

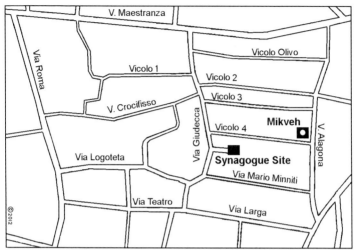

Giudecca (Jewish Quarter) in Ortygia, Siracusa
Great synagogue site is St John's Church. Mikveh at Via Alagona 52.

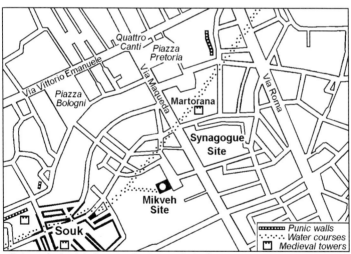

Palermo's Jewish Quarter, Souk (now Ballarò Market) and Kemonia Spring
Great synagogue site is San Nicolò da Tolentino Church. Mikveh in Palazzo Marchese.

Jewish Quarters

CHAPTER 1

Meet the Peoples

What is a Sicilian?

Ethnology gives rise to complicated questions and equally complicated answers. The advent of the use of DNA in genealogy has revived passionate discourse about ethnic identity, rekindling some old "nature versus nurture" debates we need not contemplate at length here. Having broached the subject, let's make our point by way of example, avoiding the verbose analysis that plagues the field of anthropology.

Two intelligent, promising girls, each sixteen years old, are separated by an ocean.

Amy has three Italian-born grandparents — two from Sicily — and her father is in the quintessential Mediterranean genetic haplogroup J2. Like her parents, she was born in Chicago but now lives in Los Angeles. Amy is an American citizen and speaks no Italian but is proficient in Spanish, which she studied in school. She is thinking about following her mother into teaching. Amy knows little about Italy beyond what she sees on television or the internet, but she dreams of a honeymoon in Venice someday. She has never heard, or heard of, Laura Pausini.

Rose, who lives in Siracusa, was born in Palermo as an Italian citizen; her father, like Amy's, is in haplogroup J2. Rose speaks Italian and dresses in stylish Italian clothes, and her

English is very good. She listens to Italian music and adores Laura Pausini. Her parents have a successful restaurant but Rose plans on studying medicine in Britain where her aunt lives. Then she wants to live in Italy forever. Until now, it has been the only country she has ever known. Two years before Rose was born, her parents arrived in Italy as immigrants from northern India.

Which girl, Amy or Rose, is the more "Sicilian" of the two?

That kind of question is a quandary of our pluralistic age, but in Sicily it would have been just as timely in 1200 as it was in 2000. The concept of Sicilian identity expounded in the following pages reflects nothing less than reality. In truth, the Middle Ages were not the only time that Sicily played host to a multiethnic society. Anybody traveling across the island in 700 BC (BCE) would have encountered five distinct cultures, each with its own language: Sicanian, Elymian, Sikelian, Phoenician, Greek.

What is to be our paradigm? "Ethnic" identity can be imprecise, even capricious. Medieval boundaries were fluid, and despite their paternity some of the historical figures we'll meet in these pages were actually multiethnic as well as multilingual.

Roger II was the son of a Norman father, but Adelaide del Vasto, his "Italian" mother, was descended in the male line from the Frankish Aleram family of Montferrat and in the female lines from a series of ancestresses from around central and western Europe.

Frederick II was the son of Constance, a daughter of the Norman Roger II and Beatrice of Rethel, a French noblewoman. His father was Henry VI of Hohenstaufen, son of Frederick I "Barbarossa," who was mostly German (Barbarossa's mother was Judith of Bavaria, whose Guelph dynasty was Lombard). Henry's mother, Beatrix of Burgundy, was mostly French.

In the twelfth century, of course, vague geographic demonyms like *German, French* or *Italian* denoted nothing like the nationalities of today; Germany and Italy were not even united to form nations until the nineteenth century.

The geographical origins of the populations that arrived in Sicily from circa 1200 BC (BCE) until the end of the Middle Ages are indicated in one of this book's maps. In effect, the range of influences is somewhat wider than what is shown there. The Islamic empires extended from the Iberian peninsula to what is now Pakistan, while the Norsemen and Goths came from Scandinavia and the Berbers traced their roots from regions bordering the Sahara. This meant that ideas from afar took root in Sicily, albeit more in some cases (the Arabs) than in others (the Goths). Medieval trade routes facilitated this process, leading to the introduction of an efficient system of numeration from India and the process of paper manufacture from China, both via the Arabs.

The next chapter, our historical outline, lists Sicily's most prevalent genetic haplogroups, acknowledging the groundbreaking work of geneticist Luigi Cavalli-Sforza, whose research drew correlations between genetic profiles and specific populations, work continued by his student Spencer Wells and others. In Sicily the genetic record confirms a historical record of populations accrued during the course of four millennia, much as DNA sequences substantiate the development of speciation over millions of years.

Although the focus here is culture and history, it is true that certain genetic traits were closely identified with specific populations. Before the arrival of the Normans, extremely few Sicilians had red hair, which developed long ago through a genetic mutation among Celtic and western Germanic populations; the ancient Greeks and Romans (Xenophanes, Herodotus, Cassius, Tacitus) actually mention red hair in describing these peoples. It is estimated that by the twentieth century one out of twenty Sicilians had red hair — ranging in color from titian to auburn.

Apropos coloring, the first mutation for blue eyes is thought to have occurred as recently as 10,000 BC (BCE), perhaps in only one person from whom all blue-eyed people living today are descended; it is possible that a few Sicilians had blue eyes in Neolithic times, but the number certainly increased with the arrival of the Goths, Normans and Swabians.

While a fair complexion is a decided disadvantage if one is standing under the Sicilian sun, some hereditary traits are more immediately life-threatening. Thalassemia, which affects hemoglobin production, evolved in the eastern Mediterranean and parts of Asia to protect against malaria.

The story revealed by the genetic record transcends the history of Sicily and Sicilians. Studies in population genetics confirm the age-old belief that all humans are part of the same large family tree, with roots in Africa, and here we shall examine a few of its branches. The cultural differences became more pronounced over time. By no means are Sicilians the only ones with "mixed" ancestry. Remote Roman lineages, for example, will be found in almost every place the Romans went, and the same phenomenon exists for the Goths and Fatimids. Like our tree's vernal sprigs, ethnic culture, as we understand it today, is a fairly recent development when viewed as part of the flow of collective human experience spanning many thousands of years.

Genetics aside, populations assimilate and then amalgamate over generations as individuals of the arriving (immigrant) population intermarry with those of the established (or native) one. Their descendants usually identify with both cultures or a new, "syncretic" one reflecting characteristics of each. The Normans were such a population, at once Norse and Frankish. In ancient and medieval times it was rare for an immigrating or invading population to completely displace the one it found already living in the place it colonized.

The Sicilians are descended from the peoples of at least a dozen civilizations. For the record, here is a brief introduction to a few of them, beginning with the earliest. We shall become better acquainted with the medieval populations in later chapters.

The First Sicilians: The indigenous inhabitants were the Sicanians or *Sikanoi,* whose remote ancestors, the *Proto Sicanians,* colonized Malta before 4,000 BC (BCE), where they built Europe's first megalithic temples. They developed agriculture in Sicily, Homer's "Sikania," and introduced mythology. A Sicanian temple stands atop the rocky mountain overlooking Cefalù, and there are various Sicanian archeological sites around Sicily. Early on, a few Greek outposts were established on the Ionian coast (the Mycenaeans), while an Italic civilization, the Ausones (or Ausonians), reached the Aeolian Islands. The Elymians, who readily assimilated with the Greeks, migrated from Anatolia in Asia Minor and settled in the west at Segesta (their Egesta), Erice (Eryx), Entella (outside Contessa Entellina), Hypana (possibly situated near Prizzi) and probably Iaitas (near San Giuseppe Jato). Thucydides identified the Elymians specifically as refugees from the storied city of Troy, which is usually associated with a site in Anatolia. The Sikels, or *Sikeloi,* described by Philistus of Syracuse, came from peninsular Italy and settled much of eastern Sicily, including what are now Enna, Centuripe and probably Mineo, carving the earliest necropoli at Pantalica. Sicily, or *Sikelia*, was the domain of these three distinct civilizations (Sicanians, Sikels, Elymians) until circa 750 BC, and the ethnonym *Sicilian* obviously derives from the names for two of them. The Sikels are tentatively identified by some archeologists as the Shikelish tribe of the "Sea Peoples" who attacked Egypt in 1220 BC. By around 1,000 BC, all three societies, like the Greeks to the east and the Etruscans to the north, were making use of sophisticated systems of writing using the alphabet introduced by the Phoenicians, which included most of the characters, or glyphs, in this text.

The Punic Peoples: Identified as descendants of the Canaan-ites, the seafaring Phoenicians traded as far away as Britain, and may have circumnavigated Africa, and the Lebanese and Mal-tese are thought to be their principal modern descendants. They were nautical masters of the Mediterranean, leaving traces of Egyptian art in Sicily and elsewhere. According to current es-timates, the Phoenicians probably founded Carthage, along the coast of what is now Tunisia, a few decades before 800 BC. Palermo, Solunto and Motya (Mozia near Marsala) have Phoenician walls, and so does Erice — though ancient Eryx began its life as an Elymian city. By 500 BC, the Carthaginians had inherited the territories of their Phoenician forebears in the central and western Mediterranean, in the process forging an identity of their own. Carthage was widely reputed to be the wealthiest city in the region. Where the Phoenicians had estab-lished emporia, the Carthaginians founded colonies, repopu-lating Palermo, or *Zis,* and other localities. Historians now appreciate the Phoenicians and Carthaginians more than they used to; unfortunately, the Punics suffered the fate of having much of their history written by those who conquered and de-spised them, namely the petulant Romans.

The Greeks: Their sophisticated culture largely displaced that of the Punics in the eastern Mediterranean and then Sicily. Segesta was an Elymian city that readily assimilated Greek cul-ture, and there are also standing Greek temples at Agrigento, Siracusa and Selinunte, with small amphitheatres and archeo-logical sites around Sicily. In Syracuse, the most important of the Siceliot cities, the Paleo-Christian cathedral was built around a large Greek temple whose columns support it. Sicily eventually became Rome's first "foreign" province, and with the Punic Wars fought on the island the Carthaginians were finally defeated, but Greek — not Latin — remained the chief language into the Early Middle Ages. It has been postulated that the Greeks introduced Sicily's first domesticated olive cultivars, where before there were only the native oleasters. More importantly, Archimedes formulated great theories in his native Syracuse, where Plato devised his concept of Utopia to be set in Sicily. Paul of Tarsus visited the city on his way to Naples and Rome, and the Crypt of Saint Marcian marks the site where he is thought to have preached.

The Romans: Rooted in Etruscan and Latin origins, Roman culture ravenously absorbed that of the Greeks. Sicily has rather few "purely Roman" monuments, such as those in central Catania, and a number of ground-level archeological sites like the one in Palermo. Features like Taormina's Roman walls and theatre, built around an earlier Greek amphitheatre, are the rule, but Sicily also has several oval Roman theatres. Piazza Armerina's Roman villa, with its stunning mosaic pavements, is the largest, best-preserved residence of its kind in the Roman world. Their empire vast and their contact with the greater world extensive, the Romans in the time of Augustus traded as far as southern India. The essential framework of statutory "civil" law, as opposed to common law, comes to us, through many permutations, from the Romans. Compared to many parts of the sprawling Empire, Sicily, being part of the Greek civilization that was the fount of so much Roman knowledge, did not benefit exceptionally from Rome's burgeoning influence. In AD (CE) 395, shortly after the legalization of Christianity, the Empire was split into West and East, with Sicily officially in the West yet vacillating between the two spheres of influence — Latin and Greek. With Rome's slow, torturous fall during the fifth century, the island looked to the East. First, however, it would encounter some visitors from the distant North.

The Goths and Vandals: Marking the inception of what we now call the Middle Ages, a brief Gothic interlude arose as

Rome's empire decayed into disunity and chaos. For convenience, the Vandals and Ostrogoths left most of Sicily's Roman administrative infrastructure intact, admiring many features of the society they conquered. Their tribal legal system, a precursor of common law, was quite different from the Roman legal codes, but they gradually adopted Roman ways. "Every Goth wants to be a Roman," Theodoric observed, "but only the humblest Roman wants to be a Goth." Like the Carthaginians before them, the Goths and Vandals suffered the misfortune of having their history written for them, in Latin, by their Roman detractors. For nearly a century, until 535, these Germanic peoples ruled Sicily as part of their own evanescent empires. In the wake of this interlude, what did they leave behind? Some genes for blondish hair and blue eyes.

The Byzantines: The Gothic rule of Sicily met its end at the hands of a Byzantine Greek army. Greek culture, with Constantinople (Byzantium) as its point of reference, flourished in Sicily for the next few centuries, propagating its own brand of early Christianity. Its influences are most evident in the icons created ("written") in mosaic. In Taormina there's one of the *Theotokos* in an archway beneath a tower in a main street, and of course the cathedrals of Monreale and Cefalù boast famous examples, along with Palermo's Martorana church and Palatine Chapel. Byzantine culture was linked to the Greek (Orthodox) Church, with its distinctive mysticism and spirituality. The cathedral of Siracusa is the quintessential example of a Greek temple converted into an early (Paleo-Christian) church, and that city's mikveh (Jewish ritual bath) was carved into limestone during the Byzantine period.

The Arabs: By definition, an Arab was any native speaker of Arabic or its dialects. Arab traders from Tunisia, a territory seized from the Berbers, had established small communities in Mazara and Marsala by 750. The great influx of Muslim peoples arrived in Sicily following a major Aghlabid invasion in 827 that included Berbers and even some Persians. The baths at Cefalà Diana are the most complete building of the Arab period still standing in Sicily designed in a purely Arab architectural style, and the oldest part of Taormina's Palazzo Corvaja was a Fatimid edifice. Little remains of the palace on the outskirts of Palermo known as the *Favara,* once an emir's residence. The Koranic passages inscribed in relief in several pillars conserved in Palermo — one supporting the cathedral's portico — are further examples of such rarities; they were carved for mosques. More abundant are churches and palaces erected after 1071 in the Norman-Arab style, some (like Monreale Abbey) incorporating Byzantine details. Of special note, as regards purely Arab art, are the painted *muquarnas* ceiling of the Palatine Chapel and the Islamic geometry decorating the exteriors of the apses of the cathedrals of Palermo and Monreale. It was the Arabs who introduced a simple system of numeration ("Hindu-Arabic" numerals) in Sicily. Feats of engineering left to us by the Arabs include some underground channels (kanats) in Palermo and well-constructed bridges outside Corleone, Adrano and Roccamena. The Arabs greatly influenced Sicilian agriculture, cuisine, and of course language and law. A detail not to be overlooked is that the Arab and Byzantine civilizations were the most sophisticated of medieval Europe and the Mediterranean, and Sicily's Jews were highly learned; the Normans who arrived in the eleventh century found in Fatimid Sicily a highly literate society and all the ingredients of a multicultural golden age. Most of Sicily's Muslims were Shiites, but the Maliki School of jurisprudence, which influenced common law in Norman Sicily and perhaps even in Plantagenet England, was rooted in Sunni legal principles brought to the island by the conquering Aghlabids, who were Sunnis.

The Normans: When these Norse descendants arrived in Sicily in 1061, a few years before their conquest of England, they found what seemed to be two populations living side-by-side, namely Arabs and Greeks. There was also a small but prosperous Jewish population seeded among the other two. Whatever the rapport of the Normans may have been with the Saxons they found in England, in Sicily there was (at least initially) accommodation of the pre-existing populace, and Siculo-Norman culture reflected this. With few exceptions, Norman architecture in Sicily is a Romanesque style — rather than the pure Gothic — which developed in synergy with Islamic and Byzantine movements. In Palermo (the cathedral, Zisa, Cuba, Palatine Chapel), Monreale (the abbey complex) and Cefalù (the cathedral) we see the greatest examples. Some of Sicily's castles also date from this era, when feudalism was introduced.

The Swabians: By 1200, the island's cultural influences were becoming increasingly Western. Most Christians were now "Latins" (Roman Catholic) and Islam was gradually disappearing through conversion. Cosmopolitan, multilingual, freethinking Frederick II was solidly European politically. A Hohenstaufen, he was, among other things, King of the Germans — a people then defined more by their language than by territory. In fact, Sicily's Swabian kings, who were also Holy Roman Emperors, brought many Germans, not only Swabians, to their prosperous southern kingdom. Lasting until 1266, the Swabian period was a continuation of the Normans' Golden Age. Its legal system was enlightened for its time.

The Angevins: This French dynasty ruled Sicily briefly, with Naples as its capital, from 1266 until the Vespers uprising ousted them sixteen years later. This gave rise to the phrase "Two Sicilies" because rival monarchs, Charles of Anjou in

Naples and Peter of Aragon in Palermo, claimed the same crown. Charles was the younger brother of Saint Louis, whose heart is preserved in Monreale's cathedral to remind us of Angevin rule and the last Crusades.

The Aragonese and Castilians: In 1282 Sicily became part of the empire of the "Crown of Aragon" ruled from Barcelona in Catalonia, to be claimed in 1412 by Castilian kings. Signs of medieval Aragonese-Catalan influence are abundantly evident in Sicily. The Catalan Gothic style of a few churches and residences comes to mind. In some ways the Sicilian language heard today is strikingly similar to Catalan. By 1492, with Spanish unification a *fait accompli,* Sicily, though a separate kingdom, was destined to be ruled from Madrid until the eighteenth century. Many historians date the close of the Middle Ages to 1453, coinciding with the end of the Hundred Years' War between England and France, and the capture of Constantinople by the Ottoman Turks.

The Spanish: With the unification of the various Spanish states, Castilian rule segued into that of a united Spain governed from Madrid. Perhaps the greatest visible legacy of the Spanish period is the ubiquitous Baroque present in virtually every Sicilian locality. While a native Sicilian Baroque developed around 1700, to flourish in Catania, Noto and Ragusa, most of Sicily's churches and palaces were constructed in a simpler Spanish style vaguely influenced by Italian movements. Centuries of Spanish rule shaped Sicilian society and culture in myriad ways. The Inquisition became more powerful than ever and the effects of terrible bureaucracy are still felt today. The last vestiges of common law introduced by the Arabs and Normans had all but disappeared by 1500, and in Italy today "statutory" civil law, not "case" law, forms the principal basis of the legal system. One modern benefit of the oppressive

Spanish administration is the abundance of documentary records it has left us.

The Albanians: Arriving as refugees from Ottoman expansion beginning around 1470, the Albanians established or repopulated several communities — Piana degli Albanesi, Contessa Entellina, Mezzojuso and others — where they reintroduced the Greek Orthodox faith, which in Italy was eventually absorbed into the Roman Catholic Church as an Eastern Rite. These towns, and Palermo's Martorana Church (built for the Greek Orthodox community in the twelfth century), are well-known for their religious festivals, especially around Easter, but they also preserve Arberesh, the medieval Tosk dialect of the Albanian language.

The Jews of Sicily: On the advice of the Inquisition, in 1492 the King of Spain enacted the infamous Edict of Expulsion (the "Alhambra Decree") dissolving Sicily's Jewish communities in 1493. Many Jews left while some converted to Catholicism. Their visible traces are rather few, but the mikveh of Siracusa, in that city's Jewish Quarter, is the oldest such structure known to exist in Europe.

The next chapter more precisely places these civilizations into the flow of history.

CHAPTER 2

A Historical Outline

Our focus is the Middle Ages, but no epoch invents itself. It is the result of that which precedes it. For that reason, we shall begin this survey, and our Chronology, in the mists of antiquity. What follows is by necessity concise, a synopsis. Sicily's medieval history is considered in much greater detail in subsequent chapters.

The World's Island

Sicily's earliest art dates from circa 9000 BC (BCE), when the drawings at Levanzo in the Aegadian Islands, and Addaura, outside Palermo, were rendered in caves overlooking the Mediterranean coast.

To the Romans, the Mediterranean was the sea at "the middle of the world," which, loosely translated, is what *Mediterranean* means. In time, Sicily became even more central than its location might otherwise imply.

The peopling of the Mediterranean lands began tens of thousands of years ago, when the last dwarf elephants roamed Sicily, but only in the last eight or nine thousand did it get interesting. That was when the introduction of agriculture in the Fertile Crescent led to the establishment of large "sedentary" settlements, as opposed to those based primarily on hunting and gathering.

In the Mediterranean region, some of the earliest known to us are in Anatolia in Asia Minor, where stone structures and carvings survive from as early as 9000 BC (BCE), the end of the Pleistocene. Sicily boasts no monumentality so significant as the megalithic temples and sculpture at Turkey's Göbekli Tepe, which saw hunter-gatherers become farmers in the so-called Neolithic Revolution. In Sicily the only things of note that survive from the Neolithic are a few dolmens and some interesting stone jewelry. The first Sicilian megalithic temples, as we shall see, were constructed some time later on Malta.

Agriculture's sedentism planted the seeds of social change because it left more time for the development of intellectual pursuits, including the evolution of writing systems, eventually ushering in the Bronze Age. The inception of writing was not immediate, nor was it universal. The societies of many of the Germanic, Celtic and Asiatic peoples on the fringes of the decaying Roman Empire were to some extent migratory, or at all events geographically de-centralized, and at first only a few had their own writing systems, the majority eventually relying on Latin for written communica-tion. This is one reason among many for the dearth of informa-tion about the Vandals and Huns compared to our voluminous knowledge of the Egyptians and Greeks.

Ancient historicity is sometimes open to question. Philistus, Timaeus, Diodorus Siculus and other Greek historians fash-ioned their own ideas about the origins of Sicily's "indigenous" peoples. Replete with hyperbole — Theocritus was a poet first and a historian second — their early accounts are not lacking in literary merit, and should not be dismissed out-of-hand, but they are now augmented by reliable scientific studies. Archeology, population genetics and other disciplines have disproved some of the ideas advanced by these ancient historians. Such an ob-servation may seem mundane, even quaint, but it is amazing that so many misconceptions about, in particular, the Sicanians and Elymians persist despite the research of the last few decades.

The Earliest Sicilians

The Sicanians were the earliest indigenous inhabitants whose society can be identified with a specific culture, circa 1600 BC (BCE). By 1200 BC they shared the island with the Italic *Sikeloi* (Sikels) in the east and the Elymians in the northwest. With the arrival of the Greeks, these peoples were absorbed in every way into Hellenistic society — first the Elymians, then the Sikels and, after some initial reluctance, the Sicanians. What traces did they leave behind?

Beginning around 4000 BC (BCE) the Sicanians' remote forebears (the Proto Sicanians) built Europe's first megalithic temples in Malta, where they appear to have invented the simple wheel, a stone cylinder fitted to a semicylindrical groove carved into a stone block.

We know very little about Malta's temple builders or their language, but around 2200 BC they abandoned the Maltese islands (which were later recolonized in the Punic era), apparently resettling in southeastern Sicily. Through these inventive Proto Sicanians, the Sicilians can lay a plausible claim to having the oldest society in Europe to be identified continuously from megalithic times until the modern era.

Erected about three thousand years after Malta's first megalithic structures, the mountaintop temple overlooking Cefalù is Sicanian. Upon it the Greeks built their "Temple of Artemis," leaving only the base of the original edifice. The Sikelian necropoli at Pantalica are at least as ancient, dating from 1200 BC or earlier. It is generally believed that there was a thriving Sicanian village at the site of Palermo when the Phoenicians arrived.

The seafaring Sikels are occasionally, though perhaps unreliably, identified with the Shikelish tribe of the "Sea Peoples" who attacked Egypt around 1220 BC.

The Contested Isle

The first "Greeks" to reach Sicily were the Mycenaeans and Minoans, before 1500 BC, but they didn't stay long and it seems that trade, not colonization, was their main reason for visiting. The Ausonians, an Italic people, had contact with the Aeolian Islands and Sicily's northeastern coasts. At some time not long after 800 BC, the Greeks and Phoenicians began to seriously consider settling the island, the former as an expansion of their crowded, if disunited, homeland, the latter as an extension of their vast trading network. The Phoenicians may have set up trading posts in western Sicily as early as 750 BC, though this date is a matter of contention and Motya could have already been established by that time. When most of Phoenicia itself fell to the Chaldean (or Neo-Babylonian) Empire in 612 BC, Carthage became the heir of her civilization in the central Mediterranean.

The Egyptian influence on Punic art and architecture is both logical and significant. In Sicily such Phoenician — or perhaps Egyptian — items as gold signet rings have been found, while the carvings in numerous Phoenician limestone *stelae* and terracotta *protomes* discovered on Motya bear a striking similarity to those of Egypt.

The Greeks founded Naxos, near Taormina, in 735 BC, followed by Catania, Syracuse (Siracusa), Gela, Akragas (Agrigento) and numerous smaller settlements. In the next three centuries, Sicily and the southern part of the Italian peninsula would be colonized by Greeks, earning the region the name *Magna Graecia* (Greater Greece) because it boasted more Greeks — and probably more Greek temples — than Greece itself. This was, of course, a Latin name; to the Greeks it was *Megara Hellas.*

Meanwhile, the Carthaginians took control of the Elymians' city of Eryx (Erice) and expanded the settlements established by their Phoenician forebears at Zis (Palermo) and Solus (Solunto), while further developing the port at Motya (Mozia) near Lilybaeum (now Marsala). Here the dates known to us are approximate at best, but it is clear that by 500 BC Punic civilization was Carthaginian, its focus the central and western Mediterranean.

Around this time a mint began operating at Zis, its coinage bearing the city's Punic name. With commerce came prosperity. Not every trading colony boasted its own mint, and contemporary Greek commentators regarded Carthage as the "wealthiest city in the world." Whereas previously the Greeks were content to coexist with Carthage, they now began to see the thriving metropolis and its growing empire as rivals.

It didn't help matters that the Carthaginians — like their Phoenician predecessors — had occasionally sided with other nations against the Greeks. The worst case was the series of Persian Wars fought between 499 and 450 BC. Truth be told, even in the best of times turning one Greek city against another was never very difficult. Indeed, the rivalry between Athens and Sparta has become a historical metaphor.

Although it has sometimes been described rather simplistically by historians, the relationship between the Punic societies and the various Greek city-states of the eastern Mediterranean was a complicated one. It should be remembered that Greek culture was dominant in that region (by 305 BC the ruling dynasty of Egypt was Greek) until it was overpowered, or one might say "integrated," by Rome. Yet even the Greek alphabet was patterned after that of the Phoenicians, whose surviving histories have — unfortunately — been written by their enemies. Greeks and Carthaginians alike viewed "underpopulated" Sicily as part of a "new world" to be developed.

Life in the Greek city-states could be enlightened, even democratic, but it was punctuated by periods of deleterious chaos.

Not always inappropriately, civic leaders were called *tyrants*.

Agathocles was one of the worst examples, while Dion was one of the best. But Greek Sicily also had playwrights like Aeschylus, poets like Stesichorus and philosophers such as Gorgias of Leontinoi (Lentini) and Empedocles of Akragas.

The Persian Wars presented an opportunity for the Carthaginians to encroach upon contested Greek territories in Sicily while occupying strategic stepping stones such as Malta. In 480 BC the Carthaginians, encouraged to war by Xerxes of Persia who was fighting his way into Greece, were defeated by Gelon of Syracuse at the first Battle of Himera, near today's Termini Imerese. Meanwhile, the Persians themselves were defeated at the fateful Battle of Salamis off the Greek coast.

The crushing Carthaginian defeat at Himera was especially bitter because the cosmopolitan colony, founded by Greeks some two hundred years earlier, had once been regarded as a community friendly to the Carthaginians. The Greeks of Sicily were rarely a unified federation; Selinus (Selinunte) was known to side with the Carthaginians against the Greeks of eastern Sicily. The Greeks' Himeran victory did not bring an end to their wars with the Carthaginians — a series of smaller battles followed — which the Romans were to inherit and continue in the form of the infamous Punic Wars.

For now, the Italic societies to the north of *Megara Hellas* were little more than a side show on a wider Mediterranean stage dominated by Greeks and Carthaginians. The Syracusans' naval victory at Cumae in 474 BC relegated the Etruscans to a secondary status in the regional power structure. The Greeks recognized that the Punic civilization to the south was more problematic.

Yet pockets of resistance to Greek hegemony remained even in eastern Sicily, where the Sikel leader called "Ducetius" (probably not his actual name) led a revolt of his people in 452 BC; he died a Hellenized citizen in 440.

Siceliots

The Sicilian cities also faced challenges from other Greeks far from Sicilian shores. The Athenians invaded eastern Sicily during the Peloponnesian War but were defeated at Syracuse in 413 BC. Sicily, and particularly Syracuse, remained important in the Greek world. Visiting Syracuse in 398, Plato declared that his Utopia could best be imagined, if not actually realized, in Sicily.

It was the Greeks, not the Carthaginians, whose mythology and folklore would exert the greatest influence on Sicily, and Sicily's museums (as well as Britain's) are filled with religious artefacts and statues reflecting the important culture whose language, philosophy and law came to form the very under-pinnings of Western civilization.

Greek myths associate the cult of Demeter, goddess of grain, with the city of Enna, high in the mountains of central Sicily; her daughter, Persephone, was abducted in a valley nearby. The Cyclops, the single-eyed monster that menaced Odysseus (and later Aeneas), is identified with Mount Etna. Scylla and Charybdis threatened the intrepid Odysseus at the Strait of Messina, which Hercules is said to have swum and the Argonauts are said to have sailed. When Daedalus fled Crete, it was in Sicily that he found refuge with King Kokalos of the Sicanians, an equally mythological figure. And when Artemis changed Arethusa into a spring of water to escape the river god Alpheus, the beautiful maiden emerged on the island of Ortygia, in Syracuse, where a freshwater pool bears her name.

Rome's First Province

Finally, the greatest threat to Greek Italy was to come not from Greece to the east or Carthage to the south, but from a rising power in the north. By 262 BC, the Greeks had begun to make peace with the Romans, who were eager to annex Sicily as the Empire's first province. They eventually succeeded, but only after much bloodshed in a series of wars.

The Romans were likely to invade Sicily and Tunisia sooner or later, but in the event their pretext was the Mamertine conflict. The Mamertines were Italic mercenaries hired by the Tyrant Agathocles of Syracuse. In 288 BC these skilled soldiers occupied Messina, killing the men and taking the women as wives. They were eventually subdued by the Syracusans under the Tyrant Hiero II at Mylae (Milazzo). Malcontent under Greek domination, the Mamertines appealed to both Rome and Carthage for help. Carthage responded first, negotiating with Hiero on behalf of the Mamertines, the compromise being that a Carthaginian garrison would remain in the region — though in fact it did not stay for long.

Rome could not long tolerate Carthaginian influence in northeastern Sicily, within striking distance of the Italian peninsula, and sent troops to occupy the region in 264 BC. Thus began the First Punic War, rooted in unfounded enmities as much as legitimate political concerns.

Unlike the earlier Peloponnesian War (431-404 BC), in which Sicily was at best a peripheral player (at least geographically), the island found itself pivotal in this protracted conflict between Romans and Carthaginians, even though Italian and Iberian territories, as well as Corsica and Sardinia, were also involved. To say that much was at stake would be a gross understatement. Indeed, the power that emerged victorious from the Punic Wars would determine the fate of the Mediterranean for centuries to come.

Several of the most decisive battles were fought in Sicily, a few resulting in the occupation of predominantly Greek areas as a pretext for ousting the Carthaginians, a little like destroying a living tree to rid it of a colony of termites feasting on a dead bough. From a strategic point of view, some of these attacks were more justified than others. Akragas (Agrigento) and its environs, for example, had fallen under Carthaginian control. Fearing its use as a military base, the Romans besieged the city in 262. With the defeat of the Carthaginian garrison at this metropolis, a large swathe of the island became Roman, leaving Syracuse as the only major Siceliot city in Greek hands.

What followed was an interminable series of battles for the island's western coastal cities, some of which had been founded by the Phoenicians. In most cases the Romans were initially repulsed, only to return by land and sea.

In 254, Punic Zis (Panormos or Palermo) fell to Roman forces, refusing to return to the Carthaginian fold seven years later at the urging of Hamilcar Barca, who waged guerrilla warfare to the west, around Trapani (Drepanum), Marsala (Lilybaeum) and Erice (Eryx), centers that fell to Rome definitively in 241. Among his troops were Celts, Gauls, Iberians and other peoples disaffected by the Romans.

The Romans' subjugation of the eastern regions took decades, setting a precedent for the kind of plodding, piecemeal conquest which would so bedevil medieval conquerors like the Arabs and Normans.

The defeat of Syracuse in 212 was the *coup de grâce*. While characteristically deep in thought, Archimedes, the brilliant mathematician and engineer — Syracusan by birth and one of the greatest minds of antiquity — was killed by a Roman soldier as the troops ravaged the city.

By defeating the Carthaginian leader Hannibal in 201, the ambitious Romans began to consolidate their influence in the central and western Mediterranean.

"Carthago delenda est," famously railed Cato the Elder. "Carthage must be destroyed." Cato, who spent time in Sicily,

didn't live to see the city he abhorred finally annihilated, razed to the ground by the Roman general Scipio Aemilianus following a battle in 146 BC.

But the end of the Punic Wars, and Rome's emergence as the predominant Mediterranean power, didn't mean that the island in the sun, the Empire's granary, was free from civil strife.

Diodorus Siculus recounts the story of Eunus, a slave of Syrian birth, leading a revolt in the Sicilian heartland beginning in 139 BC, occupying the area between Enna and Agrigento, where he was joined by another slave leader named Cleon. Seizing territories as far east as the Ionian coast and Taormina, their followers eventually numbered some fifteen thousand, and by some accounts even more. This formidable force defeated an army hastily mustered by the praetor Hypsaeus. It took a Roman legion, led by the consul Rupilius, to finally subdue them in 132, beginning at Taormina. A second revolt, this time under Salvius, broke out in 104 BC in the western region around Segesta.

Historians disagree about the causes of these revolts, apart from the abominable institution of slavery itself, something generally accepted in ancient times. The conflicts may have been an indirect consequence of changes in Sicilian property ownership in the wake of the expulsion of Carthaginian landlords during the Punic Wars. Not only did many native Sicilians become rich almost overnight, but Roman property speculators rushed to Sicily and purchased vast holdings for almost nothing, bringing thousands of farming slaves with them (and in the process destroying many of the forests of the interior). The slaves were treated miserably, and numerous problems ensued, culminating in these bloody "Servile Wars."

Sicilian by birth, the cruel Damophilus of Enna enjoyed the privileged Roman lifestyle and mistreated his slaves, who killed him on his own estate. Not far away, Piazza Armerina's

Roman villa (described below), though built much later, lends us an impression of the luxurious ambience of the homes of these greedy landholders.

Under Rome, Sicily was to experience an unprecedented level of exploitation by a ruling class rife with corruption. In 70 BC Cicero was called to Sicily to argue against the island's corrupt governor, Gaius Verres, who fled following the opening remarks of the great orator. The trial itself is little more than a footnote to history, but Cicero's lengthy indictment of the governor contains useful descriptions of the Sicily of those times.

There was further unrest under the occupation of the island by Sextus, Pompey's son, in 44 BC, during the civil war that followed the assassination of Julius Caesar. After the defeat of Sextus in 36 BC, Octavian levied heavy taxes on Sicily.

Serious as these problems were, Roman Sicily was prosperous and still largely Greek in customs, culture and language. Only during the reign of Augustus was a serious attempt made to introduce the Latin tongue to any meaningful extent, and then only among the privileged classes — the ruling elite and immigrants from Rome.

Around AD (CE) 59, Paul of Tarsus stopped at Syracuse to preach *en route* to Rome, and Greek was the language he spoke. There were already a few Jewish communities in Sicily, and a few followers of arcane sects and philosophers, but mythology was still the official religion.

Christianity made its first lasting inroads into Sicily sometime after AD 200, and a number of Sicilians were martyred in the century to follow: Agatha at Catania in AD 251 and, during Diocletian's persecution of Christians beginning in 303, Lucy at Syracuse. The cathedral of Syracuse is the archetypal example of a Greek temple converted into a church, and this became commonplace throughout the Empire as Christianity took hold.

In 313, Emperor Constantine lifted the prohibition against Christians as the Roman Empire shifted its focus to the East, to Greece and what is now Turkey. Thanks to its Roman legalization, Christianity, which had become Armenia's official religion in 301, spread rapidly across the Mediterranean during the next two centuries. Sicily's prosperity, with Syracuse as its cornerstone, continued unabated. A material symbol of that wealth is the "Villa del Casale," a lavish residence resplendent with mosaic pavements built outside Piazza Armerina between 330 and 360. The identity of its owner is the subject of much speculation.

In 330 Constantinople (previously Byzantium) became the capital of the Roman Empire, and five decades later Christianity became its official religion. In 378 a Roman army was defeated at the Battle of Adrianople — the Goths had been forced into Roman territory by the invading Huns — but this localized military failure at a remote eastern outpost was not immediately catastrophic for the Empire, which effectively split in 395. The eastern half, which did not initially include Sicily, survived in one form or another as the "Byzantine Empire" until 1453, a year considered by many historians to mark the end of the Middle Ages.

Barbarians

What signalled the beginning of the medieval era? So-called "Barbarian" invasions ensued as Vandals and Goths vied for control of Sicily and the Italian peninsula, though during the first stage of invasions of the island the raiders remained, at most, for a few years at a time. Like the ancient Greeks, the Goths were divided into subgroups. They came to be known as the Ostrogoths (who occupied Sicily) and the Visigoths (who settled in what are now Spain and France).

Modern scholars generally agree that there was no single reason or cause for the fall of the Roman Empire, no sole weakness or shortcoming. Rather, Rome's overextended dominion, like any other, could not respond to continuous, simultaneous assaults from every direction — often from peoples it had trained and educated in the arts of war and in every other way. Yet the old cliché that the Empire "destroyed itself from within" bears a kernel of truth.

Sicily's Gothic-Vandalic period lasted less than a hundred years, but it represented a bridge from Antiquity to the Middle Ages.

In 410, Alaric's Visigoths sacked Rome (by then the capital was Ravenna), and the "Western" Empire's precipitous Decline hastened. In 440 the Sicilians saw the first Vandal landings on Sicily under Genseric, but the rival Ostrogoths were masters of the island by 491.

"History is written by the victors" only when they have a written language. Yet it would be inaccurate and unfair to characterize the Vandals and Goths as "backward" peoples. In fact, they absorbed much learning from the Romans, who had made several attempts to assimilate some of their communities into Roman society, where the Huns were considered still more "foreign." But like the history of the Celts and Picts, theirs has been written chiefly by the Romans.

As the Western Roman Empire dissolved, Sicily's socio-economic situation improved, for there were fewer taxes to be paid and fewer intrusions in local affairs. But the island could claim no strident leaders during this period, no stirrings of nativist sentiment, no spirit of independence. The Dark Ages had begun.

The Byzantine Island

Ascending the Byzantine throne (as "Roman" Emperor)

in 527, Justinian already had his eye on Italy. Nobody in Constantinople seemed willing to assent to a jewel — and a territory of strategic importance to commercial shipping — like Sicily remaining in Ostrogoth hands. In 534 the Byzantine general Belisarius defeated the Vandals at Carthage and the following year he expelled the Ostrogoths from Sicily. The island was now officially part of the Eastern Roman, or "Byzantine," Empire. The Christian Church in Sicily fell under the direct jurisdiction of Constantinople. It would remain so for some five centuries.

But the hardy Goths did not succumb easily. The Ostrogoth leader Totila raided Sicily in 550 in an attempt to reclaim it for his people. This occupation — if it could be called that — was short-lived, actually little more than a lengthy incursion. Totila's defeat by Byzantine forces at the Battle of Taginae two years later signalled the end of Gothic influence in Italy. The next wave of northern invaders, the Longobards, who became Italy's Lombards, stayed longer.

The Byzantines eventually gained control over much of Calabria, Apulia and Basilicata. Their main sphere of influence was Italy's Adriatic coast. Ravenna and Venice were briefly in Byzantine hands, an influence reflected in the splendid mosaics of their cathedrals.

The Longobards invaded Italy *en masse* in 568 following Byzantine victories over the Ostrogoths in the Gothic War. They handily confiscated rural areas, where they introduced something vaguely resembling rudimentary feudalism. The Byzantines, for their part, were generally content to rule the more important centers, leaving the rest for the Lombards, but over the next few centuries there were occasional conflicts.

However, the decisive factor in Byzantine military strategy at this time had little to do with politics. For a generation or two, the problem was raising troops. An epidemic of bubonic plague in 541 decimated the population of the Byzantine Empire, rendering a reconquest of Italy from the Goths — and then the Longobards — all but impossible.

Significantly, the bishops in the Byzantine territories, and even in many of the Lombard ones, were under the ecclesial jurisdiction of the Patriarch of Constantinople, not the Pope of Rome. Equally important, the Byzantine cities implemented the Code of Justinian while in the Longobardic lands, at least initially, a form of Germanic law was enforced.

Sudden changes in government can be traumatic to the general populace, but in certain respects the Goths and even the Vandals — who were more than familiar with both Christianity and Roman culture — retained some of the fundamental institutions of Roman life in Sicily. Theodoric, who controlled much of Italy, left Sicily virtually undisturbed while seizing vast chunks of territory on the peninsula. To a great extent the invaders had to rely on the local Sicilian hierarchy for civil control of remote towns and rural estates. For most people the transition from Roman to Vandalic to Gothic to Byzantine rule brought few obvious changes to everyday life although, as we have said, there were at first fewer taxes. Agriculture, trades, worship and commerce continued as before, even if authority seemed less centralized than that of the Romans.

While the Lombardic regions of Italy were undergoing the shift toward feudalism, Byzantine territories like Sicily retained a social and economic order more akin to the Roman model, at least for a time. Compared to the intellectual darkness that enveloped most of Europe, Constantinople was a beacon of learning and prosperity.

The Lombards never conquered Sicily, but some arrived with the Normans in the eleventh century.

Under the Byzantine Greeks there was no question of the Church in Sicily being anything but Eastern. Moses Finley cogently stated as much in his *History of Sicily* when he wrote that, "by the second half of the seventh century the Sicilian Church was Eastern in every important respect, including the liturgy and ceremonies."

In 652 a small Arab force landed in Sicily but soon departed. Mohammed had died in 632, and the Muslims' greatest assault on the island was yet to come. For now, the northern Africans in Sicily were traders. The Emperor Constans transferred his capital to Syracuse for a few years beginning in 660. His main motive for the move was to establish a base for a Byzantine reconquest of peninsular Italy from the Lombards, but the fact that he considered the Sicilian city sufficiently important to substitute for Constantinople says much for its cultural and economic wealth.

Yes, Byzantine culture was an island of civility in an uncivilized age. Today we associate mosaics and other art with the Byzantines, but their society was much more than this, preserving much Roman and Greek learning in a changing world. Although we have no reliable figures, such evidence as can be garnered suggests that general literacy in Sicily under the Byzantine Greeks was higher than in most of Europe and that it increased further under the Arabs.

The Fatimid Emirate

Islam was the impetus for the spread of Arab power from east to west across northern Africa. The most popular modern definition of "Arab," which places any native speaker of Arabic in the same ethnic category, rings as slightly simplistic to the ears of the medievalist. But Arabic is the language of the Koran, and in its earliest years Islam was inextricably linked to Arab culture. It was also a case of the Arabs having a written language, while some of the peoples they conquered did not.

Around 670 the Arabs founded Kairouan (Qayrawan), considered the first Muslim city of northern Africa, and by 700 the place we now call Tunisia was almost entirely under Muslim Arab influence. Before long the great majority of Tunisians had converted to Islam and Arabic was the language that united them, but they were the descendants of Berbers, Carthaginians, Romans and even Vandals. For this reason, identifying the medieval Tunisians (or even the Moroccans) generically as "Arabs" is something of a simplification. Whatever one chooses to call them, there is no doubt that these peoples flourished as part of a larger Arab society.

The Muslims invaded Spain in 711, and Charles Martel stopped them at Tours in 732. Some years would pass before an invasion of Sicily was to be seriously contemplated.

In 827 Asad ibn al-Furat sailed from Tunisia with over ten thousand Arab and Berber troops, landing at Mazara in the western part of the island. Impressive as it was, this campaign was the result of Byzantine machinations and treachery as much as Arab ambitions. Euphemius, a Byzantine admiral and resident Governor of Sicily, found himself at odds with his Emperor, Michael II, and was exiled, so he offered the governorship of the island to Ziyadat Allah, the Aghlabid Emir of Kairouan, in exchange for his support. Euphemius was soon killed — reportedly by Byzantine soldiers in Sicily — and Sicily's Arab period began.

Predictably, the Arabs met less resistance in the western part of the island than they would encounter in the east. In 831 Bal'harm (Palermo) was occupied by the Aghlabids, who came to refer to the city informally as "medina" and made it their seat of power in Sicily. By the time the Normans arrived in 1071 it was the capital of one of three *de facto* emirates in Sicily, although the powerful Fatimids had wanted the island to be ruled by a single emir of the succeeding Kalbid dynasty.

This reflected a number of changes from the *status quo ante*. For over a thousand years Syracuse had been the island's most important city. Henceforth that distinction was to be reserved for Palermo.

There were several reasons for the preference of Palermo as the island's capital. It was closer than Syracuse to the Aghlabids' Tunisian capital, and farther away from the potentially troublesome Byzantines. Coming from the east, a Byzantine attack on the Syracuse area, such as the one launched by Maniakes two centuries later, would leave time to notify Palermo of an attempted invasion.

By 903 the Arabs (or "Saracens") controlled all of Sicily, and Islam was the official religion. They tolerated Christianity and Judaism in Sicily, without encouraging either. In Sicily, the Saracens were rulers rather than colonizers, masters rather than leaders. Because Islamic law could be harsh to non-believers, many Christians converted, though precise numbers are not known and in the northeastern part of the island there were Byzantine monasteries throughout the thirteenth century. However, it must be said that Arab society and culture were advanced; under the Saracens Palermo's splendor was said to rival that of Baghdad.

There were occasional conflicts between the predominantly Arab populations of Palermo, Marsala and Trapani, who controlled the island, and the Berbers who had settled in Agrigento and Sciacca to the south. To a great extent, these violent Berber revolts mirrored the situation in Tunisia, and worsened with Fatimid rule after 909. They were, in effect, anti-Fatimid riots tantamount to a localized civil war that ended only following a siege at Agrigento in 938.

Some years later, however, Emir Hassan al-Kalbi was killed during fighting at Rometta. This may have been an isolated Byzantine revolt, but the arrival of thousands of troops from Constantinople in 964 suggests, instead, that Rometta was the last city in Sicily to fall to the Arabs. Its very name means "fortress," from the Greek *erymata*.

The Aghlabids were Sunnis, a fact that influenced their legal system, but their Fatimid and Kalbid successors were Shiites.

The Arabs introduced mulberries (for silk making), oranges, rice and sugar cane. They built *kanats* under Palermo. Chess was played, Europe's first paper was made, and Hindu-Arabic numerals were used. Some of these developments originated in the Far East, but it was the Arabs who brought them to Europe and the Mediterranean.

It seemed inevitable that the Aghlabids would take control of strategic Malta, and they did so, if belatedly, in 870; the Normans would seize it in 1091, initially leaving the local Arab rulers in control.

The Fatimids moved their capital to Egypt in 948, delegating the administration of Sicily to the local Kalbids. In 967 Cairo, one of the most important Muslim-Arab cities, was founded by a Sicilian, Jawhar al-Siqilli, in the name of the Fatimids.

In Sicily today there are few visible traces of purely Islamic or Arab art and architecture — the syncretic Norman-Arab style being more evident — but the museum at Termini Imerese houses the stone Arabic inscriptions from some ninth-century Saracen palaces while Palermo's archeology museum also has some interesting Arab finds. However, Arab culinary culture lives on in the traditional Sicilian cuisine we know today. Panella (chickpea fritters), rice balls (arancine), cassata, cannoli, caponata (but without tomatoes), the stuffed herring fillets called "beccafico," and the fruity ice creams similar to sorbet all began their delicious existence in Sicily during the Arab period. Sicily's colorful street markets are part of the tradition of the Arab *souk*. One of these, Palermo's Ballarò, is still known by a variant of the Arabic name it bore a thousand years ago.

The Arabs were prolific. They founded or resettled numerous fortified towns around Sicily. Most obviously, places whose names begin with *cal* or *calta* bear the mark of Arabic: Caltagirone, Caltabellotta, Caltanissetta, Calascibetta, Calamonaci, Caltavuturo, Calatafimi. Also in this category are places whose names begin with derivatives of *gebal* (Gibilmanna, Gibellina) and *recal* (Regalbuto, Racalmuto). This expansion, and the fact that wealthier Muslims could take more than one wife, explains how Sicily's population doubled during the few centuries of Arab rule. There were also many conversions to Islam, especially of young Greek-Byzantine women marrying comparatively affluent Muslim men. These facile conversions reflect the fact that in the Mediterranean many of the social differences between Muslims, Christians and Jews were fairly subtle well into the Middle Ages. Not for nothing did visitors such as Abdullah al Idrisi and bin Jubayr observe that the vast majority of Sicilian women dressed in a similar style which both chroniclers described as the "Muslim" fashion; in fact some kind of veil was traditional among Sicily's Jews and Christians as well as its Arabs.

By the middle of the eleventh century the island's populace was divided about equally between Muslims and Christians, with Jews constituting the remaining population, less than a tenth of the total.

Land ownership was generally based on "smallholding," which is to say that most properties were large farms owned by the people who worked the land, while areas such as larger forests appertained to the emirate. Water rights were strictly controlled; rivers and lakes belonged to the government.

Arab society had its peculiarities for those who were not Muslim. Christians and Jews were taxed more heavily than Muslims, especially by the Kalbids, and there were restrictions on the number of new churches and synagogues that could be built (Palermo's cathedral and some other churches were converted to mosques). Church bells could not be rung, and Christians could not read aloud from the Bible within earshot of Muslims or display large crosses in public. Christians and

Jews could not drink wine in public, though Muslims sometimes did so in private — something the Normans observed
in the Nebrodi Mountains during the eleventh century. Jews
and Christians had to stand when Muslims entered a room and
make way for them in the souks, streets and other public
places. In Arab Sicily there was harmony and tolerance if not
absolute equality.

Following the death of Hasan as-Samsam in 1053 three
warring emirs divided control of Sicily. Ibn al Hawas ruled
northeastern Sicily (Val Demone) from Kasr'Janni (Enna), Ibn
at Timnah ruled southeastern Sicily (Val di Noto) from Syracuse and Catania, and Abdullah ibn Hawqal ruled western
Sicily (Val di Mazara), a region which included Bal'harm, from
Trapani and Mazara. During this period of political chaos and
localised power struggles the title of *emir* came to be abused,
occasionally usurped by leaders of large towns, hence when
the Normans conquered the capital in early 1072 there was a
nominal "Emir of Bal'harm" (Palermo) resident in the Favara
palace in what is now the city's Brancaccio district.

The Cosmopolitan Kingdom

The conflict among Sicily's jealous emirs prompted one of
them into contact with a band of Europeans set on the conquest of Sicily. The Normans had been in Italy for decades, as
mercenaries fighting battles for Byzantine, Lombard or Papal
patrons. From 1038 to 1043, they found themselves with the
Byzantine general George Maniakes during his brief occupation of parts of eastern Sicily. In addition to the Normans, the
Norse Varangian Guard was present, led by Harald Hardrada.

The Normans liked what they saw in Sicily, and in light of
the Great Schism of 1054 — which divided Christianity into
the "Roman" Catholic and "Greek" Orthodox churches —
Pope Nicholas II, a Frenchman who enjoyed a good rapport

with the Normans in Italy, made it understood that he wanted the island in Latin hands rather than Byzantine ones. This was not the only political consequence of the Schism, but it was the one most immediately shaped by it. Of course, Nicholas also wanted the Muslims ousted, or at least converted to Catholicism, and he made it known that the Normans could have as much of the island as they could wrest from its Arab masters, on condition that they pledge the Church in Sicily to Rome instead of Constantinople.

Only rarely are men-at-arms men of God. The Pope's offer meant that the landless knights from Normandy could have their own lands, and to win them they need only seize power from a few Arabs — and along with them perhaps a few stubborn Byzantine Greeks like Bishop Nicodemus of Palermo. It sounded simple. In fact, the conquests of the world's most contested island had never been too easy for any invader, and the Normans' experience would prove no different. Nevertheless, the temptation was too great to resist, and any questionable commitments to the Papacy could always be negotiated anew once the conquest was complete. Such was the way of the Middle Ages.

In 1061, a Norman lord named Robert de Hauteville crossed the Strait of Messina with his brothers and several hundred knights from Normandy, Lombardy and Southern Italy, defeating the local Arab garrison and establishing a foothold under cover of darkness. Unlike their Viking forebears, the Normans were unaccustomed to naval combat; even the transport of horses proved challenging. Apart from more immediate concerns, the conquest of Messina against Arab foes would serve as the blueprint for the battle at Hastings against the Saxons a few years later, and several knights actually fought at both battles.

This was Robert's second attempt to land at Messina. Though it was successful, Palermo was still far away. It was captured a decade later following another epic battle by land and sea. When the fighting was over, Sicily was again part of Europe.

In the wake of this Norman conquest, most Arabs remained, for Sicily was the only home they had ever known. A few, like the poet ibn Hamdis, who was born at Noto around 1056, chose to emigrate rather than be ruled by Christians.

At the time, anybody who might have suggested that an unruly band of brigands from Normandy could establish Europe's first truly multicultural society would have been dismissed as insane. Yet that is exactly what occurred in 1071. It was the beginning of medieval Europe's greatest social experiment.

Styled "Count of Sicily" by his knights and "Emir of Emirs" by the Arabs, Robert's younger brother, Roger, brought to his new dominion a complex, versatile feudal system. His rule also brought with it increased religious freedom, greater artistic expression and a sovereign government. There was little actual serfdom as that institution was understood in most of Europe, and even less slavery. There were mosques, synagogues and plenty of churches, English bishops and Saracen imams. The Sicilians who didn't speak Greek or Arabic spoke Norman French, and court decrees were issued in several languages, including Latin, Greek and Arabic. Benedictine monks worked alongside Muslim scribes. The Normans accepted certain Byzantine, Jewish and Muslim legal practices; Islamic law as it then existed in Sicily was fairly sophisticated, and there is evidence that it was exported to England to form the basis of early common law.

Count Roger's son, known to us as Roger II, was crowned King of Sicily in 1130 and ruled a dominion that included Sicily, most of Italy south of Rome, a piece of the Tunisian coast and some territories across the Adriatic, with Palermo as his capital. It was the wealthiest realm of Europe, whose monarch wore Byzantine robes in the manner of an Eastern Emperor and kept a private harem in the style of an Arab emir. A mosaic in Palermo's Martorana Church depicts Roger, clad in Byzantine garb, accepting his crown directly from Christ.

Roger's grandson, William II, whose mother and regent was the erudite, politically savvy Margaret of Navarre, wed Joan, daughter of Henry II of England. His cathedral complex at Monreale is the perfect synchronicity and symbiosis of Byzantine, Arab and Norman art, where a mosaic icon of Thomas Becket is the earliest holy image of the English saint.

Universal legal codes such as Roger's *Assizes of Ariano* were eventually introduced toward the middle of the twelfth century, but until then the Normans permitted each Sicilian — Christian, Muslim, Jew — to be judged by his own law. It would not be an exaggeration to describe the Kingdom of Sicily during the reign of Roger II as the most important realm of Europe and the Mediterranean, intellectually as well as politically. This halcyon era was a prosperous one. The royal revenues from Palermo alone exceeded those of all England.

As promised before the Sicilian conquest, feudalism was gradually introduced as estates were given to Norman knights and the allied Lombards (and others) who came to Sicily with them. Such an *ad vitam* and *ad personam* fief was meant to revert to the Crown following the death of its holder, but it became common practice to transmit these estates to male heirs. These men followed in their fathers' footsteps, becoming enfeoffed knights and (later) barons and lords. Here we find the early divergence of traditions — the Normans left their fiefs to their eldest sons as universal heirs while the Lombards divided their fiefs among all sons as heirs general. There were never very many Sicilian serfs tied to the land, though records survive which make it clear that at least a few were.

Sicily became a springboard for the Crusades, even if relatively few Sicilian knights participated in those undertaken during the twelfth century. Joan's brother, Richard Lionheart, came through Messina — which by now had eclipsed Syracuse as the island's second most important city — in 1190 *en route* to Palestine for the Third Crusade. The heart of Louis IX of France is preserved in Monreale Abbey, along the route to (and from) the Tunisian Crusade he undertook in 1270.

The Third Crusade occasioned the early use of heraldry, the practice of knights emblazoning their shields and surcoats with colorful symbols, called *coats of arms,* for easier identification during combat or tournaments when their faces were concealed by helmets. The practice, which came to entail a great deal of elitism and snobbery, seems to have begun at some point during the third quarter of the twelfth century. By 1200 it was widespread in western Europe, arriving a bit late in Sicily. Armorial insignia remained popular for centuries, engraved in sealing rings or carved above the doors of castles and other aristocratic residences. Coats of arms are seen on many Sicilian coins minted after 1200. The earliest royal heraldry was based on symbols already in use by specific dynasties — the Norman lion, the Swabian eagle, the Angevin fleur de lis — but most knights displayed either simple geometric designs or heraldic symbols allusive to their surnames (themselves rare outside the nobility until the fifteenth century). A knight named *Oliveri* might display an olive tree, while a man named *Arezzo* might display a hedgehog (rizzo).

Bin Jubayr described Sicily at length. The geographer Abdullah al Idrisi travelled across the island and authored what may be considered its first travel guide. He observed that castles had sprung up everywhere. Benjamin of Tudela described Sicily's Jewish communities and much more.

The Emperor Kings

In 1198 the very young Frederick II von Hohenstaufen succeeded his father, Emperor Henry VI, to the Throne of

Sicily. The Swabian dynasty were Holy Roman Emperors, and Henry's father was none other than Frederick Barbarossa. But it was through a Norman connection that Sicily came into Hohenstaufen hands, for young Frederick's mother, Constance de Hauteville, was the posthumous daughter of Roger II. Frederick ascended the Throne and ruled for more than half a century. His first wife, also Constance, who like Margaret of Navarre came from what is now Spain, was an intelligent, strong-willed woman whose presence was eminently well-suited to such an important court as Frederick's.

From Palermo's splendid royal palace, the enlightened Frederick ruled most of Italy and also parts of Germany as Holy Roman Emperor, though in truth he spent little time in Sicily. As in Norman times, rather few Sicilian knights took part in the Crusades and the other religious wars of the day, and Frederick's bloodless "crusade" to the Holy Land — for he was King of Jerusalem — was an exercise in diplomacy. His *Constitutions of Melfi* are a benchmark of medieval European law, legalizing divorce as a civil right and unequivocally outlawing rape. The freethinking Frederick was reputed to be brilliant. *Stupor Mundi* (wonder of the world) was the Latin nickname given to the most powerful man of Europe and the Mediterranean.

By the middle years of the oft-excommunicated monarch's long reign, subtle, gradual changes were taking place as Sicily's Muslims converted to Christianity. They became Roman Catholic rather than Greek Orthodox; the latter were ever fewer. Under the Normans most Sicilians had been bilingual; many spoke both Greek and Arabic, and some managed a bit of Vulgar Latin or Norman French. The vernacular language of the Sicilian Jews was a Maghrebi dialect rather similar to that spoken by the Maghrebim of Tunis. Now Sicily was being Latinized in every sense, and Ciullo of Alcamo composed poetry in the Romance language which was becoming the Sicilian vernacular. This was a new Italic tongue embellished by Arabic, Greek and Norman French borrowings, and later recognized by both Dante and Boccaccio for its literary value. Ciullo's *Dialogue* is considered the earliest true "Italian" poetry of the Middle Ages. (The Sicilian language is considered in Chapter 26.)

Siculo Arabic, the language spoken by Sicily's medieval Arabs, survives as Maltese, the only Arabic language written with the Roman alphabet.

During Frederick's reign the Catholic Church — through its bishops and abbots — emerged as the largest landholder after the king himself. This was a slow but incessant process. In addition to outright grants from the Crown, the Benedictines and other religious orders succeeded to the estates of Eastern (Orthodox) monasteries as Latin (Catholic) abbots replaced those under Constantinople's jurisdiction lost through attrition. Frederick permitted the knightly orders to found a number of preceptories and commanderies in Sicily; these were quasi-monastic institutions. The Teutonic Knights were already present during the brief reign of his father, Henry VI, after 1194. The Hospitallers of Saint John (later the "Knights of Malta") had been in Sicily during the Norman era but expanded their presence under Frederick.

It was Frederick who assigned Sicily's Templar commanderies to the Hospitallers following what he believed to be an affront by the arrogant Templars in Palestine during his Sixth Crusade in 1228.

Under Frederick the feudal (or manorial) system developed further than it had under the Normans. *Feudal towns* were controlled by their resident lords, but there were also royal or *demesnial cities* — Trapani and Agrigento but also smaller ones like Vizzini, Taormina and Calascibetta — that answered directly to the Crown and were administered by local councils of minor nobles called *jurats*. The king's justiciars, a roving court of circuit judges, sought to ensure justice around Sicily. But certain "allodial" areas seemed to be governed by neither feudal or demesnial principles.

This was the case of several Arab towns. Usually tolerant of Islam, Frederick and his German barons were unwilling to accommodate the many demands of the Muslims who still inhabited a few parts of the Sicilian interior. For some years before 1220, Ibn Abbad, a Saracen leader, had been acting as if he were an independent sovereign, only to have his ambitions thwarted by the real sovereign, who resettled some of Sicily's Muslims in Apulia. But although Sicily's Church was gradually becoming Latinized, and the Pope supported local suppression of the Muslims, the Papacy was only rarely content with Frederick's use of power. He ruled two-thirds of Italy, with the Papal State sandwiched in between, and his death in 1250 was met in Rome with a sigh of relief. The Papal choice to rule southern Italy was Charles of Anjou, the unsaintly younger brother of the king-saint, Louis IX of France.

The throne was ascended by Conrad, one of Frederick's sons, in 1250, but he died in 1254, leaving behind a young son, Conradin, in Germany. For a few years, the kingdom was ruled in young Conradin's name by Conrad's half-brother Manfred, one of Frederick's sons born outside marriage.

Frederick's legacy survives him. He founded one of Europe's first secular universities at Naples and he is credited with maintaining at least a semblance of the spirit of cultural diversity and intellectual curiosity that flourished at the court of his grandfather, Roger II. Nor was he forgotten in the Holy Roman Empire, where his building program included one of Europe's most magnificent Gothic cathedrals at Cologne — this despite a strained rapport with the local bishop.

Until the last years of the fifteenth century, the powerful

Teutonic Order, introduced in Sicily by the Hohenstaufens, maintained a commandery at Palermo's Magione Basilica, where several of these German knights are buried.

The Angevin Checkmate

Frederick's heirs proved themselves far less able than he, even if Manfred and young Conradin adroitly managed to preserve the Hohenstaufen patrimony for a few years and were willing to fight to defend it. Sicilian independence came to an effective end with Manfred's defeat and death at the hands of Charles of Anjou at the Battle of Benevento in 1266, and young Conradin's beheading following the Battle of Tagliacozzo two years later.

The new monarch sent his French justiciars, castellans and officers to Sicily, confiscating estates and giving them to his own nobles while generally trampling on the rights of the Sicilian barons. Worse yet, whatever religious or ethnic diversity still existed in Sicily during the Hohenstaufen era effectively died when Charles of Anjou became king.

During this period Italy saw the growth of two political factions — the *Ghibellines* who supported the authority of the Holy Roman Emperor represented by the Hohenstaufens, opposing the *Guelphs* who advocated the power of the Papacy and the Angevins embodied by Charles of Anjou in Naples. With the battlefield defeat of the Hohenstaufens, one might think the cause of the Ghibellines all but lost. But some of the Hohenstaufens' old friends, notably the headstrong John of Procida, kept Swabian hopes alive.

To identify the end of Sicily's multicultural experiment with a specific date, any year from 1250 to 1300 will do. But the signal year of 1282 was a turning point.

Sicilian baronial opposition to Charles seemed to vanish with the execution of brave young Conradin in 1268. The

Angevin dynasty of France ruled Sicily from Naples until 1282, when a bloody uprising, the War of the Sicilian Vespers, expelled Angevin troops.

The political reasons for this war were indeed rather complex. The local aristocracy and John of Procida were certainly involved, but so were several European monarchs and even the Pope. In some ways the Sicilian conflicts mirrored those between Guelphs and Ghibellines elsewhere in Italy. In the wake of the Vespers, during which the Sicilians had slaughtered most of the Angevins on their island, the barons offered the Crown to Peter of Aragon, who gladly accepted. Peter's wife, Constance, was the daughter of Manfred Hohenstaufen (the illegitimate son of Frederick killed at Benevento in 1266), and on that tenuous basis the Aragonese monarch was thought to be the best dynastic candidate for the Sicilian throne since his sons carried Hohenstaufen blood in their veins. This led to the island being ruled, except for brief periods, from Barcelona (and then Madrid) for the next few centuries.

That this new dynastic arrangement was antithetical to the very concept of an independent Sicily that supposedly encouraged the rebellion in the first place went unnoticed.

The Vespers, with Sicily claimed by two monarchs — Charles of Anjou and Peter of Aragon — gave rise to the ironic phrase "Two Sicilies" because until now the Kingdom of Sicily included not only the island itself but most of Italy south of Rome, and neither Charles nor Peter would renounce his claim to the Sicilian crown even though Peter alone now held it in fact. Eventually the peninsular region would be called, more appropriately, the "Kingdom of Naples." (The War of the Vespers is described in greater detail in Chapter 27.)

The "Peace of Caltabellotta," a treaty signed between Aragonese and Angevins, formally ended the hostilities in 1302, but occasional conflicts broke out between the two camps over the next few years. The Late Middle Ages found

Sicily in the Aragonese (and Spanish) orbit rather than the Italian one. Although Peter of Aragon had promised that Sicily would always have its own king (through the line of his second son) who would rule from Palermo, there were to be Aragonese kings of Sicily who rarely ventured beyond their beloved Barcelona, entrusting their authority to delegates in Sicily. These were not yet "viceroys" but the Sicilian barons were resentful of them just the same.

The Aragonese Empire

For a few decades rule by Aragon seemed a solution to most of Sicily's problems, but this "honeymoon" didn't last long. By the middle of the fourteenth century, the island kingdom had come to be seen as a colony to be exploited, this time from Barcelona instead of Naples. Significantly, the Sicilian monoculture that had taken root by then was antithetical to everything that existed on the island under the Norman and Swabian kings, though one doubts whether anybody living in Sicily at the time was consciously aware of this.

Taxation was increased. This included taxes on grain and everything else, and now there was the *collecta* or *donativo,* an arbitrary "one-time" tax which was not levied at regular intervals but could be decreed at royal whim to cover any exigency (and which still exists in Italy today as the *tassa una tantum* deducted directly from bank accounts).

Most of the forests that remained in Sicily were harvested — but rarely replanted — to provide wood for the Aragonese to build their ships, with the former woodlands turned over to grain production.

The zealous, jealous baronage, the same class that had instigated the Vespers uprising in 1282, grew ever more greedy. Yet Sicily had no *Magna Carta,* nor a true parliament (despite widespread misuse of that term to denote any gathering of nobles) to either guarantee baronial rights or to rein in the barons. That said, the Sicilian parliament — such as it was — met fairly regularly beginning around 1400.

In 1295 such a parliament was convened by Frederick, the younger brother of the absentee King James of Sicily (both were sons of King Peter of Aragon). At this session, the Sicilian baronage nominated Frederick, who was Sicilian by birth and upbringing, as their sovereign, and crowned him at Palermo the following year. His elder brother objected but could do nothing to alter the course of events. In the wake of the Vespers, this was an early example of the importance of the assent of the people, or at least that of the baronial faction, in deciding who would rule Sicily.

In 1347 ships arriving at Messina from the eastern Mediterranean brought the bubonic plague ("Black Death") to Europe. By 1400 more than twenty million Europeans had died from two major outbreaks of this disease. This catastrophe was a decisive event in western European history, eventually bringing about the end of serfdom where it still existed.

But serfs weren't the only ones to become bolder. So were chroniclers and poets. In 1353 Giovanni Boccaccio's *Decameron* mentioned Palermo's Cuba palace and King William II. This was the beginning of a serious historical critique of Sicily's rulers of the High Middle Ages.

By 1385 there were more than forty guilds in Sicily, reflecting the growth of a class of artisans and tradesmen, but little changed outside the larger towns. The nobility exercised increasing control of the countryside and the smaller towns. The worst abuse of baronial power to be seen during the Middle Ages occurred late in the fourteenth century.

A dynastic interregnum facilitated the Chiaramonte family usurping a certain degree of feudal power for some years after the death of the Catanian-born King Frederick "the Simple" in 1377. The wealth of this family known for its castle-building came from confiscated estates that had belonged to the displaced Angevin feudatories before the Vespers, but with the sovereign so far away families like the Chiaramonte, Peralta, Ventimiglia and Alagona, the so-called "Four Vicars" of the Crown, vied for local power. This internecine struggle, though not a full-fledged civil war, was nearly as destructive.

King Frederick's young daughter, Maria, was in the care of the Alagona family when he died, and the barons effectively kidnapped the girl in order to secure her marriage to a husband — and potential king — of their choosing. Eventually, Maria was abducted from Catania Castle by a rival baron, Antonio Moncada, and spirited off to Barcelona to marry her cousin, Martin, a grandson of the King of Aragon and potential heir to the Sicilian throne. The rebels were brought to justice when Martin arrived in Sicily in 1392 to ascend the Throne and restore order. For his treason, Andrew Chiaramonte, the leader of the rebels, was executed at his Palermo castle, now called the "Steri," and his lands were confiscated. His headless body is entombed in the Steri's external chapel.

Like Peter after the Vespers, Martin granted fiefs to a new influx of Aragonese barons. In conjunction with this, the king called a parliament. It wasn't the first and it would not be the last, but at all events it was not particularly effective, and it led to few real reforms except to enforce royal prerogatives.

Matters may not have been much better elsewhere in western Europe, but for the average person justice was more easily had in kingdoms where the sovereign was present to guarantee the order of law, where the prosperity of his humblest subjects was in his own interest. In this important regard Sicily compared unfavorably to the northern Italian communes (city-states) and the patchwork of small monarchies of central Europe. Aragonese policy, or perhaps the absence of a firm "Sicily program," set a terrible precedent. The exploitation of the land, its people and its economy was to continue for many centuries.

The guilds were a sign of the late-medieval development of a kind of "middle class," but there were other encouraging signs as well. During the fifteenth century a growing number of peasants and tenant farmers were able to obtain their own small parcels of land, even though the common areas of many towns were under feudal control — and even if most of these new smallholders were as illiterate as their parents. However great the power of the landed classes was, there were occasional signs of relief. Labor wages were, in theory, established by national law, and in 1446, when the baron of Calatabiano prohibited the pasturing of sheep on common land, the shepherds took their case to the Crown courts and won.

Welcome as these things were, Sicily was virtually ignored by the Renaissance, both artistically and philosophically. A prominent exception was Francesco Laurana, an early Renaissance sculptor who established a workshop in Palermo in 1466. Yet well into the 1490s, while a new architectural movement was flourishing in northern Italy, in Sicily the churches and palaces of the fifteenth century were more medieval in appearance. The Catalan Gothic movement was an example of this; it was a style popular with the Aragonese and modified only slightly to accommodate Renaissance sensibilities. In church architecture, Sicily rarely experienced the true Gothic so much as a peculiar Romanesque Gothic.

Sicily's first university was founded at Catania in 1434. In general, however, education was left to the schools of the religious orders — at first the Benedictines but then the Dominicans and later (in a few cities) the Jesuits, followed by others. These monastic schools were not all seminaries or convents; aristocrats and even some tradesmen sent their sons to them. Except for nuns and noblewomen, literacy was a male monopoly, but it was the exception for either gender.

Here we come face to face with a disturbing phenomenon.

In the two or three centuries immediately before the Angevin period, Sicily probably had a higher general rate of literacy than it did in 1400 or 1800. Sicily's Byzantines, Muslims and Jews strongly advocated literacy. Indeed, learning was a distinguishing feature of the culture of all three civilizations, something in which their people truly believed. Instead, the Catholic hierarchy accepted the illiteracy of the general populace as a simple fact of life, while Sicily's Spanish monarchs failed to recognize it as problematical.

The nobility, of course, exploited the general illiteracy of Sicily's poorer classes to its own advantage. At some point after 1300 a hopeless cycle of poverty and illiteracy began. The destitute classes grew in size while the better-educated ones stagnated. Today's *popolino,* an urban underclass, is the heir to these poor peasants. Yet the peasants were not serfs tied to the land; serfdom was never instituted universally on the island and at all events it did not last much beyond the Swabian period.

Alfonso V was crowned in 1416 and ruled for forty-two years; in 1442 the Sicilian and Neapolitan crowns were united under him. But for the most part the rulers remained in Spain; Aragon and Castile were united in 1479 to form the cornerstone of what was to become the Kingdom of Spain. Soon the Spanish kings would send governors and viceroys to administer Sicily on their behalf. Alfonso was a slightly more generous patron of learning and the arts than his immediate predecessors, and founded the University of Catania, but the Sicilians had to bear the cost of his petty wars against the maritime cities of northern Italy.

Constantinople fell to the Ottomans in 1453. The Hundred Years' War ended in the same year. The Middle Ages were at an end and the Renaissance was firmly on its course. The Sicilian-born painter Antonello da Messina was part of this new movement. So was Antonio Beccadelli, the aristocratic poet, diplomat and chronicler known as "Panormita." Both spent the greater part of their careers outside Sicily.

The nobility was little concerned for their welfare, but during this period the common people of Sicily began to assume familial surnames rather than personal ones. This made it all the easier to identify them for taxation. Until now, hereditary surnames were the perquisite of the landed classes, whose families were often known by toponyms based on the names of the fiefs they held.

Catholic zeal was becoming ever more widespread. In a prelude of things to come, over three hundred Jews were massacred in the town of Modica in 1474. Conveniently ignored by most Sicilian historians until recent years, this localized genocide was the most blatant act of violence ever perpetrated against the Jews of Sicily.

Spanish Sicily

The Spanish Inquisition was instituted in 1487, with horrific consequences. In 1492 Spain's edict against the Jews was enforced on the island, prompting widespread conversions and many emigrations. At the same time, the arrival of Columbus in America was a turning point that began to shift the focus of European power away from the Mediterranean and Sicily. With the exception of a few Orthodox Christian refugees arriving from Albania in the wake of the Turkish invasions of the Balkans, Sicily was exclusively Roman Catholic by 1500. It wasn't long before the Albanians were absorbed into the Roman Church, where they were permitted the use of their own Byzantine Rite.

The increasing influence of the Dominicans and then the Jesuits would prove political as well as theological, and not always for the better. With the Inquisition and the growing dominance of the Church in Sicilian society, divorce, a fundamental civil right upheld by Frederick's Constitutions in 1231, was

now outlawed, while crimes such as rape — though con-
demned officially — became nearly impossible to prosecute.

The lives of the common folk, the *popolino,* were as miser-
able as the hereditary ruling class could make them. The island,
which Madrid viewed as a colony in all but name, was exploited
in every imaginable way, and with it its people.

"Nobility of birth," observed Francis Bacon, "commonly
abateth industry."

The intrusive Spanish bureaucracy and its zealous taxation
spawned all manner of records, many preserved for us today.
The *riveli,* or land tax rolls, which date from the fifteenth century, are especially useful in feudal and genealogical research.
Indeed, Sicily boasts the world's best genealogical resources,
facilitating the construction of many pedigrees into the waning
years of the Middle Ages, even for families lacking connections to the aristocracy — something researchers elsewhere
can only dream of.

The Genetic Inheritance

Not surprisingly, DNA haplotyping confirms what historians have always known about the diversity of Sicily's historic
populations.

It used to be that genetic studies addressed subjects such
as specific physical traits, identifying, for example, those in the
population having blue eyes (around fifteen percent of Sicilians) or red hair (five percent), or the segment of the population carrying the gene for thalassemia (compliments of the
Phoenicians and Greeks) or multiple sclerosis (the Normans).
With gene mapping and extensive study, DNA analysis has become very sophisticated indeed.

Favism (hemolysis from G6PD deficiency) may not be
much higher among the Sicilian population than others, but it
is more frequently diagnosed because of the higher consump-

tion of fava beans in Sicily than in some other regions. Genetic factors probably account for the extreme rarity of alcoholism among Sicilians.

Of course, genes determine physical appearance. While the first major influx of genes for blond hair and blue eyes probably arrived with the Vandals and Goths, there does not seem to have been extensive intermarriage of these peoples with the existing population, which remained essentially endogamous until the ninth century. For this we must look to the Normans, perhaps the Lombards who came with them to Sicily, and of course the Germans who arrived with the Hohenstaufens. We know that, for example, Frederick II had red hair, and his matrilineal grandfather, Roger II, had reddish hair, while Frederick's paternal grandfather was nicknamed *Barbarossa* for the color of his beard.

The geneticist Luigi Luca Cavalli-Sforza wrote an entire book about amalgamation among peoples and its connection to their social culture. *Genes, People and Languages* remains a good reference for those curious about these phenomena.

What follows is only a very general approximation reflecting data from a constantly evolving field of study. It is not a gospel.

There is no single "Sicilian haplotype" or haplogroup, no "Sicilian DNA" *per se.* By percentage of the population, Sicily's Y haplogroups are approximately: J (35), R (25), I (15), K (10), H (10), Others (5). These proportions vary somewhat by locality.

Attempts to ascertain patrilineal Sicilian "ethnic" origins based on this should be undertaken with a great degree of caution because haplogroups do not correspond precisely to medieval or modern conceptions of nationality or ethnicity. At best, they are approximate. For example, J2 is identified with Greeks but also with some Germans, while R1b is identified with Normans but also with some Spaniards. The isolation of sub-clades within a major haplogroup helps to identify smaller populations in more specific geographic areas at more specific dates; as we have said, this is an ongoing field of research.

Speaking very broadly, the most frequent Y haplogroups of the world's most conquered island may be correlated generally, but not exclusively, to the following populations:

• J1 - Arabs, Berbers, Carthaginians, Jews,
• J2 (M172) - Greeks, Romans, Jews, Spaniards,
• R1b (M173) - Germans, Normans, Lombards, Aragonese, Spaniards,
• I1 & I2b - Vikings and Normans,
• I & I2a - Elymians,
• G - Arabs and Elymians,
• N - Vikings and Normans,
• E1b1b - Arabs, Berbers, others,
• K - Arabs, Greeks, Berbers, Carthaginians,
• H - Arabs,
• T - Phoenicians, Carthaginians.

What we are really identifying is common descent over many generations from a remote male ancestor. For example, everybody in the J2 haplogroup has the same patrilineal ancestor in the northern part of the Fertile Crescent around 6,000 BC (BCE). Sicilians are descended, through one line or another, from *all* of these groups.

Female lines are not to be overlooked. Matrilineal haplogroups trace mitochondrial DNA (mtDNA) through one's mother's mother's mother and so forth. Bryan Sykes identified a number of European ancestresses he named the "Seven Daughters of Eve," though he has since added greatly to this number with haplogroups on other continents. These are the haplogroups H (Helena), J (Jasmine), K (Katrine), T (Tara), U5 (Ursula), V (Velda) and X (Xenia). All seven lineages are found in Sicily.

Population genetics, researched particularly widely beginning with the Genographic Project sponsored by the National Geographic Society, dispels simplistic theories about race, societal development and ancient migrations.

The most viable hypothesis advanced regarding Haplogroup J2 and the earliest Sicilians is that it correlates with the first neolithic farmers, as opposed to simple hunter-gatherers, making their way from western Asia across the Mediterranean.

But what of the place they found? That is the subject of the following chapter.

CHAPTER 3

Land, Flora, Fauna, Cuisine

Let's cast a glance over the island's geography, natural features, population, agriculture and cuisine — then and now.

The Land

At 25,711 square kilometers (9,927 square miles), Sicily is the largest island in the Mediterranean and the largest of Italy's twenty political regions, slightly larger than Piedmont. For comparison, Wales covers 20,780 square kilometers and Massachusetts 27,340. In addition to the island of Sicily, the region includes a number of coastal and volcanic islands. For centuries Malta and Gozo were part of the Kingdom of Sicily.

The highest peak is Mount Etna, western Europe's largest active volcano, at a variable 3,329 meters (10,922 feet) above sea level, followed by rocky Pizzo Carbonara (at 1,979 meters) and several other summits in the Madonie range, and forested Mount Soro, in the Nebrodi range, at 1,847 meters. All of these peaks are covered with snow for at least two months of the year, Etna usually for three or four.

The longest river is the Salso at 144 kilometers (89 miles), rising in the Madonie Mountains and flowing southward past Enna to Licata, marking Sicily's drainage divide, or watershed. A tributary of the Simeto in western Sicily coincidentally

91

shares the same name. To supply drinking water, there are numerous man-made lakes fed by streams and springs, but Sicily boasts very few natural ones, notably salty Pergusa near Enna and a few in the Nebrodi and Etna regions. None of Sicily's rivers are navigable today. After the Salso the chief rivers – now little more than streams – are the Simeto (114 km), the Belice (107 km), the Dittaino (105 km) and the Platani (103 km). Several are of historical interest. The Platani (the Greeks' Halycos) delineated the boundary between Greeks and Carthaginians according to a treaty of 306 BC (BCE). The Simeto and the Dittaino mark the route of the Normans to the Arab city of Kasr'Janni (Enna) in 1061.

For the most part, the Sicilian landscape we see today bears only the slightest resemblance to what it was like from antiquity into the Middle Ages, no less the seventeenth century. It's not just the urban sprawl that has marred the scenery around Palermo and Catania, but the scars of a long process of overzealous deforestation and mediocre land management across the island.

The idyllic terrain of the island beloved by Phoenicians, Greeks and Romans was full of forests. In most areas they were far more expansive than they are today. Yes, Sicily's wooded mountains are still spectacular. There's Etna, which segues into the Nebrodi and Peloritans, and the Madonie to the west are not to be overlooked. There are isolated but precious jewels like the Ficuzza and Cammarata forest reserves in the Sicanian Mountains.

But by the seventeenth century the fate of the forests around Enna, Agrigento and Caltanissetta was sealed by the need for wheat to feed a growing population and the lust for wood to build ships for an expanding Spanish Empire. Then came the mining for sulphur, marble and limestone.

Most of the rivers were attenuated to streams and, finally, the seasonal "torrents" (run-offs) we have today — some of which being little more than dry creek beds for five or six months of the year.

The extensive coastline ranges from rocky cliffs to sandy beaches, and the island also offers fascinating natural features like Alcantara Gorge, fed by Etna's snows, caverns like Carburangeli and the gray mud flows formed by sporadic geysers that give Maccalube, near Aragona, its moonlike appearance.

Sicily's chief mountain ranges are distinguished in their limestone formation and, perhaps more obviously, in their vegetation. The stunning Nebrodi Mountains of northeastern Sicily seem to have endured the ages better than the other ranges. The rocky buttes capped by Sutera's monastery and the castles at Mussomeli and Caccamo resemble those that house the Metéora monasteries near Kalambaka in Greece.

In the southeastern corner of the island the Hyblaean Mountains are less imposing, rising gently above graceful slopes. Yet Cavagrande Cassibile, a scenic canyon, was formed here, and the necropoli of Pantalica were fashioned into limestone cliffs in antiquity. The wine country is a hilly region in the west, with Marsala its unofficial capital.

In addition to its larger protected areas, Sicily has a number of smaller reserves, some of which welcome human visitors. In the southeast the Vendicari Reserve lies along the Ionian coast. In the northwest the Zingaro is the most "people friendly" of the coastal reserves. Near Catania there's a reserve at the mouth of the Cyane River where papyrus still grows, and the Biviere di Gela, as well as similar reserves at the mouths of the Simeto and Platani rivers, are stops for migratory birds making their way between Africa and Europe.

The Population

At the end of the Middle Ages, circa 1500, Sicily's population was slightly more than 600,000 in 112,890 households plus a number of monasteries. In 1748 it was approximately 1,180,000. In 1861 it was estimated at 2,408,000; a century later it had doubled despite mass emigration.

In 2010 it was officially 5,048,805, comprising approximately 8.4 percent of Italy's population, being the fourth most populous of Italy's regions, surpassed by Lombardy (Milan), Lazio (Rome) and Campania (Naples). Sicily's population density was less than that of any of those regions. For comparison, Denmark's population was around 5,574,000 with a land area of 43,090 square kilometers.

Flora, Fauna, Agriculture

Much of the wild vegetation, like the papyrus, palm trees and stone pines, is typically Mediterranean, but certain conifers, including the endangered Nebrodi Fir, are similar to species found in much cooler climates. Medieval Sicily was significantly cooler than it is today. Global warming explains part of this; rampant deforestation and the gradual decline in precipitation explains the rest. Except for some unusually wet Winters every few years, Sicily's precipitation and temperatures follow a consistent pattern year after year, especially during the Summer. This makes the grape harvests remarkably constant from one season to the next.

Most of Sicily's fauna is hidden from view most of the time. There are more foxes than wolves; the latter are almost all gone. There are few hare, but rabbits abound.

A few wild cats roam the large national park on the slopes of Mount Etna and also the remote parts of the Nebrodi and Madonie; these regal hunters are similar to the striped wild cats found in the Pyrenees. The cats survive because they live in wooded areas on rugged slopes where few humans venture, but they are threatened by hybridization through crossbreeding with the ubiquitous domestic cats.

One still sees the rare beaver or squirrel (one variety of the latter is strikingly similar to the North American chipmunk) in the woods of the Madonie or Nebrodi. The wild boar that has been re-introduced into Sicily is actually a Sardinian variety, though the "domesticated" Nebrodian black swine is perhaps more boar than pig. The local deer, for which the Nebrodi were named by the Greeks (from *nebros* for fawn), were hunted to extinction long ago.

A local species of toad whose body grows to a length of almost 20 centimeters (8 inches) sometimes comes out into the rains, several varieties of frog inhabit the streams, and several varieties of gecko lizard can be seen during warm months. Hermann's tortoise also thrives in Sicily. The nocturnal hedgehog still lives here, though it is only rarely seen. Until the latter decades of the nineteenth century, several species of freshwater fish were found in the island's streams; most are now extinct.

Eagles and falcons, though rare, can sometimes be seen soaring in the thermal currents above the mountains in search of prey, and local varieties of grouse, quail and partridge live in the fields of the interior. The migratory birds already mentioned are sometimes seen along the coasts, where the purple swamp hen has been re-introduced.

In Sicily most homes were in towns, not amidst farms. Typically these were stone row houses. Every day, farmers hiked out to the fields or orchards they cultivated. The exceptions were isolated "farm houses" or the occasional bailey (baglio) for lodging when a farm was especially distant from a town or village. The English and French concepts of a rural estate, with its own manor house, church and tiny hamlet, rarely applied to Sicily.

Cuisine

Even today, there are essentially two kinds of communities among the numerous towns and cities of Sicily. Inland towns, especially those in the mountains, are in the vast majority, and in the past their economies were usually based on livestock and agriculture. The economies of coastal towns were based more on fishing, commerce and maritime trade, though agriculture also contributed to their prosperity.

These factors obviously influenced the cuisine, customs and, to some extent, the mentalities of the inhabitants of these places. Until the twentieth century, somebody who lived in Castrogiovanni (Enna), Caltanissetta or any city of the mountainous interior might rarely visit the sea or taste its fruits, but plenty of goat, lamb, pork, chicken and rabbit was available. Incredible as it may seem, somebody born and raised in Centuripe might never see a roasted squid, cuttlefish or prawn.

The fact that Italy has a greater diversity of flora than any other country in western Europe has certainly influenced its cuisine, which is nothing if not regional. Piedmont is known for its *risotto,* Lombardy for its *polenta* and the southern regions for pasta.

The vegetation of Sicily is remarkably varied. Apart from the great variety of agricultural produce — ranging from citrus fruits to grapes, olives to artichokes, pistachios to mulberries, watermelon, nuts and even truffles — numerous trees, flowering shrubs and grasses are native to Sicily, though the cactus is an American import. Oleasters will still be found, along with tender wild asparagus, cardoons and even the manna ash. Lentils were known to the Phoenicians and Greeks, and perhaps the Sicanians.

Sicily's recorded culinary history dates from Greek and Roman times. Ovid, for example, wrote about the "sweet mullet and tender eel" to be fished in Ionian waters. Pliny the Elder mentioned the lamprey as well as wine from the Etna region, local bread, delicious capers, and Sicilian cheese made from the milk of goats.

Sausage, a mainstay of Sicilian cuisine, was made in antiquity, and the Syracusan dramatist Epicharmus of Kos even wrote a play called "The Sausage."

When sources for Sicily's culinary history seem contradictory, it is usually because they are describing different periods, perhaps centuries apart. For example, deer and wild boar no longer roam Sicilian forests because these creatures have been hunted to extinction, and in the event there were fewer woodlands for them by the eighteenth century than there were in the Middle Ages. Certain species of freshwater fish no longer survive because the rivers that sustained them are now mere seasonal streams. Mulberry trees are now rare, whereas formerly they were used in silk making. Most pistachios consumed in Sicily are now imported.

It is clear that the ancient Sicilians at least knew of certain foods which were no longer available by medieval times. The extensive mosaic pavements of the Roman villa "del Casale" erected outside Piazza Armerina around AD (CE) 360 depict all manner of fruits and beasts, many virtually unknown by the Middle Ages. Some, such as the purple swamp hen already mentioned, probably were not consumed, but there is a scene of Romans on horseback chasing relatively large deer. A pictorial resource from the fourteenth century is the wooden ceiling of the Barons' Hall in Palazzo Steri in Palermo.

The Greeks traded with northern India and central Asia, and the Romans with southern India, so it is likely that certain foods and spices were introduced via those routes. Pistachios, for example, were present in Sicily in ancient times, but they are native to central Asia.

It appears that medlars and pomegranates were also introduced by the Greeks, who brought both from western Asia, but the Phoenicians probably knew of these fruits as well.

Citrons originated in India or China and were probably brought to Greece by Alexander the Great following his battles in Persia and what is now Pakistan. Here we look to information provided by another student of Aristotle. In his lengthy treatise on plants, Theophrastus, "the father of botany," mentions rice and other crops grown in his time (he died in 287 BC), and it seems that some of these were once raised in Sicily but were no longer cultivated on the island by the fifth century. In that regard, Sicily would not be unique among Italian regions; the rice known as *arborio* has been grown in the Po Valley for many centuries and may have sustained Roman soldiers in Germany.

Early literary references to lentils, pistachios, almonds and citrons are found in the Torah. During the Roman period these foods were common among Mediterranean peoples.

Durum wheat has been grown on the island since antiquity, and in the twelfth century, long before Marco Polo brought such recipes from China, the court geographer Abdullah al Idrisi described spaghetti being made at Trabia east of Palermo. Couscous, once a mainstay of the Berber diet, is popular in Trapani, Marsala and Erice.

The Arabs introduced (or re-introduced) rice in Sicily during the tenth century, along with sophisticated canals and irrigation methods. Cotton (for paper as well as fabric) and sugar cane were also cultivated during that period but, like rice, they ceased to be grown in Sicily at some point after the Middle Ages.

Edible oranges and, primarily for silk making, mulberries were also brought by the Arabs. *Arancini* (rice balls), *caponata* (aubergine salad), *panelle* (ceci fritters) and various desserts made with cane sugar come to us from Arab cuisine. The Arabs re-introduced sorbets, fruity ices and ice cream, which were Greek or Roman in origin.

By no means was the use of sugar limited to desserts. Indeed, it completely altered Sicilian cookery. There is, for example, a delicious fish recipe based on an *agrodolce* (sweet and sour) sauce made from white wine vinegar, sugar and onions, thought to have originated in Arab times.

A fishing practice dating from that era is the *mattanza,* a method for capturing large tuna in a series of "chambers" formed by giant nets. The head fisherman is accorded the Arabic title *raìs,* leader.

Tomatoes, potatoes, peppers and cocoa beans arrived with the Spaniards early in the sixteenth century; a local chocolate is still produced in Modica using the traditional method of the Aztecs. *Sfincione,* a kind of Sicilian pizza without cheese, has been made since that time; it is a thick bread topped with tomatoes, onions and anchovies.

Other foods seem to have been known in Sicily forever. Celery takes its very name from *Selinus* (Selinunte), where it grew wild. The large "Hundred Horse Chestnut" outside Sant'Alfio on the slopes of Mount Etna is one of Europe's oldest nut trees, probably planted in the Roman era.

Many foods are seasonal. *Fritella* (or *fritedda* in Sicilian), a simple dish made from artichokes, fava beans and peas, is served in Spring; *maccu,* a soup made of fava, is served in Winter (from dried beans) but there's also a fresh spring version.

The island of Pantelleria is known for its capers and Ustica for its lentils, while the Nebrodi region produces hazelnuts and truffles. Bronte is famous for its pistachios, for which the Sicilian word, *fatùk,* comes directly from Arabic.

It is generally believed, though not without scholarly contention, that the Greeks introduced olives and grapes, and hence olive oil and wine, perhaps with the first Mycenaean communities.

Today a number of olive varieties are identified taxonomically as Sicilian. Among them we find Nocellara, Biancolilla, Carolea, Moresca and Verdello, the large "Green Sicilian." Some years ago a single tree near Siracusa was genetically determined to be a *Kalamata* cultivar directly descended from original Greek stock brought to Sicily in the time of

Archimedes. Like Sicilian wines (described below), the island's olive oils are identified and marketed chiefly by *variety* rather than by geographic *appellation,* though regional appellations, or *denominazioni di origine,* do exist.

An entire volume could be dedicated to Sicilian wines and cheeses. The wine country of western Sicily is one of Italy's largest contiguous viticultural regions. It was greatly expanded with the popularity of Marsala wine during the early decades of the nineteenth century, when viticulture replaced the cultivation of wheat in some areas. (The "Places to Visit" section includes a scenic winery route.)

Until the twentieth century, most of the wine consumed in Sicily was home made and not of a very high quality compared to today's estate-bottled vintages. Much of it was rather high in alcohol and neither red or white but a light amber color.

In Sicily red wines were historically more popular than whites. The quintessentially Sicilian Nero d'Avola is the most robust of these. Sicily, where there is rarely a cloudy day from June through August, hardly ever produces a mediocre harvest, and as early as the nineteenth century some of its growers were selling Nero d'Avola in bulk as a blending grape to wineries in France to add color and body to wines deemed lacking in those qualities.

The island has several regional wine appellations but only those of the dessert wines have achieved international prestige among oenophiles, and the Sicilians themselves purchase their wines according to variety rather than geography.

Marsala is made from local varieties such as Grillo, Cataratto and Insolia — whites that can stand on their own as table wines. This fortified dessert wine, which travels well, was developed around 1800 for the British market, as the supply of Port, Sherry and Madeira was no longer sufficient to meet consumer demand. Much used in cooking, Marsala figures in some traditional Sicilian recipes, for example *zabaglione* (eggnog).

The historical influence of Sicilian viticulture transcends the Marsala market. The grape called *Zinfandel* in America is actually Primitivo, a Sicilian variety which may be of Balkan or Greek origin. It was probably introduced in the Americas by Spaniards during Sicily's centuries-long Spanish period.

The Zibibbo grape is a Muscat variety historically used in the making of Moscato wine, which can also be made from the sub-variety known locally as Moscatello, sometimes with the addition of Corinto. Owing its name to the Arabic *zabìb* (literally *raisin*), Zibibbo was much favored by the Arabs, but the grape was probably introduced in Sicily — first on Pantelleria — by the Phoenicians, who brought cultivars from Egypt.

Passito, as its name implies, is based on Appassito grapes. By tradition, vintners still use a special "dry" process in the production of Passito, so partially-dried grapes and even raisins find their way into the must. Unlike Marsala, to which alcohol (brandy) is added, Passito is not actually a "fortified" wine. Indeed, "passito" refers as much to a winemaking *process* as to a specific grape variety.

Malvasia is another grape used to make a distinctive varietal that is golden to amber in color and slightly fortified. Malvasia is cultivated in northeastern Sicily (near Messina) and on the island of Lipari, where it is used in the making of this dessert wine somewhat similar to Moscato.

Grappa, a brandy, as well as various liqueurs, were also home made in the past. Rosolio, limoncello, anisette (sambuca) and amaretto stand out. Cynar is a niche product made from artichokes.

How much of these potions did Sicilians drink? Historically, Sicilians' alcohol consumption was moderate, and it still is. Anybody who spends much time on the island will probably notice how rare alcoholism is among the Sicilians. Public insobriety is all but unknown, and very few automobile accidents result from drunk driving. Social culture is often cited in explanation of this, but genetic factors are thought to be at work too.

Most Sicilian cheeses are made from sheep's milk. Pecorino is the classic example, *pecora* meaning sheep. Made throughout Sicily, where it may be considered the most popular cheese, it is a favorite for grating over pasta. Its taste, though sharp, is often less pungent and dry than that of Caciocavallo, despite a similar flavor and texture.

Caciocavallo, once known as "Caciovacchino," is made from cow's milk. Canestrato is also made from whole cow's milk, though sometimes diluted with that of goats or sheep. Its name derives from its ageing in baskets, *canestri*. It is quite similar to Pecorino and Caciocavallo, made with the same process. Sicilians prefer to consume Canestrato as a table cheese with wine, fruit or both.

Provola, which comes in regional Sicilian varieties (Nebrodi, Ragusa, Madonie), is made from whole cow's milk. There is also a tasty smoked form, and it is the classic complement to hams and bacons. It assumes a sharp flavor when aged.

Piacentinu, famous in the province of Enna in central Sicily, is made from sheep's milk and flavored with saffron, which gives it a deep yellowish hue. The name is said to come from the Sicilian cognate of *piacere* ("to like").

Tuma and Primo Sale are known, in certain forms, as "Vastedda" in some parts of Sicily, such as the Belice Valley. Made from sheep's milk, this variation of Pecorino is usually called Tuma when fresh, Primo Sale when aged slightly and salted lightly, and Vastedda when aged longer. It is best served with ham, wines and fruits as a table cheese. It has a sweetish taste not unlike that of Provola, with a similar texture.

Maiorchino, its name possibly based on that of the island of Majorca, was supposedly introduced by the Aragonese. Made in the forested Peloritan and Nebrodi mountains of northeastern Sicily, it contains roughly equal amounts of whole milk from native breeds of cow, sheep and goat.

Ragusano, made in the province of Ragusa from cow's milk, has a mild flavor. A number of other regional Sicilian cheeses are made from goat's or sheep's milk. These include Capra (Messina), Fiore Sicano (Palermo), Cofanetto, Ericino and Caciotta degli Elimi (Trapani).

Made from sheep's milk, Ricotta (cottage cheese) is not technically a cheese but a milk product (like yogurt and feta).

Sicily is known for its pastries. Almond paste is the base for marzipan pastries; these are shaped, colored and decorated realistically to look like fruit, known as *pasta reale* or, around Palermo, *frutta di Martorana*. Ricotta cream is the filling for *cassata* cake and *cannolo* shells. *Buccellato,* a pastry of figs, nuts and berries, is Sicily's *panforte* or fruit cake. Marzipan and halva both come to us directly from Arab cookery, though the latter is no longer part of Sicilian cuisine.

Some Sicilian foods have particularly interesting links to religious tradition. The pomegranate, of course, is associated with Persephone. The artichoke, whose English and Italian names come to us from the Arabic *kharshùff,* is native to the central Mediterranean and the cardoon is a distant cousin. But the Greek and Latin words are said to derive from *Cynara,* for the maiden who Zeus transformed into a beautiful artichoke flower. The citron is coveted by Jews as the *etrog* associated with Sukkot.

In the next chapter we shall consider the history of Sicily's faith traditions.

CHAPTER 4

The Faiths

Said King William II of Sicily to his subjects following an earthquake in 1169: "Let each of you pray to the God he worships. He who has faith in his God will feel peace in his heart."

Each faith has its own ethos. One perhaps states the obvious in affirming that beliefs dictate actions and lifestyles. As we saw in the previous chapter, religious practices can even be associated with certain foods. Leaving theological intricacies to the theologians, let's concentrate on describing the principal faith traditions that shaped Sicilian life from antiquity into the Middle Ages. Purists may find this precis superficial, but its main purpose is to serve as an exordium to other chapters.

The religions practiced during the Norman period are viewed as they existed at that time. It is clear that these faiths today are not precisely what they were in the Middle Ages, even if their essential beliefs have changed little since then. In passing, it is fair to say that there is today greater distance between Catholics and Orthodox, and between Sunnis and Shiites, than there was in 1100.

As we have said, medieval faith traditions were closely identified with specific ethnic populations. Sicily's Byzantines were what we would now call Greek Orthodox, and her Arabs were Muslim, while the Normans and Germans were Roman Catholic. The faith of the Jews was part of the ancient tradition of a civilization that existed when Plato's Greeks were building temples to worship gods.

In Sicily the ubiquity of those temples is overwhelming. Segesta boasts what is probably the best-preserved temple of the Greek world.

It used to be presumed that formal religion, with its grandiose temples, first evolved in tandem with the introduction of agriculture and sedentism, but this theory has been challenged by a significant discovery near Urfa, the Greeks' Edessa, in Turkey. At Göbekli Tepe, the world's earliest megalithic temples presently known to exist were built around 9,000 BC (BCE) not, apparently, by farmers but by hunters, in what was then a verdant region teeming with wild game.

Comparatively recent archeological vestiges of the religious practices of the Proto Sicanians, Sicily's megalithic society, are known to us. In Malta, Europe's oldest temples were built by these first Sicilians as early as 4,000 BC (BCE). Some three thousand years later, their descendants built a Sicanian temple at Cefalù.

The Elymians and Sikels, moreso than the Sicanians, readily embraced Greek deities and myths. The Greeks' greatest imitators were, of course, the Romans.

Through apotheosis, a few Roman emperors became divine after death, a status famously exploited by Caesar Augustus as heir of the deified Julius Caesar and (according to some theologians) the precursor of beatification and canonization in early Christianity. But was Sicily ever a full-fledged theocracy?

Theocracy and Ecclesiocracy

In our times there is a danger of the term *theocracy* being ascribed overzealously wherever there is a state religion. Yet the attributes identifying *theocracies* and *ecclesiocracies* are nothing if not subtle and even subjective, with no clear consensus on the words' definitions. Important as religion was in ancient and medieval Sicily, no society established on the island was literally a theocracy: a state or system of government ruled by or explicitly subject to religious authority.

A disquisition addressing the question of the degree to which Sicily's Muslim emirs and Catholic kings were *expected* to submit to religious authority, as opposed to exactly which laws they applied in practice, would be a lengthy one. Fortunately, the island's Fatimid and Norman rulers chose to govern Sicily from Palermo rather than from Cairo or Rome.

However, two specific periods of Sicilian history saw powerful religious influences at work in government, shaping what today would be called "social policy."

Caliphates are usually classed as theocracies, but Sicily's ninth-century Aghlabids ruled only nominally under the Abbasid caliphs of Baghdad, and despite their encouragement of Islam they did not coerce conversions in Sicily. They also permitted Jewish communities to flourish in Tunisia. The successive Fatimids and Kalbids were, if anything, even more tolerant in this regard. For Sicily's least tolerant social policies regarding religion we must look to a particularly unenlightened era that began in the last years of the Middle Ages.

Ferdinand II of Aragon, who ruled Sicily and — with his wife Isabella — a united Spain at the end of the fifteenth century, was called "the Catholic" with good reason. Yet he did not act as a direct agent of the Papacy or the Inquisition despite his slavish adherence to both, especially in matters such as the expulsions and forced conversions of the Jews in Spain and Sicily. This unsavory policy was not restricted to Jews; Spain's Muslims were likewise expelled or forcibly converted. Ferdinand and Isabella are, of course, known for sponsoring the voyages of Christopher Columbus, and the resulting Spanish conquest brought the zeal of the Inquisition to the Americas and their native peoples. (Not surprisingly, Protestant movements failed to take root in Sicily, which was to be ruled from Spain for centuries.)

From the vantage point of a contemporary observer living in Aghlabid or Spanish Sicily, such a society would be all but indistinguishable from an actual theocracy, even if caliphs and bishops were not governing it.

Marriage Practices

Religion was important in familial life. In Sicily all medieval weddings were religious. (Not until 1820 were civil marriages introduced.)

In the Middle Ages, and indeed into the latter decades of the nineteenth century, most marriages in Sicily were contracted with the consent of the spouses' parents. These were, in effect, "arranged" marriages. Even where this was not literally the case, it was unlikely that a young woman would marry a man against her parents' wishes. Endogamy was the norm; most people married within their faith, social class and locality, though there were certainly rare exceptions to this. Marriages between second or third cousins were not altogether unusual. Sicily was not anomalous; in medieval times such practices were quite commonplace throughout Europe and the Mediterranean.

Particularly striking is the general similarity in medieval marriage practices (as opposed to wedding ceremonies) among Christians, Muslims and Jews.

Mythology

Persephone, Demeter, Arethusa, Alpheus, Aphrodite, Theseus, Daedalus, Icarus, Minos, Dionysos, Charybdis, Hades, Hercules, Jason, Thetis, Aeolus, Polyphemus, Odysseus. Their names resound in the Greek myths of antiquity, and each knew

Sicily, the Greeks' New World, intimately.

The Cyclopes and Vulcan (Hephaestus) lived on volcanic Etna, the sacred mountain of Sicily's Greeks, Aeolus dwelled in the islands north of Sicily, Scylla guarded the Strait of Messina, Persephone was abducted outside Enna, and Arethusa emerged as a spring at Syracuse.

The Sicanians, Sikels, Elymians, Phoenicians, Carthaginians and ancient Greeks were polytheistic; they created their own deities. The Romans adopted the Greek gods and myths as their own; consider that Virgil's *Aeneid* was but an imitation of Homer's *Odyssey*. Unlike the Greeks, the Romans are thought to have been essentially "pagan," rather than devoutly religious.

Not to be outshone were the Phoenicians, to whom the Greeks owe their tripartite division of sky (and mountains), sea and underworld. Zeus, Poseidon and Hades were patterned on the Canaanites' Baal, Yam and Mot. The Phoenicians' Astarte became identified with Aphrodite, the Romans' Venus.

To the myths we owe a great many cultural artefacts, including the names of a few days of the week, which in English were adapted to Norse gods like Tiw (Tuesday), Woden (Wednesday) and Thor (Thursday). In Italian they come to us from the Latin: Martedì for Mars, Mercoledì for Mercury and Giovedì for Jove or Jupiter.

A sincere belief in mythology by somebody living today could only be viewed as anachronistic, but the classical myths represent more than a quaint memory. Indeed, they were born in the same society that gave birth to the very foundations of Western literature, art, architecture, science, ethics and — after a fashion — democracy.

Perhaps ironically, the Greek culture of myths and legends has given us Sophocles, Aristotle, Plato, Aesop and (in Sicily) Archimedes, Empedocles, Theocritus, Philistus, Stesichorus, Timaeus and Aeschylus. But there is little evidence to suggest that these great thinkers considered mythology anything more than a cultural curiosity. Clearly, Greek philosophy represented a quantum leap beyond mythology, but it was not religion.

That the early Christian scriptures were written in Koine Greek rather than Latin or Aramaic reflects the wide influence of the Greeks' culture even in Roman times.

When Paul of Tarsus stated that the invisible must be understood by the visible, he was expressing an idea more Greek than Judaic. The Greeks were the first civilization to create deities in the human image, complete with human bodies and very human flaws. To the *Siceliots,* as the Sicilian Greeks are known, the myths were an inspirational element of daily life in their *Sikelia.*

The magnificent Greek temples of Sicily attest to more than a people's passion; they represent the perfect union of Humanity and Nature. After thirty centuries of progress, it is a model of harmony still worth emulating, and one that we have largely abandoned.

The Abrahamic Legacy

In the beginning there was monotheism. The difference between God and gods brought with it monumental implications for Mediterranean society.

But to opine is part of human nature, so sects and philosophies sprung up within religions almost immediately, based on belief, law and observance. There were the Pharisees, Sadducees and Essenes of Judaism, the Arians and Nazarenes of Christianity, the Sunnis and Shiites of Islam. Contestation and factionalization became part and parcel of organized religion.

Of the isolated monotheistic sects in the Roman Empire, those rooted in Judaism boasted the earliest, most cohesive tradition. Christianity and Islam followed.

For the first few decades following their Sicilian conquest, and at least until around 1110, the Normans permitted each population to be judged by its own law, norms greatly influenced by religious law. This was clear enough for the Arabs and Jews; for the Byzantines it was rooted in the Code of Justinian with a smidgen of ecclesial (canon) law, and for the Normans it was essentially feudal with some Catholic influences. The Assizes of Ariano, which incorporated elements from all of these traditions, were promulgated in 1140, definitively establishing a uniform legal system which, if not exactly "secular," accomplished progress in that direction.

Judaism

The inception of Judaism is difficult to date precisely, but Hebrew culture certainly existed by 1200 BCE (BC), and its literary traditions refer to personages such as Abraham who are thought to have lived at least several centuries before then. The historicity of an actual Abraham has been questioned.

Unlike most religions that flourished during the Bronze Age, Judaism boasted a sophisticated, rigid, written code of law governing every aspect of life. Modern skeptics posit that early figures like Moses are probably apocryphal, but few doubt that Mosaic Law, built upon the "ethical decalogue" or Ten Commandments, has been with us for a very long time, at least since 500 BCE. The Torah, which scholars believe was completed by 400 BCE, establishes Judaism as a faith and as a way of life.

Around 1000 BCE, Hebrew tribes established a monarchy in Judea, a region loosely contiguous to the present-day state of Israel. The ancient nation and its faith were inextricably linked to each other. But not all Semitic peoples of the region professed Judaism; the Phoenicians, who are usually identified with the Canaanites, were multitheists.

Greek civilization created its divinities in the human image, while Hebrew culture held that humans were created in God's image.

As a people, the Jews were never more than a small minority in Sicily; by 1492 they comprised perhaps eight percent of the island's unique multicultural mosaic.

Hebrew traders resided in Sicily during the last centuries of Roman rule. At first, these were communities of immigrants and descendants of former slaves, though it is clear that a number of local people in search of faith, as opposed to mythology, converted to Judaism. By the Middle Ages, intermarriage with Christians was not extremely unusual in Sicily.

The successive Eastern Empire was more tolerant than Rome, and the first free Jewish congregations grew after the time of Constantine the Great. Jewish temples were founded in Sicily's port cities (Palermo, Messina, Syracuse) around the same time that the first Christian churches were openly established. The central Mediterranean region's oldest known synagogue, discovered at Bova Marina in Calabria, was built during the fourth century.

Sicily's Jews lived more or less undisturbed until the fifteenth century. The year 1492 signalled the unification of Spain, the beginning of the European conquest of America and the Inquisition's final banishment of Jews from Spanish territories, including Sicily. Given until early 1493 to decide, many of the island's Jews, being Sicilian in almost every cultural sense, chose conversion (Sicily's *anusim* are descendants of those *neofiti,* similar to the *conversos* and *marranos* of Spain), and a number of Sicilian surnames reflect Jewish origins, or at least acknowledge a Jewish presence (Siino from Sion, Rabbino from Rabbi).

Contemporary estimates of the number of Jewish Sicilians indicate that the Jewish populations of Palermo, Messina, Siracusa — where Europe's oldest existing mikveh is preserved in Ortygia — and several other cities were sizeable in 1492. In Palermo, the Jewish Quarter was located in the area between Piazza Ballarò and Via Roma; there is solid evidence that the first metal merchants in the district of what is now Via dei Calderai were Jewish, and a synagogue stood near what is now Vicolo Meschita.

The conversion of the Jews, coming as it did through decrees and zealously enforced policies at a specific date, has left us with more identifiable traces than the conversions from Islam (see below) two centuries earlier. There are, for example, notarial records written from 1493 until around 1520 listing the names of former Jews and their property, and a few baptismal acts of converts. We also find certain surnames and given names of this period which are identified almost exclusively with Jews.

The culture of Sicily's earliest medieval Jews is best described as *Maghrebi*. Beginning in the Aragonese period (from 1282) it was subjected to Sephardi influences. The history of Sicily's Jews is described at greater length in Chapter 7.

Islam

Islam was founded by Mohammed, considered by Muslims to be the last Prophet of God. The Prophet Mohammed, who died in the Arabian city of Medina in 632, is believed to have restored to perfection a faith that was brought forth by many predecessors over the centuries but invariably corrupted. Islam considers Abraham to be the father of the Arabs and all Semitic peoples, regarding Jesus as a messenger of God. Written in Arabic, the Koran, the holy book of Islam, is considered the literal word of God, so any translation into another language is at best an interpretation. Islam brought religious law and obedience to tribal peoples living in isolated desert regions on the edge of the Byzantine Empire. Islam, like Judaism, is intended as a way of life.

Although it bears influences of the earlier Abrahamic faiths described here, Islam does not follow a direct line from either.

Conversely, Jesus was born a Jew in Judea and Christianity accepts most of the fundamental tenets of Judaism as they were taught until around the time of the *Pax Romana* of Augustus.

Nevertheless, some Muslim customs (veiling, fasting) were essentially similar to practices that had been known among Middle Eastern Jews and Christians, and certain of Islam's Koranic scriptures and precepts were not completely divorced from Judeo-Christian ones. Fasting (during Ramadan), almsgiving (zakat), pilgrimage and even Mohammed's visit by the angel Gabriel are essential elements of Islam. Islam shares the Jewish proscription on the consumption of pork.

The Muslims respected Jews and Christians as "people of the book," while considering their faith imperfect.

Islam remained united so long as Mohammed was alive, but then it divided into sects which exist to this day.

Initially, this was not a dispute about fundamental principles of faith but a more prosaic debate over who would lead. After Mohammed's death, some Muslims recognized his cousin (and son-in-law), Ali, as the spiritual leader of Islam, and these followers became known as Shiites (or Shia). Those who chose to follow Abu Bakr, Mohammed's father-in-law, as *caliph* (the religious and civil leader of Islam), became known as Sunnis.

The rift deepened following the death of Hussein, Ali's son and successor, at the hands of Sunni troops in 680. As time passed, different ideas about the nature and structure of Islam emerged. Shia believers came to accept earthly religious authorities, such as *ayatollahs,* as Allah's representatives, while Sunnis emphasized prayer and belief. In time, further differences arose over various questions of religious practice and law, and a number of sub-sects of Islam were founded in much the same manner that Protestant churches grew out of Catholicism, but that need not concern us here. (Worldwide, the great majority of today's Muslims are Sunnis.)

Sicily's Islamic tradition was overwhelmingly Shiite. The

Aghlabids, who ruled Sicily until 909, were Sunnis who were only nominally subject to the Abbasid caliph in Baghdad. (Like the Umayyads, the Abbasids were Sunni.) The Kalbid dynasty, which ruled Sicily from 948 until 1053, was officially subject to the Fatimids. Based at Madiyah (in Tunisia) and then, from 969, at Cairo, the Fatimids were Shiites whose caliphate extended from Morocco to Syria and included the holy cities of Mecca and Medina in Arabia.

The Fatimids embraced an early form of Ismailism, a specific "branch" of Shia with particular ideas about interpretation of the message of the Koran. *Zahir,* for example, points to the exoteric, or "obvious" lessons of the Koran that may be readily appreciated by any believer, as opposed to the esoteric understood by only a few. Quasi-materialist perspectives of this kind were linked to the Fatimids' appreciation of science and reason, and the value they placed on individual meritocracy over ancestry as the basis of a person's worth in society. The effects of such views on daily life might be subtle, making any extrapolation difficult at this distance of time. However, Fatimid pragmatism goes a long way to explain the Siculo-Arab concept of equal justice and — in areas such as commerce — equal opportunity for all.

In Palermo alone, there were over a hundred mosques with Koranic schools, and hundreds of imams, when the Normans arrived.

A body of evidence suggests that Islamic law of the Maliki School as it existed in twelfth-century Sicily influenced the early development of English common law (a theory considered in Chapter 25). By the time of the Vespers War (1282), there were extremely few professed Muslims in Sicily. Frederick II had exiled some of them to Lucera in Apulia for armed insurrection in 1246.

Sicily's Muslims converted a number of churches to mosques, perhaps including Saint John of the Hermits near the Norman Palace. The Normans, in turn, rebuilt some of these as churches.

Like many Jews in 1493, most of Sicily's Muslims converted to Catholicism during the twelfth and thirteenth centuries, a fact borne witness by artefacts such as the Gospels written in Arabic in Palermo during this period.

In medieval Sicily, Islam was inextricably bound to Arab culture. Most of the Muslims in Sicily were these "Saracens" or the descendants of Berbers. More precisely, many were the descendants of Sicilian women who had wed the conquering Arabs, each of whom, under Koranic law, could take as many as four wives.

During Arab rule, many churches and synagogues survived (though new ones could not be built), and not every Sicilian woman chose to wed a Muslim despite the economic advantages implicit in such a marriage. As recently as the thirteenth century, there were Muslims at the royal court — pontiffs cynically referred to Frederick II, who spoke Arabic, as a "baptized sultan" — and the Muslim towns in Sicily were essentially Arabic in every way, not unlike the Muslim towns in Spain.

There is compelling evidence to suggest that Frederick II considered his Muslim guards, soldiers and archers more loyal than many of his unruly Christian knights and barons.

Some interesting traces of the Muslim conversion to Catholicism after 1200 are known to us. There are, for example, lists of Catholic Sicilians of the thirteenth century bearing Christian names, with their parentage indicated giving their fathers' Muslim names. We find, for instance, "Tommaso, son of Abdullah."

Arab architects designed churches in what has come to be known as the "Norman-Arab" style, and an Arabic inscription is visible around the high cupola of the Martorana Church in Palermo.

Tangible evidence of Sicily's mosques is scant at best. In a corner of the interior of Palermo Cathedral, in the sacristy above the crypt, is a piece of the muquarnas ceiling that was probably part of the Great Friday Mosque, itself built upon a Paleo-Christian basilica in the ninth century. Outside, a pillar that was once part of a mosque supports the portico. It is inscribed in relief with passages from the Koran in Arabic. The importance of Islam in Arab society is considered further in Chapter 9.

Christianity

Christians believe that Jesus Christ was the Messiah, the Son of God. Jesus was crucified around AD (CE) 33 to atone for humanity's sins and is believed to have risen from the dead, ascending into heaven. The four gospels of the Bible's New Testament recount the life, words and works of Jesus. Other scriptures, most prominently the letters of Paul of Tarsus, complement these gospels, establishing the framework of Christianity. The Jewish scriptures are accepted according to Christian interpretation as the Old Testament. Christianity, like the other Abrahamic faiths, is intended as a way of life.

The importance of its derivation from Judaism cannot be overstated. Not for nothing has the term "Judeo-Christian" become part of our modern vernacular. Indeed, for some time after the death of Jesus, the Roman leadership regarded the Christians as little more than an eccentric sect of Judaism that happened to appeal to Greeks and other Gentiles.

Early in the fourth century, leaders (bishops) of the Church established the canons and the creed, and decided which scriptures would become part of the New Testament and which books (such as certain "gnostic" gospels) would be excluded. They also addressed widespread but mistaken beliefs that threatened to divide the Church, most notably Arianism (see Chapter 5), a doctrine which took root among the Germanic peoples.

There is thought to have been a tiny Christian community in Syracuse when Paul, the "Apostle to the Gentiles," preached there, though in his time the Christians were still a covert sect persecuted by the Empire. Armenia made Christianity its official religion in 301; Rome legalized its practice twelve years later.

A number of Greek and Roman temples were eventually converted into churches; Siracusa Cathedral, formerly the Temple of Athena, is the most magnificent example still standing. The essence of the oldest historical Church in Sicily is rooted in the Byzantine East, in the tradition which is today preserved in the Orthodox Church. The Normans arrived just a few years after the Great Schism (1054), in which the Patriarch of Rome (the Pope) separated from communion with the other patriarchs of the Church. That is the subject of Chapter 11.

Eastern Orthodoxy

The Norman kings, whose Italian conquests were sanctioned by the Popes of Rome, are generally viewed, theologically speaking, as "Latinizers." Yet, during the reign of Roger I the Archimandrite Nilos Doxopatrios authored a manuscript refuting the supremacy claimed by the Roman Pontiff.

The cathedral of Cefalù is distinctly Romanesque, with certain Gothic elements, while the cathedral of Monreale, and the churches of the Martorana (Palermo) and the Annunciation (Messina) are more similar to what one might encounter in Greece.

Despite eclectic styles, all were constructed during the same period. The Martorana, in fact, was built specifically as an Orthodox place of worship, and Monreale's cathedral originally had an icon screen.

The Schism's theological implications became evident over time as the Western Church itself evolved. Superficially, statues replaced icons, and the liturgy was altered. The mosaic icons in the Martorana, the Palatine Chapel, Monreale Abbey and Cefalù Cathedral reflect a Byzantine heritage. They also indicate an Orthodox presence for some time after the arrival of the Normans.

In social matters, the Schism paved the way for a more Italianate (and Papal) orientation which, in retrospect, brought Sicily's unique medieval interfaith experiment to an early demise. Yet Byzantine monasteries in northeastern Sicily's rugged Nebrodi Mountains continued to thrive into the fourteenth century.

There came a new influx of Orthodox Christians into southern Italy with the Albanian immigration of the fifteenth century. These parishes soon became known as "Uniate" because they entered into union with Rome. Today, their liturgy and customs are Orthodox but in fact these are Byzantine Rite parishes of the Catholic Church.

Compared to the disappearances of Islam and Judaism, the insidious transition of Orthodoxy to Catholicism was so subtle as to be all but invisible to most faithful until the middle years of the thirteenth century.

Byzantine culture, of which Orthodoxy was an integral part, is described at greater length in Chapter 6, where a few surviving Orthodox churches are mentioned.

Roman Catholicism

Sicily's early kings enjoyed the title and function of Apostolic, or "Papal," Legate, though as a fundamental principle of belief the Sicilian Crown was granted not by any Pope but emanated from God Himself. Ecclesiastical Sicily gravitated toward Rome very slowly indeed; occasional excommunication was something the Norman and Swabian kings took in stride. The new dioceses founded in Sicily during the Norman period, in places like Monreale and Patti, were under the canonical jurisdiction of Rome and probably used the Gallican Rite initially. Some of the new bishops were Normans; Bishop Walter "Offamilias" was a cousin of the royal Hautevilles. Sicily's Eastern tradition didn't vanish immediately, but like the Normans themselves it was all but forgotten within a few centuries. Byzantine Venice, Bari and Ravenna suffered the same fate.

How was Catholicism different from Orthodoxy? There were theological matters, such as the controversial *filioque* passage in the Creed, while the ecclesiastical primacy of one man (the Pope) also distinguished Catholics from their Orthodox brethren, whose patriarchal leadership was collegial. The Crusades were a Catholic phenomenon. In Sicily, Latin's replacement of Greek as the liturgical language represented perhaps the least significant alteration, but liturgy itself changed radically from that which existed in Byzantine times, and with it the role of the clergy.

Even the churches were different. The icon screen was omitted, and statues of saints (as opposed to the icons or simple bas-reliefs of earlier times) became increasingly commonplace in Western churches, where the Gothic, the Baroque and the Italian Romanesque supplanted the austere ecclesiastical architecture of the East. Statues and stained-glass windows are not something one expects to see in an Orthodox church.

Catholic culture is overwhelmingly Latin. The Papal appellation *Pontifex Maximus* is a Roman title once reserved to the highest priest of pagan Rome — one of many perpetual reminders that the Western Church was built upon the society of the Western Empire.

It could be argued, perhaps cogently, that the Christians of East and West always had their subtle differences, with Westerners cultivating a particular appreciation of the ideas of scholars like Augustine of Hippo (354-430), and the chasm merely widened after the Schism. Over time, the doctrines of Original Sin and the Immaculate Conception were introduced. Purgatory, indulgences and other Latin ideas rooted in late-medieval Western theology further distinguished Catholicism. The eloquent words of the nature-loving Francis of Assisi are appreciated today, with the environment at risk, but in the thirteenth century the "philosophical" theology espoused by Thomas of Aquinas carried more weight among intellectuals. To this day, the Orthodox churches are unencumbered by these later doctrines and dogmas.

In 1123 and 1139 the First and Second Lateran Councils made celibacy mandatory for Catholic clerics. Until then Catholic priests were permitted to take wives before ordination, and Orthodox priests (but not monks) still are. In more recent times, numerous bulls and encyclicals have brought to Catholicism a certain "legalism" lacking in Orthodoxy.

One of the antipodean differences between East and West had little to do with theology as such. Under the auspices of the Catholic Church, the Renaissance, in all its glory, fostered a fundamental change in creative and philosophical thought (Humanism), bringing about the true end of the Middle Ages.

Despite this great leap forward by a few artists and intellectuals, the vast majority of people living during the Renaissance in what is now Italy could not read or write, and their predicament was little improved by the time the country was unified in the nineteenth century. It must be said, however, that the situation was not much better in predominantly Orthodox countries like Greece and Russia.

Yet another schism, the Reformation, would challenge some of Catholicism's dearest tenets.

CHAPTER 5

The Vandals and Goths

Rome prospered for a thousand years, adopting various forms of government over the centuries. Its fall marked the beginning of what modern historians call the *Middle Ages,* and in the disarray a number of societies encroached upon what had once been Imperial territory. Among them were the Celts, Picts, Huns and various tribes described by Julius Caesar and other Romans. Two of these societies had a direct impact on Sicily.

They cannot be said to have influenced Sicily to the extent of the Greeks or the Romans, but the Vandals and Goths controlled the island for a brief interlude — just under a century — that ushered in a new era. Little visible evidence of the Vandals or Goths remains, though they probably intermarried with Sicilians to some extent and altered the gene pool. In Sicily their legacy is essentially a question of historical record and an important transitional period.

Here we shall consider their civilizations together, for they were contemporary and sometimes occupied bordering territory, and evidence suggests that the Vandals spoke the Goths' language. However, their societies and cultures were distinct, and it is quite possible that neither group would enjoy being placed in the same chapter with the other.

As we have said, most of what we know about the Vandals

and Goths comes to us from the Romans. In the days of Julius Caesar, who died in 44 BC (BCE) and Tacitus, who was born in AD (CE) 56, there were large European tribes known as the Celtae and Germani who controlled the regions to the north of the sprawling Empire. While they were but two of many such tribes, their influence was widespread, particularly in language, so most cultures in western and central Europe came to be described generically as "Celtic" while those to the north and east of these, including what are now the German, Baltic and Slavic regions, came to be called "Germanic." Imprecise they may be, but these vague Roman definitions shall serve our purpose.

The word *Barbarian* derived from a Greek term descriptive of bearded foreigners (the word *barbaros* meaning "bearded"). The Romans used the term to refer to peoples beyond the Empire's borders, whether or not their warriors wore beards. Common nouns like *barbarian* and *vandal* acquired their meanings due to the Latin influence on English, French, Italian and other languages.

Bearing the exemplar of Tacitus' *Germania* as their banner, historians are justified in recognizing in Germanic tribal practices the precursor to "common law," something we shall consider in Chapter 25. For the most part, however, these legal ideas did not survive except in residual form among such peoples as the Longobards and Saxons, and even those societies looked to Roman-style legal codes for the underpinnings of their jurisprudence.

The Goths and Vandals seem to have made no effort to introduce their legal system in Sicily, and in the long interlude from 600 to 900 it vanished except for a few isolated practices around Europe; Ireland's Brehon law, for example, bore lingering similarities to Celtic and Germanic ideas. The common law that has come to us is the product of twelfth-century Anglo-Norman principles which may have been influenced by

Muslim law.

Yet various social practices known to us seem to have originated with Germanic or Celtic ones. For example, when a man
wed a woman from a neighboring tribe — or a separate village
of the same tribe — he would bring with him, for protection,
a close male friend as his "best man." (In the early Church,
conversely, the "best man" was a *witness,* hence the Italian term
testimone at civil as well as religious weddings.) Here we see that
the Germanic concept of marriage itself differed somewhat
from what was prevalent among the Romans, Greeks, Jews
and early Christians, though by the beginning of the fifth century this was tempered by the introduction of Christianity
among the various Germanic peoples.

Certain articles of clothing, such as trousers, were probably
introduced into Roman society through contact with the Celts
or Germans.

Not a great deal of Gothic and Vandalic architecture survives except for monuments such as Theodoric's mausoleum
in Ravenna, the Ostrogoths' capital from 493 until 552. The
art left to us by the Vandals and Ostrogoths consists largely
of jewelry and small objects such as detailed figurines fash-
ioned of gold or silver, rings, belt buckles, necklaces, religious
articles like jewelled crucifixes, and of course coins. (The Visigoths in Spain left us more than the Ostrogoths in Italy.)

The Germanic languages, which include English, are of
course the greatest modern legacy of the ancient and early-
medieval peoples collectively known as "German" or "Germanic."

A tribe might settle in a certain area, but rarely was there a
"sedentary" capital city characterized by grandiose stone buildings. The law courts, for example, were simple councils of elders gathered to adjudicate specific cases. There was little
writing except, through later contact with the Romans, Latin.
Instead, specific individuals memorized legal decisions that

had been rendered. Certain principles of feudalism can be traced to earlier concepts which developed among the Germanic peoples.

Some of the greatest Germanic leaders, such as Arminius (Hermann), had been trained by the Romans, who permitted people on the fringe of the Empire to obtain citizenship.

In AD (CE) 9, Arminius and his Germans won a decisive battle against the Romans in the Teutoburg Forest. In response, the Romans constructed a wall between two great rivers to protect this part of the Empire from "Barbarians," a tactic which was successful in Scotland a century later when Hadrian's Wall was erected to keep out the Picts. But the tribal peoples rarely stayed united for very long, and the union of communities formed by the intrepid Arminius soon dissolved into the old, internecine rivalries.

A few centuries later, during a period coinciding with a series of troubles in the Roman Empire, several powerful tribes, usually identified as Germanic, emerged in the eastern part of Europe. The remote geographic origins of many Nordic, Germanic and Slavic tribes are not known precisely, but we have general indications.

The Vandals, who probably originated as an identifiable people in what is now Sweden, settled in Galicia, a region straddling the border between the modern nations of Ukraine and Poland. By 400, they had begun to migrate westward in response to the threat of the Huns, a nomadic Asiatic people. The Vandals, a people on the march, were eventually joined by the Alans, from Ossetia, and other tribes. In 406 they crossed the Rhine and raided Gaul (France). In 409 they entered Spain, though they did not settle there in substantial numbers. These were their first serious forays into the Roman Empire. The Vandals do not seem to have been much more destructive than other tribes, but to be called a "vandal" is not very flattering.

Much that is known about the Goths comes to us from the *Getica,* an embellished account written by the Roman Jordanes circa 551.

The Goths seem to have migrated from Scandinavia to Pomerania, on the Baltic Sea, then southward to the region just north of the Black Sea. The Goths came to be identified as two populations, the *Ostrogoths* ("East Goths" of the Black Sea area who eventually reached Sicily) and the *Visigoths* ("West Goths" of the Lower Danube who later occupied Spain but not Sicily). In AD 376, the Romans permitted the Visigoths to settle south of the Danube, effectively constituting a foreign state within the Empire.

It was to prove a fragile peace. In 378 a Roman army was defeated by Goth forces at the Battle of Adrianople, now Edirne in European Turkey near the borders of Greece and Bulgaria. The victory of the Goth cavalry has occasionally been attributed to stirrups which facilitated a mounted charge with a lance. Historians now doubt that the Goths made use of the stirrup at this early date, but there is little doubt that the battle itself was a bitter turning point for the Romans, and a harbinger of things to come.

By this time Christianity was the most important religion among Romans. It wasn't long before the Goths and Vandals, who imitated Rome in so many ways, adopted Christianity. However, in embracing Arianism, a doctrine that came to be considered heretical, they set themselves apart from most other Christians.

Before 383, Wulfila, who was educated in the Byzantine east, translated the Bible into Gothic using a script of his own invention. A later copy, the *Codex Argenteus,* is the earliest written example of the Goths' language. The characters used are an uncial variation of Greek not unlike the Cyrillic alphabet devised for Slavonic by Cyril and Methodius a few centuries later, now used for Russian.

While the introduction of writing was inevitable, it brought with it reliance on the written word, and as it happens few oral traditions of the Germanic peoples of the fifth and sixth centuries were recorded to be handed down to us. Consequently, we know much more about Punic and Roman mythology and literature than we do about the earliest Norse and Germanic myths — the *Edda* was written long after the *Odyssey*. But Germanic (and Norse) mythology has given us fairies, elves, dwarfs, trolls, valkyries, various talking animals and giant, mystical trees. Medieval fairy tales owe much to this tradition.

Children's stories of this kind were not an ersatz invention, but a reflection of the existing social environment. The hierarchy of medieval European society, with its kings, nobles and peasants, is largely the fruit of Germanic social norms widespread by 700, a model epitomized by the rule of Charlemagne. Except for the persistence of quaint literary archetypes like the fairy tale princess, such institutions tend to be dismissed as anachronisms in our republican age. Yet ten hereditary monarchies survive in Europe in the twenty-first century. Monarchies were closely connected to political power as recently as the era of the calamitous First World War.

That bloody conflict is but a single example of Christians warring against each other. The first major battles between large armies composed primarily of Christians were the clashes of the Goths and Vandals with the Romans.

Rome was sacked by Visigoths under Alaric in 410, though by then the city was no longer the capital of the Western Empire, which was governed from Ravenna. Spain eventually fell to the Visigoths, and a few of the oldest Spanish noble families claim descent from them.

Having invaded France and Visigothic Spain, and having been driven from both, the Vandals migrated into northern Africa. In 429, they annexed several Roman provinces to their upstart kingdom, which from 430 was based in the area around

Carthage. Nearing the end of his life, the early Christian thinker Augustine of Hippo saw his homeland fall to the Vandals, who soon dominated trade and transport in their part of the Mediterranean. The best known Vandal leader was Genseric (Gaiseric), who ruled from 428 to 477.

The Huns invaded Gaul in 451, only to be repulsed by a joint Roman-Germanic army at a decisive battle near Troyes. But this alliance against a common foe would prove transient.

Genseric's Vandals first landed in Sicily in force in 440 in what was essentially a major looting expedition, without establishing a lasting presence. A year later, the Byzantines launched an effective counterattack meant to discourage Vandalic expansionism. Only decades later would the Vandals achieve complete dominion over Sicily, and they were not to enjoy it for long. In the meantime they turned their attention to Rome, which they sacked in 455, following in the footsteps of the Visigoths forty-five years earlier.

Rome perhaps failed to meet their expectations, for the beleaguered city that the invaders found on the Tiber was but a shadow of its former self.

The Byzantines, as we have seen, made occasional efforts to assist their Western Roman allies in defending Sicily against the Vandals, if only in the interest of guarding their own western frontier.

The Vandals eventually agreed to a fragile peace with what was left of the crumbling Western Roman Empire. This held up until 461, when Genseric exploited a change in Roman leadership as a pretext for breaking the truce. Returning *en masse* to raid Sicily in that year, the Vandals gradually established a permanent presence, completely occupying the island by around 468. Here the Vandals encountered a prosperous economy but — in one of the first major acts of anti-Semitism by Christians — they destroyed the synagogue at Syracuse. It was for this kind of *vandalism* that they would become infamous.

Meanwhile, the Ostrogoths and their Germanic confederates finally decided to put an end to declining Rome's empty pretensions. It was all but anticlimactic when Odoacer, a German (like Arminius before him) formerly in the service of Rome, deposed the last Western Emperor in 476. Meanwhile, Genseric, King of the Vandals, then aged about eighty-six, was making "perpetual" peace with the "Byzantine" Eastern Romans of Constantinople.

Odoacer's successor was another "Barbarian" educated in Roman society. Theodoric "the Great" was an Ostrogoth raised in Constantinople. He and his people had been eyeing strategic Sicily for years, but only in 488 did they finally make a major landing on the island. Here the Ostrogoths encountered resistance from the entrenched Vandals, but they emerged victorious in 491 following a three-year campaign.

Most of the vanquished Vandals in Sicily probably returned "home" to Africa while some simply assimilated with the new occupiers and remained. Considering how Romanized the Ostrogoths' culture had become, it is unsurprising that Theodoric's government in Sicily, such as it was, would be essentially Roman in form. "Every Goth wants to be a Roman, but only the humblest Roman wants to be a Goth," he is said to have commented.

Historians now recognize that many of the invasions in the declining Western Roman Empire were not continuous wars but steady migrations punctuated by the occasional battle. In certain isolated (rural) communities the change of government may not even have been evident for months or years. This appears to have been true of the migrations into Sicily, where evidence suggests that the Ostrogoths were better administrators than the Vandals, and it partly explains a particular historiographical phenomenon.

Some accounts — and even maps — of Gothic and Vandalic rule in Sicily are confusing if not contradictory. That is because, like the Carthaginians and Greeks a thousand years earlier, one or the other controlled specific *parts* of the contested island at certain times. (This pattern of plodding conquest was to be repeated by the Arabs and Normans.)

As we have seen, the Vandals' first major invasion of Sicily (in 440) failed to achieve absolute control, their ambitions being thwarted by a Byzantine force the following year. But while their initial Sicilian adventure was hardly a conquest, the Vandals' African base so close to the island made it easy for some of them to return to western Sicily from time to time over the next twenty years, even before the new wave of "declared" raids commenced in 461.

In the typical scenario, a party of fifty or sixty Vandals would come ashore in an unguarded area of western Sicily, making its way beyond the coast to raid a few unprotected villages of the hinterland in search of plunder and women. Enough of these episodes are recorded for us to know that they occurred. Five centuries later, the Vikings were making use of similar tactics, which by then were a normal part of medieval warfare.

As we have said, the Ostrogoths were masters of the island by 491. By 493, making the Romans' Ravenna their capital, they ruled not only Sicily but the Italian peninsula and parts of what are now Austria, Switzerland, Croatia, Slovenia and southeastern France.

The kindred Visigoths, meanwhile, had settled in eastern Spain and part of southwestern France, where Alaric II issued his *Breviarium* of Roman law, the *Lex Romana Visigothorum,* in 506.

Observing developments from Constantinople, the Byzantines were not happy to see the Ostrogoths in control of so much Italian territory, but they were equally concerned about the vagarious Vandals. The Emperor Justinian was particularly annoyed to learn that his friend, the Vandal king Hilderic, was deposed by Gelimer in 530.

The Vandals in north Africa were handily defeated by an army led by the Byzantine general Belisarius during a bloody war in 533 and 534. Gelimer was deposed and the ephemeral Vandalic kingdom was banished to the pages of history. In the process, the Vandals' homeland was annexed as a province of the Byzantine Empire.

In Sicily the formidable Ostrogoths' day of reckoning was soon to dawn. Unlike the Vandals, they saw it coming. Nevertheless, in 535 Belisarius conquered the island from them and it, too, was now ruled from Constantinople.

Totila, an Ostrogoth leader, invaded Sicily in 550 but the Byzantines reclaimed complete control following his defeat at Taginae, in Umbria, two years later. This squelched any subsequent "Barbarian" pretensions to rule Sicily. Indeed, Ostrogothic and Vandalic civilization effectively came to an end after this "Gothic War," though the Visigoths continued to flourish in Spain.

These victories incidentally dealt a veritable death blow to Arianism, which thereafter survived only in a few lingering pockets of resistance. This movement was dividing the Church.

The first major theological conflict of Christianity, Arianism challenged, among other things, the full status of Jesus Christ as part of the triune God. This doctrinal error, declared heretical by the Council of Nicea in 325, provided the Romans of East and West with a religious pretext for condemning the Vandals and Goths moralistically. In the Vandal Kingdom the majority of native (Roman) believers were permitted to worship in "Nicene" churches, while most Vandals were Arians. This divided Christians socially based on religious belief. The defeat of the Vandals and Ostrogoths was as significant theologically as it was politically. Indeed, it was an early example of how religion and politics were to be inextricably linked throughout the Middle Ages.

The fate of peninsular Italy was tied to the ambitions of another Germanic civilization, the Longobards, which originated in the northernmost part of Germany along the Elbe. Following the Byzantines' victory over the Ostrogoths, the Longobards, or "long beards," occupied most of the peninsula except for a few Byzantine cities. They never conquered Sicily, but some of their descendants, the Lombards, arrived with the Normans during the eleventh century.

Perhaps the "Barbarians" were not always so barbaric as they were depicted in the past. Perhaps their evanescent society had much to offer. But the social order had changed. The era we now call the *Middle Ages* had well and truly arrived.

CHAPTER 6

The Byzantine Greeks

Born of the Eastern Roman Empire that emerged after AD
(CE) 395, the Byzantine Empire lasted throughout the Middle
Ages — its official language initially Latin but its culture and
vernacular tongue Greek. During Europe's "Dark Ages," the
two or three centuries following the fall of Roman Italy around
476, Constantinople (the former Byzantium) shone like a beacon in a sea of darkness.

The Byzantine Empire did not portend great changes.
Rather, it preserved older Greek and Roman traditions while
fostering new "Byzantine Greek" ones. It emerged as the most
important and influential Christianized region of the Early
Middle Ages.

It was the Roman Emperor Constantine I "the Great," a
charismatic leader of eastern origins, who legalized Christianity
in the Roman Empire early in the fourth century. In many
ways, this early form of worship was very similar to what is
still preserved in the Orthodox Churches, the Roman Catholic
Church having altered much of its theology and liturgy since
the eleventh century (more about this later). The defining
Byzantine artistic movements were Christian ones.

Ethnically, the earliest Byzantines were essentially Greek,
with Italic, Balkan, Armenian, Slavic and western Asian strains.
By the ninth century, Sicily stood at the western edge of this

empire. To the east, the bourgeoning Kievan Rus culture of the next century was an outgrowth of Byzantine civilization around the Black Sea, personified in the rule of Vladimir the Great, who Christianized much of what is now Russia and Ukraine, and wed the daughter of Eastern Emperor Basil II. By then, however, Sicily was part of the Fatimid Empire ruled by the Kalbid dynasty.

The Byzantines' Roman culture, such as it was, merits explanation.

The Latin language never made great inroads into Greece proper or any of the Mediterranean regions to the east of Sicily. Here the vernacular, and the language of much literature, was Greek. Not without reason, the Christian scriptures were written in Koine Greek rather than Latin, the latter rightly regarded as a "foreign" tongue.

Greek was the scholarly second language of the better educated Romans in Italy and Gaul. In the words of Horace, the greatest Roman poet of his time: *Graecia capta ferum victorem cepit et artis intulit agresti Latio.* "Conquered Greece has conquered the brutish victor by bringing her arts to rustic Latium."

Over time, Latin was introduced as the official language in the eastern reaches of Rome's expansive Empire. Some historians even suggest that the Roman elite in some eastern provinces made use of Latin as if it were an esoteric code that could not be understood by the subject population.

Latin remained the official language of the Eastern Roman ("Byzantine") Empire until 620, when Greek was restored for that purpose. This may have been part of a general trend to reintroduce "native" languages in the wake of Rome's fall. Unlike the Germanic peoples, whose ancient languages were not written, the languages of the Greeks and Hebrews had been written since at least 1000 BC (BCE).

Linguistically and culturally, Byzantine society was not very different from that of Sicily in the fifth century. Throughout most of its history, the Byzantine Empire was a monarchy — albeit not always a strictly hereditary or absolute one — having legislative bodies and other democratic institutions considered exceptional for their time. Over the centuries, Byzantine society and culture greatly influenced eastern Europe, and particularly (as we have said) the Kievan state which became Russia, as well as the cultures of the Caucasus to the east of the Black Sea, facilitating the introduction of Christianity in Armenia, Georgia and elsewhere.

In AD 324, when Constantine became Emperor of the Roman Empire, Byzantium was little more than a Greek town on the European side of the Bosporus strait. In 330, he made it the capital of the entire Empire. Byzantium was eventually renamed Constantinople and is now Turkish Istanbul.

Constantine convoked the Council of Nicea in 325. With the participation of numerous bishops from across the Empire, it selected the New Testament scriptures to accurately reflect Church teaching (the so-called "Gnostic Gospels" were excluded from consideration), establishing the Canon of early Christianity still followed by Orthodox, Catholics and Anglicans today.

Straddling Europe and Asia, Byzantium was destined to play a key role in early-medieval history. In 395, when the Empire was divided into east and west, this growing city became the capital of the Eastern Roman Empire and resisted the raids of "Barbarians" — the Huns and Germanic tribes described in the previous chapter — that eroded the Empire in the West (what are today Italy, Switzerland, France, Germany, Britain, Spain, Portugal, Algeria, Morocco and Tunisia).

The Byzantine Empire was geographically its largest under Justinian I (ruled 527-565), who, as we saw in the last chapter, extended it to include Sicily, Tunisia and parts of peninsular Italy, seizing power from the Ostrogoths and Vandals.

The "Plague of Justinian," an outbreak of bubonic plague in 541, decimated the population of the Byzantine Empire, rendering the military reconquest of Italy from the Goths (and then the Longobards) nearly impossible.

Greek was the earliest liturgical language of the Sicilians. Not for nothing did the invading Normans, landing in Sicily in 1061, refer to half the inhabitants as "Greeks." This was not the classical tongue spoken by Socrates and Archimedes but an evolving, medieval "vulgar" Greek. The precursor of Italian and Sicilian was the Latin Vulgate.

The *Code of Justinian* is the basis for legal systems still used today, but in his own time Justinian himself was perceived as an extremist whose defense of Christianity led to overt intolerance of other faiths. His policy, though exceptional in the Byzantine Empire in successive years, resulted in the persecution of heretics, pagans and Jews.

Byzantine art was a major influence in Sicily and elsewhere. Often, as in Christian iconography, it was more representational than realistic. Geometric motifs were common, and the use of mosaic was highly developed. What we see in Sicily is similar in style to Komnenian mosaic, which may be its chief influence. Churches and palaces were usually built in the Romanesque style based loosely on the structure of ancient Greek temples, sometimes with cupolas (domes). Crafts such as jewelry making and silk weaving flourished. Works of literature, drama and history were widely appreciated.

In Sicily, the few centuries of Byzantine rule were peaceful and prosperous, although taxation was rather high. The Byzantine artistic influence lasted well into the Arab and Norman eras.

It was noted earlier that the stirrup probably was not used at the Battle of Adrianople in 378. But within two centuries it had made its way into the Byzantine Empire and Italy, thanks to its introduction by the Avars, and it facilitated more efficient mounted warfare. The horseborne warrior could now attack while holding a lance with lesser risk of being unseated. This led to the development of more effective cavalry units, paving the way for knights a few centuries later.

By 600, the Lombards had occupied most of the Italian peninsula. A few cities, like Venice, achieved short-lived independence, while others, like Bari, remained Byzantine culturally. Despite a tenuous truce in 603, what followed south of Rome for the next few centuries was a continuous, back-and-forth tug of war between Byzantines and Lombards. With the exception of a few localities, such as Salerno, the Byzantines usually controlled Bari and the larger cities, especially in the peninsular regions of Apulia and Calabria, leaving the hinterland to the Lombards.

In 915, faced with encroachment by yet another power, the Byzantines joined forces with the Lombards and the Papacy to expel an Arab settlement that had been established at the mouth of the Garigliano River south of Rome. But politics makes strange bedfellows, and this was little more than a transitory alliance, the expedient application of a classic dictum: "The enemy of my enemy is my friend."

The Papacy retained its influence around Rome, owing much to the efforts of Pope Gregory the Great, who desired independence from the collegial traditions espoused by the other patriarchs. Such developments in Italy did not immediately affect Sicily, where the Byzantine Emperor Constans II decided to establish his capital in 660. Syracuse, still the island's most important city, became his residence until his untimely assassination in 668. The Emperor's tyrannical demeanor and costly maintenance did not endear him to the Sicilians. Nor were his motives altogether altruistic; Syracuse served as his base for a failed attempt to reconquer peninsular Italy from the Longobards.

The capital city of Syracuse boasted a large Jewish community, and its chief mikveh, Europe's oldest surviving ritual bath, was carved into limestone during this period in the Ortygia district.

Islam was growing, and by 642 Muslim armies controlled Egypt, Syria and Palestine. By 652, Muslim pirates based in Tunisia were undertaking isolated raids on the Sicilian coast. By 750, the Byzantine Empire, though influential, was greatly reduced in size, encompassing Asia Minor (Turkey), Greece, Sicily, parts of the Balkans and some coastal settlements on the Black Sea.

With Islam's inexorable advance westward through Arab efforts, Carthage fell in 689. Muslim conquest often resulted in mass conversion of the conquered. In keeping with Koranic principles, the religious freedom of Jews and Christians was usually respected, but Muslims were accorded greater civil rights. Within two decades, several islands under Sicilian influence (notably Pantelleria) were occupied. Though the Sicilians traded with the Arabs and Berbers, coastal raids became commonplace. These diminished somewhat after 750 owing to internal struggles among the Muslims.

By 800, there were Arab merchants living in several Sicilian cities, such as Mazara and Marsala. In 805 and again in 813, the Governor of Sicily signed trade treaties with the Aghlabids of Tunisia.

Matters in Constantinople were not so serene. In 827, the Emperor ordered the arrest of Euphemius, Governor of Sicily and a distinguished general. This prompted a revolt in which the general declared himself Emperor. Faced with further dissension, Euphemius sought help from the Aghlabid Emir, offering him Sicily (a profitable source of tax revenue) in return. The Emir accepted, and soon a multiethnic force of at least ten thousand Berbers, Arabs, Persians, and Iberians occupied the western Sicilian city of Mazara.

Bal'harm (Palermo), formerly Panormus, was taken in 831

and soon became the capital of what, two centuries later, was the island's principal emirate. Syracuse fell only in 878, and Taormina in 902. The isolated Byzantine stronghold of Rometta seems to have resisted — at least sporadically — until 965, when it capitulated following a lengthy siege during which it received substantial reinforcements from Constantinople. Appropriately, its name means "fortress," from the Greek *erymata,* and its Byzantine walls can still be seen today.

Beginning in 867, the Emperor Basil and his descendants promoted a period of particular prosperity and scholarship in Constantinople. Little by little, alchemy was beginning to give way to chemistry, astrology to astronomy. The Empire continued to exist as an important force in the Mediterranean, but as only a shadow of its former self. Some Italian cities remained under Byzantine control, at least nominally, but Sicily was lost forever. Constantinople fell to the Turks in 1453, a date considered by many scholars to mark the end of the Middle Ages.

Byzantine rule did not result in a mass "colonization" of Sicily like those of the ancient Greeks or medieval Arabs, but there was certainly immigration and trade. Constantinople's lasting effects in Sicily far transcended her waning political influence.

Sources of information on the Byzantine Empire and its rapport with the Normans are not lacking. Of particular note is the *Alexiad,* written by Anna Comnena (or Komnene) around 1148. This lengthy work highlights the increasing differences between West and East, Latins and Greeks, during that period.

Byzantine culture was not simply a question of Byzantine rule and the Greek language. In Sicily and elsewhere, Byzantine society and culture melded with Arabic culture. Indeed, Arabic and Islamic art and society were greatly influenced by Byzantium. Mosques were constructed, often with the help of

Byzantine craftsmen, and in Sicily the Church, formally under the Patriarchate of Constantinople from 732, remained solidly Greek Orthodox into the early years of Norman rule, when the beginnings of Latinization took place.

The Schism between the Patriarch of Rome and the patriarchs of the East occurred in 1054, when Sicily was ruled by Muslim emirs. This is described elsewhere; what is significant is that the first, gravest effects of the division in the Church were felt in Sicily.

Here it must be emphasized that the Greek Orthodox Church was an integral part of Byzantine society, perhaps moreso even than the Roman Catholic Church in western Europe.

Differences between the Latin and Greek ecclesiastical spheres festered long before the Schism. One of the reasons the Normans arriving a few years later met as much resistance from Byzantines as Arabs was because the Orthodox justly feared Rome's intervention in their liturgy.

The Normans conquered Messina in 1061 and took Palermo a decade later. In Sicily, the introduction of Latin clergy, and the use of the Latin language in liturgy, were gradually introduced in the decades following. By the time Frederick II ascended the Throne as a young man early in the thirteenth century, little remained of Orthodoxy in Sicily except a few monasteries in the Nebrodi and Peloritan mountains. Greek, Arabic and Norman French were giving way to a new Latin tongue: Sicilian.

Yet, in the context of a society made up of several important cultures, Byzantine art flourished in Sicily well into the thirteenth century. In the popular mind, mosaic is the art form most immediately associated with the Byzantines.

Bearing the marks of Orthodoxy, several of the Normans' earliest Latin churches, resplendent in mosaic icons and other Byzantine elements, look more Eastern than Western. The

Palatine Chapel, and the cathedrals of Monreale and Cefalù, come to mind — each bears in its apse a striking mosaic icon of Christ Pantocrator.

Of particular interest among surviving churches built specifically as Greek Orthodox (not Roman Catholic) are the Martorana of Palermo, the Cuba di Santa Domenica outside Castiglione di Sicilia near Taormina, and Santissimo Salvatore (Santa Maria dei Cerei) at Rometta in the Nebrodi Mountains. The oldest surviving part of Messina's Annunziata dei Catalani, specifically the apse and cupola, was part of an Orthodox church. Despite its Romanesque layout, Santi Pietro e Paolo at Casalvecchio Siculo (also near Taormina) may have been Orthodox originally. Such churches also survive in Sardinia, Calabria and Puglia.

An everyday example of an Italian Catholic practice that survives from Byzantine times can be seen during the celebration of Mass in certain parish churches in small towns in Sicily, Calabria and Basilicata. This is the congregants' raising of both arms, palms facing forward, during prayer, rather than simply folding the hands together; this variation of the *orans* posture is a very old Greek custom popularized at the dawn of Christianity. If Saint Paul prayed when he visited Sicily, this is how he did it, for the outstretched arms and open hands "reaching up to God" originated with Hebrew prayer. The folded-hands position popular in parts of western Europe by the twelfth century was originally a sign of servility associated with Roman slaves or shackled prisoners.

As we have seen, the ancient Greeks traded overland with northern India and central Asia, and the Romans established maritime trade with southern India. The impetus of these eastward efforts is difficult to gauge, and in the event it was eclipsed by Muslim achievements, but it may have resulted in the introduction of certain Asian cultivars, such as pistachios and citrons, in Sicily.

CHAPTER 7

The Jews

In the Middle Ages the ethnonym *Jew* referred not simply to a religion, Judaism, but to those descended from Jews whose Semitic origin was rooted in the ancient society and culture of the Hebrews and Israelites. The religious and ethnic identity were one and the same.

It is often overlooked that Judaism, with its monotheism and moral code, forms the framework of subsequent Western faiths; if there had been no Judaism, the Christianity and Islam we know would not exist.

The first Jews of Sicily were present in Greek times; archeological evidence suggests that a community of the Samaritan sect flourished in Syracuse. Some Jews arrived following Pompey's sack of Jerusalem in 63 BCE (BC). It has been suggested that the infamous Crassus, famous for defeating the slave army led by Spartacus, deported a number of Jews to Sicily, where they were enslaved, but evidence of this is sketchy.

It is thought that while in Syracuse, Paul of Tarsus preached to Jews as well as Greeks and Romans. Of particular note, a few Jews arrived as slaves following the Siege of Jerusalem around a decade later in CE (AD) 70 during the First Jewish-Roman War (The Great Revolt), commemorated in Rome's Arch of Titus, where one of the earliest depictions of a menorah appears as a spoil of war. Jewish prisoners were pressed into service to build the Colosseum.

However, the greatest influx arrived in Sicily during the decades immediately after 135, in the wake of the Romans' complete expulsion of the Jews from Jerusalem after Bar Kokhba's Revolt (which began in 132) during the rule of the Emperor Hadrian. Thus whatever semblance of Jewish independence had ever existed under the Romans was lost. This led to the *Diaspora,* from the Greek word for a "scattering" or dispersion.

Though Syracuse had been a Roman city since 212 BCE, its culture and principal language were Greek throughout the Roman period. With the arrival of the Jewish refugees, Aramaic was added to its linguistic mix. Most of the city's Jews resided in their own quarter in Ortygia, where for many centuries their lives were governed by their own law. Many were traders.

Remains of one of the oldest synagogues in Europe have been discovered near the Calabrian town of Bova Marina. Built during the fourth century, it has a mosaic pavement displaying a menorah flanked by an *etrog* (citron) and a *shofar* (horn).

In 598 the Patriarch of the West, Pope Gregory the Great, with the Papal bull *Sicut Judeis,* ordered Sicily's bishops to protect the island's Jews from persecution and forced conversions.

By the time the Arabs arrived there were flourishing Jewish communities in Messina, Panormus (Palermo), Syracuse, Mazara and elsewhere. Many cities had a *giudecca,* or Jewish quarter.

A synagogue erected in Palermo around 1020 is mentioned in a document of 1094 describing its location along a river. Another — or perhaps the same one — is mentioned in passing in a document of 1302; this was located in the Kasr district near the royal palace, and it is sometimes identified with the site of the Church of Saint James (San Giacomo dei Militari) that once stood here, near the Papireto River. The great synagogue standing in 1492 was located northward, near the Kemonia River, by then diverted into a subterranean channel.

The Jews of medieval Sicily had a close cultural affinity to the Maghrebim of northern Africa and, later, the Sephardim (of Spain). In Sicily their spoken language was a Maghrebi tongue somewhat similar to Siculo Arabic, itself now preserved as Maltese. (The term *Mizrahim* originally referred to Jews in Arab areas of the eastern Mediterranean, while *Maghrebim* denoted the culture of the Jews of western regions such as Tunisia and Morocco.)

Over time, the idea took hold that every man in the congregation should be able to read from the Torah. This was not necessarily a ceremonial rite of passage to adulthood (the *bar mitzvah* we know today was a later development), but it reflected the great value placed on literacy in the Jewish community.

At this distance of time, it is difficult to characterize precisely the liturgical practice of the Sicilian Jews over the centuries. Clearly, they had a Sephardic orientation by the fifteenth century. There seems to have been no use of the Italian Rite favored by the Jews of Rome. The Sicilian Jews who migrated to Rome after 1492 established in their synagogue of that city a congregation of Sephardic tradition.

The status of the Jews was generally protected until the fifteenth century. The "Ordinance of the Jews of the Crown of Aragon," signed in 1354, while it did not involve Sicily's Jews directly (it dealt with Aragon, Valencia and Catalonia), indicates the willingness of the Aragonese kings to address the concerns of this minority population.

Unfortunately, the main branch of the Aragonese dynasty died out during a crucial period, to be succeeded in 1412 by the more zealously Catholic Trastámara dynasty of Castile.

An incident that presaged things to come was the massacre of over three hundred Jews in the town of Modica in August 1474, an atrocity instigated by a priest's zealous sermon "urging" them to pray in a church with Catholics. This was, in effect, a localized genocide.

The infamous Spanish edict, the Alhambra Decree, of 1492 brought to an end the Jewish presence in Sicily the following year. (A few months' "grace" was added to facilitate the collection of a final levy of taxes on the island's Jewish population.) It outlawed the practice of the Jewish religion, and though a number of Jews left Sicily, perhaps half converted to Catholicism and stayed, like the *conversos* in Spain. In Sicily these converts were called *neofiti*.

By the 1520s, acts of baptism and marriage in Sicilian churches near formerly Jewish communities listed a number of families bearing surnames such as *de Simone* (son of Simon), *Siino* (Sion) and *Mosé* (Moses), and baptismal names such as Isacco, Beniamino, Abramo, Iasué and Davide, formerly rare among Sicilian Christians.

Apropos surnames, here are at least a few which in many cases are associated with Jewish families: Tintura (literally "dyer"), Bottega (shop), Ebreo (Jew), Giosuè (Joshua), Giobbe (Job), Ziino (Zion), Saia (Isaiah), Isacco and Sacco (Isaac), Giudeo and Iudeo (Jew), Iudecca and Giudica ("from the Jewish quarter"), Giuda (Judas), Iacoppo (Jacob).

In 1493, most *anusim* (who forcibly converted to Catholicism) simply assumed surnames already in common use among Sicily's Catholics, whether based on a phonetic similarity to their previous (Jewish) names or an approximate translation. Some assumed given (Christian) names having no Judaic roots or references and gave such names to their children: Francesco, Calogero, Cristina or Caterina rather than Beniamino, Zaccaria, Sara or Rebecca.

Most Sicilians have Jewish ancestors through one line or another.

The Sicilian Jews never constituted a dominant or colonizing class, but their contribution to the fabric — literally — of

Sicilian society was important. Many medieval Sicilian communities had Jewish populations, and many medieval Jews were involved in fabric dying and (less frequently) weaving.

By the time of the edict, Sicily was essentially Roman Catholic except for a few Albanian Orthodox churches. In 1492 the Jewish Sicilians were a small but important part of the island's population, as much as eight percent by some estimates. They were hardly "outsiders" in any conventional sense of that word.

The Normans were tolerant and even protective of the Jewish population, and the same might be said of the Swabians. Indeed, the Jews of Sicily experienced little overt antagonism from their fellow islanders until the fourteenth century. Sicily's Christians certainly understood the differences between Muslims and Jews, but both were Semitic peoples whose way of life, at least superficially, sometimes seemed quite similar. We should consider, for example, that in Norman times even many Christian women wore veils in public — covering some of their hair but not their faces. (This information comes to us from bin Jubayr and other visitors.)

The infamous edict of 1492 was issued in an atmosphere of zeal in a time when Catholicism's reactionary influences (particularly the Inquisition) had displaced those of the tolerant twelfth century. The Moors had finally been defeated in Spain, and the Jews were a convenient target. Easy prey, it could be said. Christianized Jews were allegedly the focus of a riot in Palermo in 1516, and even if the account is merely anecdotal it proves that Sicilians descended from Jews were still identified as such a generation after the edict.

In 1493 a number of Sicilian Jews settled in Calabria, but in 1541 an edict similar to the Alhambra Decree took effect in that region.

It appears that by 1492 the Jews of Palermo constituted the largest Jewish community in Sicily, followed by that of Siracusa, whose mikveh, Europe's oldest Jewish ritual bath, is described in the next chapter.

Much of our knowledge of Mediterranean Jews, including those of Sicily, in the twelfth century comes from Benjamin of Tudela, an Iberian contemporary of Abdullah al Idrisi. In addition to visiting Sicily, Benjamin also described many Gentile groups, and mentioned China. He estimated that there were at least two hundred Jewish families in Messina in the 1170s. That Frederick II employed Jews at court to translate Greek and Arabic works implies a high level of literacy among Jewish Sicilians.

In the early 1060s Sicily's Jews often made common cause with the Arabs against the Normans, as at the Battle of Messina and subsequent campaigns in the Nebrodi Mountains. Estimates vary widely, but as recently as 1490 there may have been as many as 40,000 Jews in Sicily. Of the Jews who then departed for Rome, Ancona, Venice, Malta or elsewhere, some adopted surnames such as *Palermo* or *Messina* in reference to their city of birth — though this is not to imply that all Italians bearing such surnames are descended patrilineally from Jewish forebears.

At the threshold of the sixteenth century, Sicily's Jews constituted the largest intellectual class of what was becoming a largely illiterate society, and in some cities — particularly Palermo — they lived near or among the high nobility. A few decades following the expulsions, an unsuccessful effort was made to coax the émigrés into returning.

Few visible traces of Sicily's Jewish heritage remain beyond a handful of inscriptions and small structures scattered around the island — though there is abundant documentary evidence. Judaic law constituted one of the four civil codes imposed by Robert de Hauteville and his brother Roger, the others being Catholic, Greek (Orthodox) and Islamic. It is believed that a few localised Catholic religious traditions in Sicily and Calabria are based on Jewish ones. There are also culinary traditions which appear to be rooted in kosher observance.

Most Sicilian Jews were involved in craft or trade but at least a few lent money. Frederick II made usury a crime for most private citizens but Jews could lend money at up to ten percent interest. This implies that during the thirteenth century Jewish Sicilians enjoyed the special fiscal trust of the civil authorities.

Into the fifteenth century, the Jews exercised a virtual monopoly over the medical profession in Sicily. Many held land, and at least a few were the holders of feudal property such as manors (smaller than baronies), effectively making up a tiny part of the kingdom's aristocracy.

The cuisine favored by Sicily's medieval Jews seems to have been rather similar to Arab cuisine. The dearth of medieval Sicilian pork recipes probably reflects the Muslim and Jewish proscriptions on its consumption.

Localities that had medieval Jewish populations include: Palermo and Siracusa (the largest Jewish communities in 1492), Acireale, Agira, Agrigento, Alcamo, Bivona, Caccamo, Calascibetta, Caltabellotta, Caltanissetta, Cammarata, Castelbuono, Castiglione, Castronovo, Castroreale, Catania, Caucana, Cefalù, Comiso, Castrogiovanni (Enna), Monte San Giuliano (Erice), Gela, Lentini, Lipari, Marsala, Mazara, Messina, Naro, Noto, Ragusa, Polizzi Generosa, Ragusa, Randazzo, Salemi, San Fratello, San Marco d'Alunzio, Santa Croce di Camerina, Sciacca, Scicli, Siculiana, Taormina, Termini Imerese, Trapani. This is not a complete list; some smaller towns had Jewish communities. Interestingly, many of these localities were *demesnial* ("free" or royal), appertaining directly to the Crown, rather than *feudal,* held by a count or baron.

Most converts to Christianity continued to live in their historically Jewish neighborhoods after conversion.

There is greater evidence of the past in some towns than in others. In Agira, an *aron kodesh* (holy ark) in austere Gothic style dated 1454 is preserved in the Santissimo Salvatore

Church, having been retrieved from the site of the local synagogue, now the Santissima Croce Oratory, where it was part of the altar. In Siculiana a Jewish tombstone dated 1478 forms part of the altar of the mother church. The locations of a number of synagogues are known; most became the sites of churches but a few are the sites of the residences of aristocratic families; in Caltabellotta the synagogue stood where Palazzo Caruso was built.

One of our best sources for the history of Judaism in Italy during this period is Rabbi Obadiah ben Abraham "of Bertinoro," a great scholar of his age.

Maps of the Jewish quarters of Syracuse and Palermo, indicating sites of the most important synagogues and mikvehs known to us, are included in the map section of this volume. The mikveh of Syracuse (see the next chapter) is located at Via Alagona 52; a synagogue was located nearby at what is now Saint John the Baptist Church. Once fed by a kanat from the Kemonia River, the remains of the mikveh of Palermo are located in what is now Palazzo Marchese in Piazza dei Santissimi Quaranta Martiri del Casalotto, a square at the end of the street of the same name off Via Maqueda, across from the Church of San Nicolò da Tolentino, site of the great synagogue. (The present structure was built in the Catalan Gothic style above the mikveh late in the fifteenth century and little is left of the original bath.) There were probably other mikvehs and synagogues in these cities.

Traces of Sicily's Judaic heritage are few and precious, and a few are conserved beyond Sicilian shores. Left behind in Cammarata by the departing congregation in 1493, the jewelled Torah *rimonim* of the town's synagogue are conserved at a museum in Palma de Majorca. Fashioned of silver, they are thought to be the oldest Torah finials presently preserved anywhere in the world. Prophetically, one bears the Hebrew inscription: "These rimonim are sacred to the Lord, belonging to the synagogue of the Jews of Cammarata. May the Lord protect it."

CHAPTER 8

The Mikveh of Siracusa

The island of Ortygia is an ancient district of Siracusa (Syracuse) that was inhabited into the Middle Ages, long after most areas of equal antiquity (now the archeological park on the edge of the "modern" city) had been abandoned. It is here, among graceful limestone palaces, castles, churches and houses, that we find many of the city's rare treasures. A few have been rediscovered following centuries passed — literally — in the dark. One is the *mikveh* in the *Giudecca,* the city's Jewish quarter until 1493.

Indeed, this is the oldest *mikveh* (or *mikvah* or *miqwa*) known to survive in Europe. By definition, a *mikveh* is a ritual bath, consisting of at least one pool but perhaps several. The mikveh is an important part of Jewish tradition, and it was the inspiration — or at least the precedent — for analogous practices in Christianity (Baptism) and then Islam (Ghusl). Whereas *Baptism* is a sacrament that is performed only once (originally by *full immersion* as it is still practiced in the Eastern Orthodox Churches), *Ghusl* customs are more similar to Judaic practice. Obviously, one form or another of ritual bathing is a shared legacy of all three Abrahamic faiths.

In Judaism, ritual bathing, or *ablution*, in the form of *tevilah* (full-body immersion) in fresh water, may date from Mosaic times, and has certainly been practiced since the period when the Book of Leviticus was authored, before 322 BC (BCE). Both the *Mishnah* and the *Talmud* refer to the practice, and many Jewish rituals are rooted in this era.

The Jewish congregation of Syracuse was probably the first to be established in Sicily, and one of the first few in what is now Italy. Judaism was present here long before the arrival of Christianity on Sicilian shores.

As we mentioned in the last chapter, the greatest influx of Jews took place in the decades immediately after AD (CE) 135, in the wake of the Romans' complete expulsion of the Jews from the holy city of Jerusalem following Bar Kokhba's Revolt.

The mikveh of Siracusa dates from the Byzantine period following the fall of the "western" Roman empire to invading forces in the fifth century. In 535, the Byzantine general Belisarius seized control of Sicily from the Goths.

In 655 Ortygia's Jews finally obtained permission to rebuild the synagogue that had been destroyed by the Vandals. Was their mikveh also destroyed by the invaders, or was it spared? The latter hypothesis leaves open the possibility that the hypogeum we see today already existed in 535 when the Byzantines arrived. At all events, it was almost certainly in use when the Emperor Constans ruled the Byzantine Empire from Syracuse from 660 until 668.

Another noteworthy hypogeum in the central Mediterranean designed for religious use, and in that sense comparable to the Syracusan Mikveh, is the much-larger al-Saflieni Hypogeum carved on Malta beginning around 3300 BC. A mikveh is, of course, a sacred site, though not a place of worship.

A spring supplies water to the mikveh's five immersion pools. It is thought that the same underground spring feeds the Fount of Arethusa. There is even a vent running from the hypogeum's ceiling to ground level. Medieval oil lamps were discovered during the excavations.

The mikveh was used most often by women, especially following menstruation or childbirth, but also just before marriage. Men sometimes bathed in it to achieve purity following intimate relations with their wives, and bridegrooms bathed just before marriage. Immersion was part of the rite of conversion to Judaism by Gentiles (in this way Baptism is very similar to *tevileh*), and priests bathed during consecration and in preparation for performing certain rites. Bathing in a mikveh was required after contact with a corpse. The purpose of immersion in the mikveh was not physical cleansing (one must be clean before entering) but achieving spiritual purity or renewal.

In medieval Judaism the mikveh was just as important as the synagogue. Customarily, a new Jewish community would invest in its mikveh before allocating funds for the synagogue or Torah scroll.

It is possible that a synagogue once stood atop the Syracusan mikveh. A known synagogue (there eventually may have been two or more as the Jewish community grew) was located nearby on the site of Saint John the Baptist Church. A Hebrew inscription found at this site reads: "To the synagogue of Syracuse, founded in justice and faith."

Full of medieval buildings, the Giudecca of Syracuse is a labyrinth of narrow medieval streets and walkways. The Jewish market is thought to have stood where Saint Philip's Church was erected.

The mikveh of Syracuse has a total of five immersion pools. There are three large triangular pools in the main chamber, where there is also a round pool that serves as a reservoir. On each side of the main chamber is a small side chamber having a square pool; these were used by priests or other important individuals, exclusively male. There were probably days the mikveh was open to women, and others for men. Historically, wine vessels and eating utensils, if acquired from a Gentile, had to be immersed in a mikveh before their first use by Jews. Here we are describing usages from Sicily's Byzantine period until the fifteenth century.

By the middle of the fifteenth century Sicily's Church, like Spain's, was less tolerant of the Jews than it had ever been, and by then the Jewish minority was being coerced to live in specific quarters of larger cities and towns, whereas until that time they usually did so by choice.

During the Late Middle Ages (circa 1400), by the most reliable estimates, as much as one-quarter of Ortygia's population, or as many as 5,000 families, was Jewish, and most lived in the Giudecca. More than half of these families left Sicily in 1493. Those who remained became Christians. It would seem that these converts, whatever their number, chose not to reveal the existence of the mikveh. At some point their secret was forgotten. In many cases churches were built on the sites of synagogues during the next century, just as they had been constructed on the sites of mosques during the thirteenth century when Sicily's last Muslims converted to Catholicism.

Somehow, Syracuse's Jews managed to bury this mikveh, in Via Alagona (there may have been another one), in soil and coarse sand without being discovered by the Spanish authorities. Incredibly, the Inquisition seemed ignorant of the mikveh's subterranean existence, partly because changes in government (viceroys) were frequent, and though the Giudecca was not a completely walled community, Gentiles were not permitted in the mikveh and few ever entered a synagogue.

It is believed that the Bianca (or Bianchi) family that resided in the house above the hypogeum during the sixteenth century was *anusim,* having converted from Judaism to Christianity. Discovered only some five centuries later, the "secret" mikveh is still fed by its original water supply. Its discovery and excavation is perhaps the most fascinating part of its story, one of the things that makes it a rare find.

In Sicily there are the remains of several mikvehs other than the one in Siracusa. Of particular note is the mikveh under Palazzo Marchese, a Catalan Gothic palace in Palermo's *Giudecca,* once fed by the springs of the Kemonia River nearby. This is located in Piazza dei Santissimi Quaranta Martiri, reached from a street of the same name across Via Maqueda from the site of the synagogue (now the San Nicolò church).

Unlike other early-medieval mikvehs excavated in Europe (Cologne's comes to mind), the "Casa Bianca" mikveh has actually been used by members of the Jewish congregation in recent years. As one of the oldest mikvehs in use, it is much more than an archeological curiosity. It is a *living* legacy.

The Syracusan Mikveh is located beneath a beautiful seventeenth century residence which is now a hotel at Via Alagona 52. Like the hotel itself, the hypogeum is privately owned and administered (more efficiently than most of Sicily's publicly-operated historical sites). Guided visits are scheduled most days for a nominal admission fee. Access to the subterranean chamber is via a series of stone steps, conditions which should be taken into careful consideration by those having mobility limitations or problems in enclosed areas.

See this book's map section for maps of the Jewish quarters of Siracusa and Palermo, with these holy places indicated.

CHAPTER 9

The Arabs

They ruled Sicily for just two centuries and a few decades but their influence was nothing short of monumental. Under their administration, the island's population doubled as dozens of towns were founded and cities repopulated. The Arabs changed Sicilian agriculture and cuisine. Their scientific and engineering achievements were remarkable. More significantly, they changed society itself. To this day, some Sicilian social attitudes reflect the profound influence — often in subtle ways — of the Arabs who ruled a thousand years ago but who, with the Greeks and others, were the ancestors of today's Sicilians.

The Arabs, who in medieval times were sometimes called "Saracens" or (particularly in Spain) "Moors," have been identified since antiquity; their antecedents are mentioned in Assyrian records dated to circa 850 BC (BCE). Until the Middle Ages, however, they were not unified as a people.

In the Early Middle Ages, it was Islam that united the Arabs and established the framework of Islamic law, which may have influenced European legal principles as far away as the Norman Kingdom of England and its common law. Initially, most Muslims were Arabs, and during the Arab rule of Sicily their Islamic faith was closely identified with them.

The rapid growth of Arab culture could be said to parallel the dissemination of Islam. Except for some poetry, the first major work of literature published entirely in Arabic was the Koran (Quran), the holy book of Islam, and one may loosely define Arabs by the regions where Arabic was spoken in the Middle Ages and afterwards, rather than linking them to specific countries.

Arabs were one of many Semitic peoples of the Middle East. The Berbers of northwest Africa and the Sahara — the Maghreb — were not Arabs originally, though they converted to Islam, adopted Arabic as their language and assimilated with Arab society. Most parts of Sicily were conquered by Arabs, but certain areas along the southern coast were settled by people who, strictly speaking, were Muslim Berbers. Like many Berbers, some Arabs were nomadic. It was Islam that united them.

With the emergence of the Byzantine Empire, groups of Arabs lived in bordering areas in the Arabian peninsula and parts of what are now Iraq, Kuwait, Jordan and Egypt. Their language, Arabic, is a Semitic tongue of various dialects related to Hebrew and Ethiopic, written in script from right to left.

Mohammed, the Prophet of Islam, was born in Mecca around AD (CE) 570 and his religious community at Medina eventually grew to dominate the entire Arabian peninsula. Following Mohammed's death in 632, caliphs (civil and religious leaders) succeeded him and Islam itself split into what became two major sects, the Sunnis and the Shiites. Three families from Mohammed's tribe ruled the expanding Arabian empire for the next few centuries, namely the Umayyads (661-750), the Abbasids (750-850) and the Alids (the Fatimid dynasty in northern Africa from 909 to 1171). In practice, certain regions, including Sicily, were locally controlled by particular, minor families, sometimes under local emirs; there were several emirates in Sicily when the Normans arrived in 1061.

Initially, the Arabs aspired to little more than some productive land in coastal areas and around the Fertile Crescent of the Middle East, on the edge of the prosperous Byzantine Empire, but within decades of Mohammed's death their ambitions were greater. With the growth of their society supported by conversions to Islam, the wealth sought by Arabs was precisely that which the Koran (3:14) discouraged: "The desire for women and sons, the thirst for gold and silver, spirited horses, and the possession of cattle and land, in fact all the pleasures of worldly life." That Sicily offered all of these in abundance was known through contact with Arab traders in the south and west of the island, in cities such as Sciacca, Mazara and what came to be known as Marsala, for *Mars el'Allah,* the "Port of Allah."

By 650, the Arabs were making their way westward through Libya and Tunisia, and what remained of the city of Carthage was destroyed in 698. The Byzantines had already lost these areas, but they retained control of Sicily, despite numerous raids by Arab pirates, until 827. In that year, the duplicitous Euphemius, a Byzantine admiral and resident Governor of Sicily who found himself at odds with his Emperor in Constantinople, offered the governorship of the island to Ziyadat Allah, the Aghlabid Emir of Al Qayrawan (Kairouan in Tunisia) in exchange for his support. This fiasco led to the landing of over ten thousand Arab and Berber troops at Mazara in the western part of Sicily. Euphemius was soon disposed of — killed by Byzantine officers loyal to Emperor Michael II — and Sicily's Arab period had begun.

Three Arab dynasties ruled Sicily: first the *Aghlabids* (a "minor" clan based in Tunisia which had broken away from the Abbasids of Baghdad), then, from 909, the *Fatimids,* who entrusted much of their authority to the local *Kalbids* in 948. In that year, Hassan al-Kalbi became the first Emir of All Sicily. By 969, the Fatimid dynasty (descended from the Prophet's daughter, Fatima) were moving their geographic center of power to Cairo, leaving their Tunisian capitals (Madiyah and Al Kairouan) and western territories to the care of what in Europe would be called "vassals." It would be fair to describe Kalbid rule as a continuation of the Fatimid dominion. The Fatimids were, in effect, the Kalbids' suzerains.

Islam spread quickly across the Mediterranean but in Sicily the Arabs' conquest was a slow one. Panormus, which was to become the capital of an emirate as Bal'harm (Palermo) in 948, fell in 831. Messina was taken the following year. Enna (the Arabs' Kasr'Janni, also an emirate) was conquered in 858. With the violent fall of Syracuse in 878, the conquest was essentially complete, though Taormina and several other mountaintop communities held out into the next century. That a large Byzantine force arrived from Constantinople to assist besieged Rometta in 964 suggests that the Arabs had yet to achieve complete control over Sicily by that late date.

There were also internecine conflicts. Into the middle years of the tenth century, the ruling Fatimids had to suppress a long series of open revolts by the disgruntled Berbers of Sciacca and Agrigento — a bloody conflict that bore all the marks of a localized civil war.

In Islam, collections of *hadiths* containing *sunnahs,* or "laws," were very important. The Aghlabids, who brought Maliki law to Sicily, were Sunnis. Their successors, the Fatimids and Kalbids, though Shiites, retained in Sicily certain institutions usually identified with Sunni law and government. Nevertheless, sectarian differences provided a convenient pretext for the Fatimids to exploit popular grievances rooted in Sunni practices to overthrow the Aghlabids in Africa and Sicily.

Some of the more reliable descriptions of the Fatimid world during this period come to us from Mohammed al Maqdisi, who was born in Jerusalem around 945. Having prevailed over the Aghlabids, the Fatimids introduced some principles that were progressive, if not radical, for their time, both scientifically and socially. Indeed, when medievalists refer generically to Islam's enlightened golden age, it is usually Fatimid culture they are describing. How did the Fatimids' rise to this intellectual apex come about?

A certain openness may have been rooted in the Fatimids' Ismaili beliefs, but this is difficult to quantify. We are on more solid ground in affirming that the Fatimids generally favored personal meritocracy over nepotism and cronyism. That is to say that they usually considered the intellectual and ethical merit of an individual over factors such as ancestry or social class. In practice, this meant that in the normal course of affairs a particularly dishonest or ignorant man could not presume any special privilege simply because his father or grandfather was a paragon of virtue or intellect. Fairness extended to other areas as well.

In the realm of commerce, a man seeking to establish a small enterprise would be given the same opportunity as somebody already operating a larger business in the same field.

This had obvious implications in law, where a man or woman of humble origins could expect the same justice meted out to somebody from a distinguished family. It also meant that education was available to most children rather than a select few, and there were schools for girls as well as boys. When he visited Palermo in late 1184, bin Jubayr described buildings similar in style to those of Cordoba, encountering so many mosques that they were "impossible to count."

But their ubiquity was not all that he observed. Most of the mosques, he noted, also served as schools. As a result of this effort to educate its children, Fatimid society boasted an unprecedented level of literacy, among both genders.

This was more than an anomaly. Koranic injunction emphatically encouraged reading. In practice, reading was taught specifically so that the faithful could study the Koran, even where this meant reading Arabic instead of the local spoken language. Moreover, as Arabic numeration rendered arithmetic relatively simple, its mastery was easier than what had existed under the Romans and Byzantines.

Here the implications are enormous, for learning and literacy facilitated great social mobility for individuals and quantum leaps of progress for society as a whole. Sicily's Kalbids continued the social and educational traditions established by their suzerains the Fatimids.

Frederick II founded one of Europe's first universities, an institution in Naples, and this was probably inspired by the Fatimid arrangement then in vogue in Cairo and elsewhere. The *dar al-hikma,* or "house of wisdom," may very well be the basis for the secular university as we know it, as opposed to monastic schools, which were also centers of learning (but mostly for clerics). A major *dar al-hikma* probably existed in Palermo at one time, but such information as is known to us cannot confirm this.

As we have said elsewhere, the Arabs were not the only educated population in Fatimid Sicily. The Jews were highly literate by longstanding tradition as it was presumed that Jewish men could read from the Torah; only rarely did one meet an illiterate Jew. Literacy was also high among the Byzantines, but most of their schools were monastic and exclusively male.

We usually associate the work of scribes with monasteries, but these religious communities were not the only ones to pursue this important work. A number of manuscripts recording the work of great thinkers were preserved (in Greek) in the Byzantine Empire. Some were translated into Arabic. Euclid's *Division of Figures* is an oft-cited example. In a few cases, the Arabic editions were the sources of later (Latin) translations when the Greek copies were lost or destroyed.

Advances in mathematics were facilitated by the use of the Arabic, or Hindu-Arabic, numerals mentioned earlier, which trace their origin to Brahmi and Sanskrit. In Baghdad, the ninth-century Persian mathematician Abdallah Mohammed al Khwarizmi made use of this numeration system to simplify Diophantus' algebra, whose modern name comes to us from the Arabic *al-jabr wa'l muqabalah.* Hindu-Arabic numerals are not merely a simpler writing system than Roman numerals;

they more clearly isolate concepts such as fractions and *zero,* whose Medieval Latin form, *zephirum,* derives from the Arabic *sifr,* "cipher," from a Sanskrit word. Khwarizmi's studies also encompassed trigonometry, astronomy and geography.

Leonardo Fibonacci introduced this system in northern Italy and much of Europe in the thirteenth century, but by then it was already used in Sicily, thanks to the Fatimids and Kalbids, and in Spain, where Hindu-Arabic numerals appear in the *Codex Vigilanus* compiled in 881.

Byzantine society, culture and government were closely identified with Christianity, and the law was based largely — though not entirely — on Judeo-Christian principles. Islam was likewise a way of life that could not easily be separated from society itself.

The Arabs divided Sicily into three large administrative areas: Val di Mazara (the largest) in the west, Val Demone in the northeast, Val di Noto in the southeast. The word *val* did not refer to a valley, as is often presumed today, but to a *district.* Sicily was almost half Muslim by 1061 when the Normans captured Messina.

Arab administration, if not especially enlightened, was not very harsh by medieval standards, but it was far from egalitarian. Sicily's Christians and Jews were highly taxed, and one could not recite from the Bible or Talmud within earshot of Muslims. Christian and Jewish women (who like Muslim women wore veils or scarves in public) could not share the public baths with Muslim women. These *dhimmi* had to rise to their feet in the presence of Muslims. New churches and synagogues could not be built, nor Muslims converted to other faiths.

Indeed, a number of churches were converted to mosques, including the cathedral of Palermo. A column of the cathedral's fifteenth-century portico bearing the inscription of a verse from a Koranic sura was obtained from the remains of a mosque, but by then the architects failed to recognize the decorative script as Arabic.

A great degree of religious tolerance prevailed; there were no forced conversions to Islam. Yet a new social order evolved. Except for some merchants and sailors, there had been few Muslim Arabs in Sicily before 827, but Byzantine legal strictures imposed upon them, and upon the Jews living across the island, cannot be said to have been as rigid as those imposed upon non-Muslims by the Arabs after about 850. At first, however, many Sicilians probably welcomed the prospect of change because they had been overtaxed and over-governed by their Byzantine rulers.

The Arabs introduced superior irrigation systems using canals and *norias* (water wheels); some of their underground *qanats* (kanats) still flow deep beneath Palermo, where one fed the *mikveh* (Jewish bath) into the fifteenth century, and *gébbia,* a Sicilian word still in use, comes to us from the Arabic for "reservoir."

Along these lines, the Arabs built the baths at Cefalà Diana. Constructed during the tenth century, this is the largest purely Arab structure still extant in Sicily. Similarly, Taormina's Palazzo Corvaja was erected during the Arab period, but parts of it have been altered over time.

The Arabs established the Sicilian silk industry, and later, at the court of the Norman monarch Roger II, great Arab thinkers like the geographer Abdullah al Idrisi were welcomed.

Agriculture became more varied and more efficient, with the widespread introduction of rice, sugar cane, cotton and oranges. This, in turn, influenced Sicilian cuisine. Many of the most popular Sicilian foods trace their origins to the Arab period. In Sicily the Arabs appreciated the native artichoke, whose name comes to us from the Arabic *kharshùff,* and introduced it in other parts of their expanding empire. The Arabs also introduced the cultivation of henna. The process of distillation, important in chemistry and in the making of spirits, was developed by the Arabs.

Dozens of towns were founded or resettled during the Arab epoch, and *souks* (suks, or outdoor markets) became more common than before. In Palermo one of the largest souks became what is today the Ballarò street market (shown on the map of the city's Jewish Quarter in our map section). Located just outside the Punic wall, it probably dates from the ninth-century Arab conquest of what was then a largely depopulated city. Its Sicilian name is thought to derive from the Arabic phrase *Suk al Balari*. This may refer to much of the produce coming from *Bahlara* (or Ba'lat), a farming village near Monreale.

Bal'harm (Palermo), which was often referred to simply as "medina" ("the city"), was repopulated and became one of the largest, wealthiest Arab cities after Baghdad and Cordoba (Cordova), and one of the most splendid. Despite later estimates of a greater population, there were probably fewer than two hundred thousand residents in and around Palermo by 1050. Precise estimates are impossible. When he visited in the tenth century, ibn Hawqal estimated the number of halal butcher shops in Palermo at around one hundred fifty. As the emirate's capital and commercial center, it eclipsed Syracuse in size and affluence.

Construction on Bal'harm's Khalesa district along the coast was begun in 937 by Khalid Ibn Ishaq, who was then Governor of Sicily. It is thought that what is now Via Alloro was the main street leading to this area from the higher al-Kasr quarter, where the Norman Palace now stands.

Bal'harm was the official residence of the Governors and Emirs of All Sicily, and al Khalesa (now the Kalsa district) was its administrative center. As we've mentioned, in 948 the Fatimids granted a degree of autonomy to the Kalbid dynasty, whose last "governor" (effectively a hereditary emir), Hasan II (or Al-Samsan), ruled until 1053. By then, Enna, Trapani, Taormina and Syracuse were also self-declared, localized "emirates."

The early Sicilian vernacular, such as it was, was in constant evolution. Arabic was a major influence on Sicilian, which later emerged as a Romance (Latin) language peppered with Arabic borrowings, although the poetic tongue of Ciullo of Alcamo bore little resemblance to the guttural Modern Sicilian heard today.

Until the arrival of the Arabs, the most widely spoken language in Sicily was a medieval dialect of Greek. Under the Arabs, Sicily became a polyglot community; some localities were more Greek-speaking while others were predominantly Arabic-speaking. Mosques stood alongside churches and synagogues, and most Sicilians were bilingual.

Arab Sicily emerged as one of Europe's most prosperous regions — intellectually, artistically and economically. Contemporaneously, Moorish Spain was comparable to Sicily in these respects, but in Sicily the Arabs were able to build upon a Byzantine foundation more sophisticated than the essentially Visigothic culture of the Iberian lands. For the most part, the Sicilian Arabs coexisted peacefully with the peoples of the Italian peninsula. These were Lombards (Longobard descendants) and Byzantines in Calabria, Basilicata and Apulia, where Bari was the largest city.

As we have seen, the Romans traded with southern India during the *Pax Romana* of Augustus. In the Byzantines' empire, Sicily enjoyed some contact with the East, but as part of a larger Arab empire having greater contact with India through better-developed trade routes, Far Eastern developments such as paper (see below) and, as we have mentioned, "Arabic" (Hindu-Arabic) numerals arrived. So did important inventions like the spherical astrolabe and an improved compass. At the court of Frederick II, Michael Scot (born 1175) translated *On the Sphere* by the Arab astronomer Al-Bitruji, or Alpetragius, who died circa 1204. Under the Arabs, Sicily and Spain found their populations advanced compared to those of England and

Continental northern Europe.

Sicily's most famous Muslim leader was Jawhar as-Siqilli ("the Sicilian"), about whom little is known. Born around 910, he was the founder of Cairo. Jawhar was a Christian sold into slavery in youth. The young man, soon known as Abul Hussain Jawhar bin Abdullah, or al-Katib, was taken to Tunisia, where Caliph Ismail al-Mansur took him under his tutelage. Ismail's son and heir, al-Muizz (953-975), freed Jawhar and made him his scribe. From this humble rank he eventually became a military adviser and, finally, a *visir,* a kind of Fatimid general.

With the allied Zirids, the Fatimids under Jawhar conquered Moroccan lands to the west, expanding to Fez and then the Atlantic coast. Cordoba's Umayyads retained control of the important centers of Sabtah (Ceuta), birthplace of Abdullah al Idrisi, and Tangier. Jawhar later led the Fatimid expansion eastward toward Egypt, defeating the Ishidids at Giza and occupying lands around the Nile valley. He administered Egypt on behalf of the Fatimids until 972.

He founded Al-Qahira (Cairo) on the site of a small village in 969, and it became the seat of the Fatimid caliphate. Jawhar died in 992.

Meanwhile, Byzantium hadn't forgotten Sicily, and in 1038 George Maniakes, at the head of an army of Byzantine-Greeks, Normans, Vikings and Lombards, attempted an invasion of the island. (See the next chapter.) By the 1050s, the Pope, and some Norman knights from this failed adventure, were casting a long glance toward Sicily with an eye to conquest. This desire was later fuelled by dissension among the island's Arabs, leading to support by the Emir of Syracuse for the Normans against the emirates of Enna and Palermo. Most of these internal problems developed after the ruling Fatimids moved their capital from Tunisia to Egypt, where they established Cairo near ancient Memphis.

The Normans conquered Messina in 1061 and reached the

gates of Palermo a decade later, removing from power the local Emir, Yusuf ibn Abdallah, but respecting Arab customs. Their conquest of Arab Sicily was slower than their conquest of Saxon England, which began in 1066 with the Battle of Hastings. Kasr'Janni was still ruled by its Emir, Ibn Al-Hawas, who held out for years. His successor, Ibn Hamud, surrendered, and converted to Christianity, only in 1087.

While the Muslim-Arab influence continued well into the Norman era — particularly in art and architecture — it was not to endure. The Normans gradually "Latinized" Sicily, and this social process served to lay the groundwork for the introduction of Roman Catholicism as opposed to the preservation of Greek Orthodoxy. Widespread conversion ensued, and by the 1280s there were few, if any, Muslims in Sicily. Yet, the mass influx of north-African Arabs and Berbers was the greatest immigration to Sicily since that of the ancient Greeks.

While Norman government and law in Sicily were essentially European, introducing institutions such as the feudal system, at first they were profoundly influenced by Islamic practices. Many statutes were universal, but in the first few decades of Norman rule each Sicilian — Muslim, Christian, Jew —was judged by the laws of his or her own faith.

When did the various Sicilian localities cease to be Arab? There was not an immediate change. Following the Norman conquest, complete Latinization, fostered largely by the Roman Church, its clergy and liturgy, took the better part of two centuries, and even then there remained pockets of Byzantine influence in northeastern Sicily's Nebrodi Mountains.

For an impression of the Siculo Arabic language we may look to Malta, where it survives as Maltese.

Had the Normans not conquered Sicily, the place might have evolved into an essentially Arab society not unlike that which survived in some parts of Spain into the fifteenth century, and the Sicilian vernacular language (as we know it) would have evolved later and perhaps differently.

To the modern mind, it may come as a revelation that eleventh-century Sicily had Islamic schools that taught reading, writing and simple arithmetic to some forty percent of the island's young children, both male and female, while another eight percent — the children of Jews — were equally literate.

As general functional literacy in the fledgling, nineteenth-century Kingdom of Italy hovered around twenty percent, we cannot but conclude that literacy was far higher in the Sicily of imams and rabbis in 1061, when the Normans arrived, than it was in the united Italy of Catholic kings in 1861.

The Arabs made the world a smaller place. Enlightened and advanced as the Byzantines were, the Arabs, whose vast network of Muslim emirates and caliphates stretched its tentacles eastward as far as Pakistan, brought Europe into more frequent contact with India and China.

As we have said, a useful product introduced in this manner was paper. This Chinese invention made its way to Samarkand (in present-day Uzbekistan), an important city on the Silk Road, and by 795 there was a flourishing paper factory in Baghdad. The use of paper sowed the seeds for wider literacy and scholarship because it was easier to produce in quantity than parchment, and far more economical. The plethora of books in the Muslim world owes a great deal to this simple innovation.

The boys and girls in Sicily's medieval schools could conserve their written exercises and hone their writing skills away from school, a practice that could not exist prior to the use of paper. Yes, homework, the bane of every student's existence, owes its birth to the introduction of paper in schools.

Mohammed al-Qasim ibn Hawqal, who visited Sicily in 972, listed paper making among the island's craft industries, and here was an obvious link to the cultivation of cotton and linen. The earliest Sicilian paper manuscript preserved for us is a deed issued by Roger I in 1102, which may be the oldest paper document of Europe. (Citing paper's fragility, Frederick II resumed the use of parchment and vellum for public documents.) That Marco Polo was unfamiliar with paper before his visit to China, where he found paper currency in use, indicates that the Venetians were not yet making paper in the thirteenth century.

In connection with this, the Arabs devised the banking instrument known as the *check,* the paper *saqq* used by traders. This was popularized by the Knights Templar, whose sophisticated network of preceptories and commanderies facilitated the novel method of letters of credit to transfer money. Essentially, a sealed document (a "check") issued by one commandery could be exchanged for actual funds (coinage) by another. In this way checking, as it came to be known and used in modern times, was introduced across Europe.

Certain curiosities, some of which were known to the ancient Romans, became familiar again in Europe thanks to contact with the Arab world, particularly after 1200. In the zoo of Frederick II, for example, were camels, elephants, panthers and what was probably the first giraffe (from the Arabic *zarafa*) ever seen in Europe. This last is referred to in early heraldry as the *camel leopard,* hence its Latin name, *giraffa camelopardalis.* These were gifts of Malik al Kamil, the Sultan of Egypt, with whom Frederick negotiated his treaty in Jerusalem.

In forging trade, the Arabs established links to the East far eclipsing those enjoyed by the Romans. Yes, in the popular mind medieval Arab society has come to be identified principally with Islam. Day to day, however, its main thrust was what in our times would be called "international commerce." The adventuresome Marco Polo is justly deserving of praise, but the Arab world was full of itinerant merchants like him.

The golden emirate is gone but the fruits of its achievements are hardly forgotten.

CHAPTER 10

George Maniakes

The Mediterranean world of the eleventh century was a complicated place, with several ambitious powers vying for territory.

In the East the Byzantines were trying to hold on to their dwindling Empire against the Muslim onslaught. Most of the Iberian peninsula, plus Sicily and the African coast, were ruled by Arabs and Berbers. Loyal only to the highest bidder, the Normans were working their way through southern Italy while their distant kin the Norsemen (or Vikings) took an eastern route through Russia and Ukraine to serve as mercenaries for anybody ruling from Constantinople. Over in Spain, meanwhile, El Cid and other descendants of the Visigothic nobility were attempting to reclaim territory from the Moors (Muslim Arabs from north-western Africa).

In this mix loyalties were often fickle and internecine quarrels were frequent. One Byzantine Greek military commander might fight another, while one emir could view another as a rival. In 1054 the Great Schism (see the next chapter) divided the Christians, and by 1095 some zealous European Catholics were raising armies for a full-scale invasion of Palestine.

Such was the world of George Maniakes, a distinguished general in the service of the Byzantine Emperor Michael IV. Little is known of his early life, but by 1030 Maniakes was fighting the Muslims at the important city of Aleppo in what is now northern Syria. The next year he went on to capture Edessa, to the east in upper Mesopotamia, from the Seljuk Turks.

A Norse force led by Harald Hardrada, who would later become King of Norway, formed Michael's Varangian Guard. With some Normans under the command of William, a brother of Robert and Roger of Hauteville, and a Lombard contingent from Italy, Maniakes launched a series of assaults on Sicily, which was then under Arab control. The last major Byzantine force to land in Sicily fought a battle at the siege of Rometta in 964.

From 1038 until 1040, Maniakes' motley crew of mercenaries defeated Arab forces in south-eastern Sicily. Here the jewel in the crown was the city of Syracuse, traditionally a bulwark of Greek civilization. Though surpassed by Bal'harm (Palermo) in wealth and importance, Syracuse was still a gateway to the East.

It was in Sicily that the knight William Hauteville earned his nickname, "Iron Arm," reputedly by killing the Emir of Syracuse with a sword in single combat. For now, George Maniakes was satisfied to conquer Syracuse, controlling it from the coastal fortress on the island of Ortygia that still bears his name, but though he was appointed *catapan* of Italy his victory was to prove an ephemeral one.

The chroniclers tell us that Maniakes publicly insulted Harduin, the Lombard leader, who consequently decided to withdraw to peninsular Italy. William and the Normans decided to follow the Lombards — even though back on the mainland the two factions were rarely on very amicable terms with each other or with the Byzantines. Worse, Harald and most of his intrepid Norsemen also abandoned Maniakes.

This made it difficult for Maniakes to defend the piece of Sicily he had acquired. He likewise offended Stephen, his admiral, who had important connections back in Constantinople. Clearly, Maniakes was no paragon of tact and no master of politics.

In Maniakes' absence, the Crown had passed to the opportunistic Constantine IX, who failed to appreciate the general's accomplishments in Sicily or elsewhere. The general was recalled to the capital in 1042 and Syracuse once again fell into Arab hands.

More importantly to posterity, their service to Maniakes convinced the Normans that Sicily was indeed within their reach, and that its emirs were far from invincible. The Hautevilles would return to Syracuse in 1085, led by William's younger brother Roger.

In the end, it was a personal feud that led to Maniakes' fall from grace. A certain Romanos Scleros, like Maniakes, was a wealthy landholder in Asia Minor and the two had fought over land. It was said that Scleros urged his beautiful, lusty sister to influence the Emperor Constantine to act against George Maniakes. This was typical of the blunders and intrigues that would cost the Byzantines an empire. The avaricious Scleros ransacked Maniakes' home in the general's absence.

Next, greedy Scleros demanded that Maniakes concede him control of Apulia, the heel of the Italian peninsula. Maniakes killed Scleros and, having been declared Emperor by his loyal troops, including the remaining Norsemen, attempted to take Constantinople. He was killed at the ensuing Battle of Thessalonika in 1043.

At this distance of time, it is difficult to form a clear portrait of George Maniakes. Seen in the best light, he was a capable, visionary military leader who was not appreciated in his own country.

Maniace Castle stands on a coastal site in Ortygia that was already fortified by the Arabs before George Maniakes arrived. Greatly expanded by Frederick II, the fortress we see today is essentially a thirteenth-century structure. Peter of Aragon used this as one of his bases during the Vespers War in 1282.

As it happens, George Maniakes is little more than a foot-note to history, but a remarkable one.

CHAPTER 11

The Great Schism

Every day hundreds of people — most of them foreigners — visit the church in central Palermo now known as the *Martorana,* and the curious among them may even stop by the more austere Church of San Cataldo next door. Few realize what this pairing represents, for the churches, each dating from the middle of the twelfth century, were built for different communities whose individuality (from each other) had only recently been defined.

The walls of the Martorana are covered in mosaic icons, its original floor plan a simple "cross-in-square" (or Greek cross) beneath a single dome, around the exterior of which is an Arabic inscription. The Martorana was, in fact, built as a Greek Orthodox church dedicated to Saint Nicholas, its charter of 1143 written in Greek and Arabic. It was completed in 1151.

Constructed in a fairly similar Norman-Arab style, San Cataldo has a long nave and very simple Romanesque arches. Resembling a mosque, it was consecrated as a Roman Catholic church around 1160.

Elsewhere in Sicily there are churches reflecting eclectic architectural influences. Monreale Abbey, for example, is at once Norman, Arab and Byzantine, but while it initially had an *iconostasis* that cathedral was founded as a Benedictine church. Syracuse Cathedral, built around an ancient Greek temple, is a good example of a Paleo-Christian structure, though greatly modified over the centuries. There are few Sicilian churches remaining which were built explicitly for the diminishing Orthodox communities following what has come to be known as the *Great Schism*.

Fomented for several centuries, the Great Schism of 1054 separated the Western "Roman" or "Latin" church from Eastern "Greek" or "Byzantine" Christianity, and it was a historic development inextricably linked to the Normans' conquest of southern Italy. What was the Schism and how did it alter the course of Sicilian history? How are its effects still felt today?

While a detailed examination of the theological differences between what are today the Roman Catholic and Eastern Orthodox churches is beyond the scope of this concise exposition, it is best to explain the background of the dispute.

Discord

The Emperor Constantine legalized Christianity across the Roman Empire and the new religion spread rapidly, but in 395, in view of increasing decay, the Empire split into the West, ruled from Rome, and the East, ruled from Constantinople (Byzantium, now Istanbul). Preserving its great culture and traditions, the eastern half (or "Byzantine Empire") survived until 1453.

Officially, Sicily was part of the Western Empire from 395, but following the fall of centralized power in Italy a few years later a period of foreign rule by Vandals and Goths ensued on the island. In 535 it was annexed to the Byzantine Empire.

When the Roman Empire was whole, Latin was the official tongue, but even in Italy Greek enjoyed prestige as the second language of learned people and it was the popular vernacular in the Balkans, Sicily and the eastern Mediterranean. With the Empire divided, and the western part descending into chaos and ignorance, language became divisive. Misunderstandings grew more frequent because many in the West spoke no Greek, while few Greeks bothered to learn Latin. At the dawn of the Middle Ages, the distance between Rome and Constantinople wasn't only linguistic; geography itself imposed a definite obstacle, especially now that a central Imperial government no longer controlled the entire Mediterranean.

The Patriarchs, beginning with the Patriarch of Constantinople, recognized the Patriarch of "the West" (in Rome) as "the first among equals." The early Church was collegial; canon law and other matters were decided by groups of bishops rather than a single Patriarch, and that is how ecumenical councils — the Council of Nicea in 325 was the first — determined fundamental ecclesial beliefs and matters such as which gospels were to be included in the Canon. Even among today's Orthodox, the Patriarch of Constantinople is not a "Pope."

The *Codex Sinaiticus,* the earliest complete record of the canonical Gospels known to us, was written in Koine Greek between 330 and 360 (the contemporary *Codex Vaticanus* includes Old Testament books as well).

In much of western Europe the liturgy was celebrated not in Greek but in Latin, often in the Gallican Rite. By the Middle Ages, Christians in regions from the German-speaking territories westward had very little exposure to the influence of Constantinople even though the Byzantine Empire fostered and preserved the greatest learning in Christendom during this period.

By the eighth century the ecclesiastical jurisdictions of Rome and Constantinople certainly had their differences based on local practices. The Iconoclast Controversy (regarding the nature and veneration of icons) was settled by the Seventh Ecumenical Council in 787, but though the Church remained united Rome still insisted on jurisdiction over Sicily and some Balkan territories. In general, Rome wanted the Latin-speaking territories, but Sicily was mostly Greek-speaking in the ninth century when the Arab occupation began; for a few years after 660 the Eastern Emperor Constans actually established his capital at Syracuse.

Beyond questions of territorial jurisdiction (in the middle of the ninth century Rome contested a Byzantine episcopal appointment in Syracuse even though Sicily was outside Papal authority) there were conflicts over certain theological teachings and liturgical usages. In the East, for example, the theology of Augustine of Hippo was little appreciated, while Rome's use of unleavened bread in the Eucharist differed from the Greeks' leavened bread. An indicatory difference was the infamous debate over the *filioque,* Rome's use of a phrase in the Creed which seemed to alter the traditional concept of the Trinity.

Theological forces in Rome's jurisdiction — particularly among the Franks under Charlemagne and his heirs in what are now France, Germany and northern Italy — advocated for Papal authority over Constantinople, something unlikely to be approved by the various patriarchates of the East (Constantinople as well as Antioch, Alexandria and Jerusalem). This "Latin" view was unsurprising if, in the secular realm, the Pope considered himself a king maker who could crown the likes of Charlemagne and other monarchs.

Except for a few lengthy intervals, the patriarchs of the East commemorated (and prayed for) the Patriarch of the West and vice versa. These *diptychs* were seen as a sign that communion existed, however tenuously.

Finally, in 1054, Papal emissaries to Constantinople presented an egregious letter of excommunication to the Patriarch of that city. Apart from the fact that the Pope issuing the letter had died during the emissaries' trek eastward, theoretically nullifying the validity of any correspondence, the Patriarch of Rome had no authority to excommunicate or even command his brother in Constantinople. (Only nine centuries later, in 1965, did the patriarchates of Rome and Constantinople lift the mutual excommunications of the eleventh century.)

Despite the acrimony, bilateral efforts to mend the torn fabric of a divided Christianity continued into the next century. By the Second Crusade in 1147, "Latins" (Roman Catholics) were becoming highly suspicious of Constantinople's coexistence with Islam. In the words of historian Steven Runciman, "it was after the Second Crusade that the ordinary Westerner began to regard the Eastern Christian as being something less than a fellow Christian."

In Constantinople, the "Massacre of the Latins" of 1182 was ostensibly targeted at Italian mercantile power epitomized by the maritime republics' encroaching activities in that city, but the Italians' Roman Catholic faith itself provoked a certain degree of Greek hostility. By the Fourth Crusade (1204), with its bloody sack of Constantinople, hopes of a reconciliation were all but destroyed. The following year a Latin army was defeated at Adrianople (now Edirne in Turkey near the borders of Greece and Bulgaria) and in the next few decades the Teutonic Knights attempted to conquer "heretical" Orthodox republics such as Novgorod in Russia. Enmity had become a defining characteristic of the relationship between East and West, and it forebode many troubles.

Sicily

In 1054, with Sicily under Arab rule, best estimates are that around forty-five percent of the population was Christian, an equal percentage Muslim and perhaps ten percent Jewish. While many towns had mixed populations, distribution of these groups across Sicily was slightly uneven. Some towns in the east had more Greek Christians, while the areas to the west were more heavily Muslim.

The Normans began their conquest of Sicily in 1061, having already conquered most of peninsular Italy south of Rome. At the beginning of the eleventh century, this peninsular region was predominantly Lombard with a few pockets of Papal and Byzantine influence. The Papacy occasionally encouraged the Normans' conquest of southern Italy as part of its attempt to seize control of the churches which had been loyal to Constantinople.

In Sicily, the Popes saw in the Normans an opportunity to oust or convert the Muslims while Latinizing the Greek Church. Upon conquering Palermo, one of the first things the Normans did was to exile the Greek Bishop, Nicodemus, to a small church outside the city, replacing him with a Latin. Apart from this gesture, the conversion of Sicily's Christians from Greek to Latin was actually a slow, gradual process. Indeed, one can hardly speak of any real "conversion" so much as a slow transition. Over time, Greek bishops were replaced with Latin ones while Greek liturgy was replaced by Latin liturgy. This incidentally accelerated development of a Latin-based Sicilian language.

Their subsequent forays into the Balkans and the Greek islands did little to endear the Normans to the Byzantines. Bohemond, a son of Robert "Guiscard" de Hauteville and brother of Roger I, participated in the First Crusade (1098), one effect of which was installation of Roman clergy in Palestine and other areas seized from the Muslims, but the Crusades were not an exclusively Norman affair. Over time, Sicily's Normans supported them only rarely. More significant for Italy's Greek community was the Council of Bari convened by Pope Urban II in the same year as the First Crusade. This formally established that the Greek Church in Apulia would be integrated into the Roman one.

In 1143 Nilos Doxopatrios, an Orthodox cleric of Palermo, authored a theological treatise supporting the Eastern (Orthodox) Church over the Roman (Catholic) influences introduced by the Normans. This alone tells us that the Latinizing was taking root.

In the Orthodox Church there are distinct monastic communities but no large monastic orders. It was the Normans who introduced the first religious order in Sicily, endowing the Benedictines with monastic churches such as Saint John of the Hermits (in Palermo) and, of course, Monreale Abbey. Later, the military-religious orders were introduced, namely the Teutonic Knights (at the Magione in Palermo), the Templars and the Hospitallers or Knights of Malta. These orders of knighthood were Roman Catholic.

By the end of the reign of Frederick II (1250), Orthodoxy, such as it was, can be said to have been preserved only in a few churches around the island and a handful of monasteries in the Nebrodi Mountains. Two centuries later, beginning around 1470, thousands of Albanian refugees began to arrive in Sicily fleeing the Ottoman Turks. They reintroduced Orthodoxy. Within decades, however, they were integrated into a "uniate" Church preserving Orthodox liturgy but loyal to Rome — one of several Eastern Rites to be established within Catholicism in an attempt to convince Orthodox to embrace a "tolerant" or even "Byzantinized" Roman Church. In Mezzojuso a Greek Rite church founded by Albanians stands next to the Latin Rite one, and in 1935 the Martorana was given to the Albanian-Catholic diocese of Piana degli Albanesi.

Europe

While the Orthodox Church changed little over the centuries following the Schism, the Catholic Church underwent what can only be described as substantial mutations. Its theology became more rigidly legalistic and — under the influence of theologians such as Thomas Aquinas — rather more semantic and "philosophical" than it was before the Schism. Artistic and architectural movements such as the Gothic and the Baroque reflected, or at least complemented, such theological trends.

Orthodox teachings differ greatly from Catholic ones regarding doctrines on what Catholics refer to as Original Sin, Free Will and the Immaculate Conception as well as concepts such as Purgatory. In practice, the Orthodox (and most Eastern Rite Catholics) administer certain sacraments, such as the Eucharist (Holy Communion) and Chrismation (Confirmation) in infancy, and permit married men to become priests — something tolerated in the Catholic Church until the Lateran Councils of the twelfth century. Nevertheless, the Catholic Church recognizes Orthodox orders (sacraments) and apostolic succession.

Specific Orthodox views regarding certain aspects of the sacraments (and matters such as divorce in relation to marriage) differ somewhat from those of the Catholic Church, and Orthodox Canon Law (based on the determinations of Ecumenical Councils) is essentially unchanged since the Middle Ages while the more complex Catholic Code of Canon Law was fully revised most recently in the twentieth century.

It should be remembered that until 1054 Rome approached all of these matters from essentially the same perspective as Constantinople; the inescapable fact is that in the West subsequent changes were far more pervasive than in the East, and most were more significant than the introduction of (for example) stained glass windows and statues in beautiful Gothic cathedrals. As it is understood today, Papal Primacy, a doctrine based on a Western interpretation of scripture (Jesus' reference to Peter in Matthew 16:18), was formalized in Rome only long after the Schism. Phenomena such as rampant anti-semitism never reached the level of intolerance in the East that arose in the West, bolstered by such developments as the Inquisition.

As a generality, the Orthodox do not venerate Catholic saints canonized after 1054 (Saint Louis, Saint Francis of Assisi and Saint Thomas Becket, for example) while the Catholics do not venerate those canonized by the Orthodox after that date.

Even after the onslaught of the Renaissance, Italians could readily see the vestiges of Byzantine culture in the churches of Venice, Ravenna and Palermo, and perhaps in the presence of the newly-arrived Albanians.

Despite Byzantine and Orthodox influences in Sicily, the last Norman kings, the two Williams, sometimes bowed to the Papacy's incessant pressure to subdue Constantinople. In 1185, William II launched an ill-fated naval expedition intended to bring the Byzantine Empire — and especially the Orthodox Church — under Western control.

The War of the Vespers (described in Chapter 27) spared Constantinople a similar invasion planned for 1282, when the conflict in Sicily diverted the fleet and troops intended for use by King Charles of Naples in a conquest of the Byzantine Empire. Like the failed expedition of 1185, this conquest would have imposed Roman Catholicism in the East, bringing about the effective end of the Greek Orthodox Church.

Historical Views

For a series of events that occurred a millennium ago, the Great Schism remains a highly contentious topic, especially for vehement Catholic and Orthodox apologists. Catholics generally prefer to say that it was the Easterners who left the "Catholic" Church based in Rome, while Orthodox believe that the Westerners left the "Orthodox" Church and its other four patriarchs.

Further Reading

One of the more objective (neutral) general histories of the Great Schism is Steven Runciman's book, *The Eastern Schism*. Author of *The Sicilian Vespers,* he was also an expert on the Crusades. John Julius Norwich wrote an insightful chapter (numbered 8) about the events of 1054 in *The Normans in the South*. Both authors have written extensively about the Byzantine Empire as well. A pragmatic theological treatment of the underlying issues is to be found in John Meyendorff's *Orthodoxy and Catholicity.*

CHAPTER 12

The Normans

The Normans were the first Northern Europeans to firmly establish themselves in Sicily, something the Goths and Vandals failed to achieve. From Ireland to Tunisia, their conquests are the stuff of legends.

To call them "Vikings" (Norsemen) is to oversimplify the culture of the medieval Normans, for their society and heritage were as Frankish as they were Norse. The ethnonym *Norman* refers to the residual Norse and Frankish civilization of Normandy. Much as the Lombards of Lombardy were not purely Longobardic, the Normans of Normandy were not purely Norse. In fact, they were descended not only from Vikings but from Franks, Celts and Romans, and their principal language was a dialect of French. The Normans were Christians, and their feudal society was highly evolved in its government, art, architecture and literature, which during the twelfth century profoundly influenced not only Normandy but England and southern Italy.

The Norsemen were Scandinavian adventurers who rose to power in the ninth century, raiding the coasts of northwestern Europe in places like England and Ireland, and sailing as far as what is now Canada. One group ventured overland and along rivers into the Baltics and Russia to the Black Sea. Constantinople's Varangian Guard consisted of Vikings led by Harald Sigurdsson ("Hardrada") who fought alongside Normans with George Maniakes in Sicily. The Vikings were initially pagans, and their colorful mythology has given us the English names of several days of the week (Wednesday for Woden, Thursday for Thor), following an earlier Roman custom of naming the days for gods (as in the Italian Mercoledì for Mercury and Giovedì for Jove or Jupiter).

The Franks were a Germanic tribe which settled in Gaul (France and southern Belgium) during the decline of the Roman Empire. The Romans abandoned part of Belgium to the Franks in AD (CE) 358. By 507, much of France was united under the Christianized Frankish king Clovis. This included what is now Normandy.

By 900, Vikings were raiding this region but also establishing outposts there, taking local women as wives. In antiquity, the region of the Seine and Eure valleys had been Celtic. It fell under Roman control through the efforts of Julius Caesar. The Franks had ruled not only in the person of Clovis, but later under the reign of Charlemagne. In 909, Charles III "the Simple" ceded Normandy to the Norse chieftain Hrolf (Rollo), who became a Christian.

Immigration rapidly increased, and by 1000, following several generations of intermarriage of Norse with the "native" Frankish-Celtic population, a distinct ethnic culture emerged. In the decades to follow, Norman knights arrived in Italy, first as pilgrims and then as mercenaries, taking part — on whichever side offered better wages — in the wars between Byzantines and Lombards. In some cases, these knights were the younger sons of nobles who (under Frankish law) could not inherit lands destined for eldest sons. In others, they were simply wandering men-at-arms, soldiers of fortune.

The physical appearance of the great majority of the first Normans to arrive in Sicily differed somewhat from that of most of the Sicilians they met. The Normans had slightly lighter complexions easily scorched by Sicilian sunshine. Most had blond or reddish hair, and blue or green eyes. On average, they were perhaps an inch or two taller than the Sicilians. Initially, this made the Normans seem rather foreign.

The early decades of the eleventh century found Norman adventurers turning up in various parts of Europe. Raoul and Roger of Tosny, for example, fought in northern Spain for a few years but eventually returned to their native Normandy. In Italy there were isolated instances of Norman fighting Norman, one for Byzantines and the other for Lombards.

In general, the Normans of England were somewhat higher-born than their compatriots in Italy, their toponymic surnames typically based on familial fiefs in Normandy. Like the conquest of England, the Normans' conquest of Italy was characterized by social and political motivations, though it was much slower than the English campaign. The Patriarchs of Rome (the Popes) resented Byzantine influence in Italy, while the power of the Lombards was viewed as a nuisance.

Whereas the competition between Saxons and Normans for England was largely a question of a certain Saxon nativism versus Norman greed, the campaign against the Sicilian Arabs had at least some of the makings of a "holy war," whether justified or not. The Papacy made it clear that bringing Sicily to Latin Christendom — separating its Orthodox Christians from Constantinople's influence — was at least as important as reducing the influence of Islam on the island. In the event, the Normans did not Latinize Sicily rapidly enough for Papal tastes, nor did they overtly seek to convert the island's Muslims. In fact, they were often at odds with the Popes.

In 1054, the Church divided. The Great Schism (described in the last chapter) left the Latin "Roman" West distinctive of the Byzantine "Greek" East, resulting in the churches described in today's lexicon as "Catholic" and "Orthodox." In truth, of course, the conflict had been brewing for centuries, transcending theological ideas.

In 1061, having assumed control of much of southern Italy, a Norman force crossed into Sicily at Messina and seized the city from its Arab garrison during a major raid conducted on a night in May.

The Sicilian conquest now underway was arduous, tedious and wholly discouraging. Consolidating Norman power here would be difficult indeed. In 1066, a Norman force, including some knights who had fought in the Italian campaigns, won the Battle of Hastings (based in part on tactics learned at Messina), establishing the Norman presence in England. London was taken soon afterward.

In Sicily, on the other hand, the de Hauteville brothers, Robert "Guiscard" and Roger, reached Palermo only in late 1071, decisively winning it early the next year. While Saxon lords paid fealty to William "the Conqueror" of England almost immediately, it took Roger and his knights more than a decade following the Battle of Palermo to bring the entire island under Norman control; Emir Ibn Hamud of Kasr'Janni surrendered only in 1087. It was worth the effort. Their Mediterranean jewel was more important — and far wealthier — than William's rainy realm in the North Sea; revenues from the city of Palermo alone eclipsed those of all England.

For all that, the Normans were not the first northern European invaders to reach Sicilian shores during the Middle Ages. As we have seen, that distinction belongs to the Vandals and Goths, whose rule was short-lived and left few visible traces. By contrast, vestiges of Norman Sicily are everywhere to be found.

Sicilian society was infinitely more sophisticated than what the Normans encountered in England or even mainland Italy. The polyglot culture of the Arabs and Byzantines was a prosperous intellectual, artistic and economic environment at the center of the most important region of the "Western World" — the Mediterranean. It was a geographic crossroads between north and south, east and west. The beautiful Romanesque architectural style of Normandy (Cefalù's cathedral is based on Caen's Saint Etienne), so important in changing the face of Saxon England, was welcome in Sicily, but it merely embellished what the Byzantines and Arabs already had. The "Norman-Arab" style of art and architecture was unique, combining Byzantine, Moorish, Provençal and northern European movements in a new expression of aesthetics.

More important than this was the evolution of the social fabric of Norman Sicily, adapting essentially Arab institutions, including law as well as art and literature, to European realities. Throughout the Norman era (roughly from 1070 to 1200), ethnic and religious equality were generally accepted as integral parts of Sicilian society. Though there were conflicts, multicultural coexistence usually prevailed. The Church, but also the Sicilian language, was gradually Latinized. European institutions such as feudalism were introduced. In effect, Norman Sicily became part of Europe rather than northern Africa (under the Arabs) or western Asia (under the Byzantines).

On a purely humanistic level, its multicultural orientation was important enough, but Sicily's emergence as one of Europe's most important regions ushered in a "golden age" which continued into the "Swabian" era (of Frederick II von Hohenstaufen) during the first half of the thirteenth century. It was Sicily's finest hour. The twelfth century saw the island become a kingdom under Roger II, whose realm included not only Sicily but most of Italy south of Rome. The Norman government included clerics and administrators from England and Normandy. At court were great thinkers like Idrisi, an Arab geographer, and Thomas Brown, an Anglo-Norman known to Sicily's Arabs as "Qaid al Brun."

Nowadays, "new world" nations such as Canada, the United States and Australia seem to represent the epitome of tolerant, multicultural societies. In the Middle Ages, however, the concept was a novel one. True, the Roman Empire had embraced many cultures, but it could be argued that Norman Sicily supported a truer equality than most places offered, and it was more benevolent than ancient Rome.

Slavery was all but abolished, and serfdom was never as prevalent as it was in England, France or Germany, while literacy and freedom of speech came to be considered every Sicilian's birthright. For a few decades, the Normans' system of justice allowed separate — but equal — jurisdictions based on Koranic law for Muslims, Judaic law for Jews, Byzantine Greek law for Byzantines and Norman feudal law for Normans. Important documents were multilingual. True, a Latin (and Roman Catholic) orientation prevailed by 1200, but into the reign of Frederick II an egalitarian society existed. At least for a time, it was a successful experiment, and a necessary one.

Despite its ethnic diversity, or perhaps because of it, Norman Sicily evolved into an enduring "nation" with Sicilians as its "people." In other Italian regions such developments were literally centuries away. In time, the territory ruled by the Normans, contiguous to ancient Magna Graecia, became known to Italians simply as *il Regno* ("the Kingdom"). Palermo, the Arabs' Bal'harm, was the capital of this realm and later, under Frederick II, the unofficial administrative capital of his entire Holy Roman Empire. The period beginning with the arrival of the Normans in 1061 and ending with the death of their descendant, Frederick, in 1250, was a brief but remarkable, shining moment in European history.

The Normans retained most of the institutions of Arab society. After all, there was no need to change things which functioned well. Some everyday sights, like the souks (street markets) and Romanesque windows, still exist, of course, but throughout the twelfth century it was the Arabs' institutions that truly distinguished Sicily from other Norman territories, particularly England. Instead of abolishing existing policies and practices, the Normans built upon what already existed, adapting these as they found necessary. Coming as it did from renegades and mercenaries who just a few decades earlier were pillaging the Italian countryside, this was enlightened rule.

We do not know how many Normans settled in Sicily. Most were men, most were knights or other soldiers, and many were feudatories, effectively constituting the earliest medieval Sicilian landed aristocracy. Most married Sicilian-born women. The best estimate of the Norman migration places it at fewer than eight thousand persons arriving between 1061 and 1161, but even this is highly speculative. It certainly was not a mass immigration comparable to those of the Arabs (Saracens) or ancient Greeks, but a constant influx. The first Norman incursions into Sicily were measured in hundreds of Norman knights accompanied by greater numbers of non-Norman infantry, and not all of them remained on the island. Except for Benedictine and diocesan clergy, there were rather few men of learning among the Norman arrivals.

To this day red-haired Sicilians are referred to as "Normans." Most red-haired and blue-eyed Sicilians owe their coloring to the medieval Normans or the Lombards who often accompanied them, if not the Vandals and Goths.

Change did not come overnight. Some localities were more Orthodox Christian and Greek-speaking while others were predominantly Muslim and Arabic-speaking. Mosques stood alongside churches and synagogues. The Norman vassals and knights, though Christian, were Roman Catholic. True, some isolated Orthodox monasteries in the northeast of Sicily survived this process for a time, but most of Sicily's greatest Norman churches, though boasting some superficially Byzantine elements, were founded (or rebuilt) as Latin (Roman Catholic) ones.

The Norman era lasted through four rulers (two Rogers succeeded by two Williams), followed by two Swabians. Frederick II, whose mother was a daughter of Roger II, could be said to have continued the Norman tradition, but he was a Hohenstaufen and not a Hauteville. In the event, the "home rule" of Sicily from its own capital effectively ended with his death in the middle of the thirteenth century, to return only intermittently thereafter. Henceforth, the island — though a kingdom — was to be governed, for the most part, from Naples or from cities even further afield. The Sicily of the Normans represents a unique time in history which, like all such periods, was all too brief.

Fortunately, its monuments and its lessons endure.

CHAPTER 13

Roger I and Judith

If the growth of the identity of a Sicilian people could be attributed to the influence of a single historical figure, the eleventh-century ruler Roger I would be a good candidate. This is not to suggest that the social and political unification of the Sicilians had never been attempted before his time, but the arrival of the Normans marked a significant turning point in the island's complex history.

It was a complicated evolution over some twenty centuries, for if the native Sicanians lacked anything resembling a nation, Sicily's Greeks were perpetually at war with other Greeks and the odious Carthaginians. The Romans, who inherited the rivalry with Carthage from the Greeks (leading to the Punic Wars), managed to unite Sicily as a province, but one doubts whether Sicily's Greeks ever truly thought of themselves as Romans. The Byzantines continued the Roman tradition, but with a Greek cultural flavor. Arab Sicily, in the end, consisted of several emirates along the contested fringes of the Fatimid empire. Despite their great success in making Sicily prosper, the Arabs never achieved a completely egalitarian society, something the Normans accomplished with Greek, Arab and Jewish help.

Religious tolerance, of course, was at best incidental to the attitudes of the first Norman adventurers who arrived in Italy during the eleventh century. In practice, these ostensibly Christian mercenaries fought for whoever paid them, be it a Byzantine Greek or a member of the Lombard feudal nobility, and perhaps occasionally a Pope of Rome. Prominent among the knights were the many sons of the Norman lord Tancred of Hauteville. Too numerous to inherit their father's estate in the Cotentin, they sought their fortunes abroad.

The Count of Sicily

By 1042, the Normans of Italy had their own capital city, Melfi. Twelve years later, the Great Schism provided a solid pretext for the conquest of Sicily.

Arriving in Italy around 1056, the future Count Roger was born in Normandy around 1031 to Fredisenda, second wife of Tancred Hauteville. Roger wed (firstly) in 1061 the valiant Norman lady Judith of Evreux, who eventually bore four daughters but no surviving sons. He then married, in 1077, Eremburga of Mortain, who bore eight daughters. Roger's third wife, Adelaide del Vasto of Savona, who he wed in 1087, was mother of Simon and the future Roger II, first King of Sicily.

In its earliest stages, the conquest of Sicily was complicated by a brief quarrel between Roger and his elder brother, Robert, in 1062, a dispute rooted in questions of wealth and territory.

The Battle of Palermo led to Norman control of perhaps half the island in early 1072, but Noto, the last Arab stronghold, was taken only in 1091, and in that year, with little resistance, Malta was also conquered; indeed Malta and Gozo remained part of the Kingdom of Sicily until the last years of the eighteenth century, when the Knights of Saint John, who owed fealty to the Sicilian kings, were expelled by the French. At Count Roger's death in 1101, Sicily was a unified territory — though not yet a kingdom — which could boast its own identity.

In terms of government and law, Roger's rule in Sicily was far more effective than Robert's in mainland Italy. The feudal investitures of 1072 and 1092 found Norman, French and Italian vassals bound to Roger. From 1098, the Apostolic Legateship allowed him a voice in the appointment of bishops in new Latin (Roman Catholic) bishoprics around Sicily — part of the gradual trend toward Latinization as henceforth the establishment of Greek Orthodox monasteries and parishes was to be virtually unknown. In the event, most of mainland Italy south of Rome became part of the Kingdom of Sicily under Roger's successor.

Under Roger's rule, the Muslims kept their mosques, kadis, and freedom to trade, particularly in the cities. In rural areas, some were subject to the new Norman lords (enfeoffed knights who were vassals of the king). While serfdom was introduced it was not as widespread or enduring in Sicily as in, for example, the Norman realms of Normandy or England.

However, Roger always drew a good part of his infantry from the loyal Muslims. Visiting him at the Siege of Capua in 1098, Saint Anselm observed that "the brownish tents of the Arabs were innumerable." Clearly, Arab institutions and culture were preserved throughout Roger's reign, and into that of his great-grandson, Frederick II. An incidental example is the *tarì* coin, its name taken from an Arabic word. (In fact, this coinage, alongside the *onza,* was used until the end of the Kingdom of the Two Sicilies in 1861.)

Roger's respect for the Arabs as soldiers reflected his esteem for them in his civil administration. It may seem a paradox that into the twelfth century the Arab troops were often more loyal to the Hautevilles than were many "kindred" Norman knights and nobles. True enough, the Arabs' collective destiny depended on their European leader being kindly disposed to the Muslim population (Roger himself never embarked on Crusade though some Normans did, including his nephew, Bohemond of Taranto), but Roger cultivated Arab support for his own reasons. To his Arab subjects, he was Emir of Emirs and highly respected. Economically speaking, Arab Sicily had been somewhat isolated from Europe; now, under the Normans, commerce expanded, making the island's Arab merchants richer than ever.

Envy characterized the Norman ranks. Why, thought many knights, should the Hautevilles be the leaders when back in Normandy they were just another landed clan? A few of the Lombard vassals imported from mainland Italy might be equally cynical. Prudently, Roger and his immediate heirs maintained Melfi, the Calabrian town of Mileto, and San Marco d'Alunzio in Sicily's Nebrodi region as faithful — and fortified — enclaves well into the twelfth century. One never knew when a revolt might occur, and the most dangerous kind was usually sparked among the Norman population. Beautiful as Palermo was, it was always expedient to have a place to retreat to in time of danger. Medieval kings travelled often, and Roger was almost always on the move. His children, meanwhile, were raised at San Marco, a refuge far from the chaos and potential peril of the cities.

Roger is a good example of the medieval ruler as a warrior knight whose success depended on military prowess and efficient conquest. Like the Franks and Saxons, the Normans were fighters first and Christians second. It might not be too bizarre (though certainly anachronistic) to compare them to a violent motorcycle gang on horseback. They were exceptional, of course, in what they accomplished in Italy. In London, William was already a powerful monarch by the time the Hautevilles arrived in Palermo; in Sicily it would take another generation for the Norman knights to become kings.

How did Sicilian life change under Roger I? Under the Arabs, no (new) churches could be constructed. Precedence was generally given to Arabs (or to Greek-Sicilians who converted to Islam) for public positions, though the Fatimids were fairer in this regard than the Aghlabids and Kalbids. Christians had to make way for Muslims in public places, and rise when a Muslim entered a room. Special taxes were levied upon non-Muslims, namely Christians and Jews. Certain services were forbidden, or at least restricted, to non-Muslims; for example, Christian and Jewish women could only use the public baths during restricted hours, and never with Muslim women. While Christian and Jewish women were not required to wear veils (though some did wear scarves), their behavior in public, especially in matters of modesty in dress, had to comply to Muslim norms. This situation could hardly be considered religious persecution, but the Normans treated Sicilians of all faiths equally, and in fact (into the reign of Roger II) permitted Christian, Muslim and Jew each to be judged by the laws of his own religion. In practice, specific aspects of Islamic law came to be woven into the fabric of society. In effect, society moved beyond the mere "tolerance" of Sicily's Arab period toward genuine equality among the people. There were still serfs tied to the land, but slavery *per se* was eventually abolished.

Rather few buildings remain which can be attributed to Count Roger's thirty-year reign. He expanded coastal Milazzo Castle and other Arab fortresses around the island. He enlarged Palermo's al-Kasr fortress, which became the Normans' royal palace; this had been an Arab castle erected upon Phoenician walls. The "crypt" of the Palatine Chapel founded by Roger II is, in fact, the palace's original chapel, built and consecrated during the last years of the eleventh century; the newer one above it dates from 1140.

Roger died at Mileto in June 1101 aged seventy, of natural causes, succeeded by his son Simon, who died before the age of majority, to be succeeded by Roger II in 1105. We shall meet the second Roger in the next chapter.

Judith of Evreux

Judith was Roger's first wife and perhaps his most-beloved spouse. The two had met in Normandy a few years before Roger, then a young knight, departed for Italy.

Fair Judith was born in Normandy around 1036. In 1060, her elder half-brother (through her mother) and guardian, Robert of Grantmesnil, abbot of an important monastery, found himself at odds with his old friend William of Normandy, the future "William the Conqueror." Robert had been William's esquire and was knighted by him, but the friendship had gone sour.

This had nothing to do with Judith, whose father was William's first cousin. In 1061 Robert travelled to Rome to seek the support of Pope Alexander II, bringing along Judith, and two of her siblings with a number of monks. In Italy he was consoled with the gift of various monasteries and estates from the Hautevilles. Later, he would receive the episcopal see of Troina, where Roger found himself in December.

Hearing of the arrival of Judith and her siblings in Calabria, Roger wasted no time making his way to the tiny town of San Martino d'Agri to meet them. There he and Judith were betrothed. They were then married at Mileto, where the wedding was celebrated with a grand feast and music in lavish Norman fashion.

But it wasn't long before Roger had to return to Sicily, leaving his tearful bride behind in Mileto. The piecemeal conquest of the island's Nebrodi region continued over the next year. Troina, where Roger had left a garrison, was to cause further problems, and in August of 1062 he returned to the high town, which his knights had abandoned. This time he was accompanied by Judith.

At Troina his force of several hundred spent a few weeks building fortifications. Then he left Judith in charge while he went off to campaign in the region with the larger part of his mounted contingent.

Troina's population was about evenly divided between Arabs and Greeks. The latter took particular offense to the Normans' Latin liturgy and, it seems, the ways of some young knights with the local women. That, of course, did not mean that the Greeks themselves were particularly chivalrous.

Emboldened, they sought to abduct Judith, attempting to make her their hostage, but failed when some Norman knights came to her aid. What ensued was more than a skirmish.

A few messengers managed to escape the mêlée to reach Roger at Nicosia. By the time he returned, the situation had worsened; a number of Arabs from the surrounding country had joined the Greeks, forcing the Normans into a corner of the town.

The Normans retreated to some streets near the castle, where they quickly erected makeshift barricades. Caught unawares and under armed, they found themselves trapped, yet their besiegers lacked the capacity to overpower them. The dogged siege was to last for four long months.

Troina is over a thousand meters above sea level and in the eleventh century it was surrounded by dense forests of conifers — stone pines and the Nebrodi fir. The climate was cooler then, and the town was blanketed by snow for several months of the year. Lacking provisions and warm clothing, Roger and his hardy knights were to endure one of the coldest Winters in Sicilian memory.

The weeks dragged on, the Normans butchering their horses for food. Judith and Roger shared a flimsy blanket of wool. By January, the coldest month of the season, food was running short.

One particularly cold night, the Normans noticed that the Arab sentinels were consuming a great deal of wine, probably in the hope of staying warm. The drunken guards were soon sound asleep and the Normans attacked.

The deep snow muffled the knights' footsteps as they took back the town. By morning, Troina was again theirs. The leaders of the uprising were hanged and a feast followed.

The ordeal was not everybody's idea of a honeymoon, but Judith had proven her mettle and her husband would live to fight another day. Troina became a Norman stronghold. Indeed, Judith governed the town in her husband's absence for long periods over the next several years.

This, however, was not the only town fortified by the Normans during this period. They erected their first Sicilian castle at Aluntium, where some of Roger's children were born. Today it is San Marco d'Alunzio, and it would be a rural refuge of the Norman kings for a century.

Judith died young in 1076, having given birth to four daughters but — as far as we know — no sons. She was the very embodiment of the stalwart woman of the Middle Ages.

Sadly, much of Troina and its castle was destroyed during a later battle between Americans and Germans in the Summer of 1943.

CHAPTER 14

Roger II and Elvira

Only when Sicily became a kingdom did the rest of Europe officially take notice. Roger II was a son of Roger I, Great Count of Sicily (see the last chapter).

Born in December of 1095, young Roger was educated by erudite Greek and Arab tutors, with the occasional Italian or Anglo-Norman visitor. At court Norman French was spoken in addition to Greek and Arabic. The boy boasted a natural ability in languages, arts and, to some extent, sciences. He was naturally curious, and comfortable among the common people, whose languages and dialects he mastered. He spent some of his early years at San Marco d'Alunzio, in the Nebrodi Mountains, and was knighted in 1112 in the original palatine chapel (now the "crypt chapel") of the Norman Palace of Palermo. This ceremony brought Roger into public life.

Whereas his father and uncle were warrior knights, Roger II, who succeeded his elder brother, Simon (1093-1105), in 1105 and effectively ruled Sicily from 1112, spent much of his time in administration at Palermo, with the occasional foray into peninsular Italy to convince unruly Norman vassals of his feudal authority as their overlord.

In 1127, he succeeded a cousin, William (a grandson of Robert Guiscard), as Duke of Apulia, and was soon recognized by Pope Honorius II as ruler of other southern Italian

territories. Italian territories.

dominions. The Papal succession to Honorius was disputed, with one rival pontiff, Anacletus II, recognizing Roger's rights while another, Innocent II, did not. The Capuan and Neapolitan dominions were also contested, particularly by certain Lombard and Norman lords.

King Roger

Roger was crowned as the first King of Sicily in Palermo Cathedral in 1130, with Anacletus' blessing, and by late 1139, following the death of Anacletus (in 1138), the monarch's uncontested authority was recognized by Innocent II. Fearing Roger's growing political power, the Holy Roman and Byzantine emperors conspired to join forces, meeting to discuss ways to thwart the new king's geopolitical influence.

In 1118, Roger wed Elvira (about whom more below), who died in 1135, daughter of Alfonso VI of Castile. In 1149 he wed his second wife, Sibyl of Burgundy (died 1151). Two years later, he married his third and last wife, the much younger Beatrice of Rethel.

A contemporary mosaic icon in Palermo's Martorana church depicts a brown-haired, brown-eyed Roger being crowned directly by Christ, thus reflecting the belief that, apart from being the Pope's "Apostolic Legate" in Sicily, his royal authority emanated directly from God. The crown worn by Roger is distinctly Byzantine in style. Here East met West.

Twelfth-century society was rife with kingly despots, many mired in ignorance. Never the conformist, Roger stood above this morass of mediocrity.

Roger's reign fostered close connections between the Sicilian (or southern Italian) and English kingdoms, though Roger's authority was more akin to that of a Byzantine emperor or Arab emir than a European monarch. As the King of Sicily spoke Arabic, kept a harem (officially maidens charged with silk weaving), and frequently found himself at odds with the Roman Church, Roger was nicknamed "the baptized sultan" by Papal sycophants. His grandson Frederick II would earn the same appellation.

The fact that both sovereigns refused to conduct open Crusades against the Muslims only engendered greater suspicion in Rome. Like Frederick, Roger was an independent-minded intellectual, regarded as one of the most enlightened rulers of his age. To characterize him as a freethinker might not be inappropriate. His Assizes of Ariano, a legal code established in 1140, set forth a system of feudal law within a centralized form of government.

Freedom of worship was preserved, with mosques, synagogues, Byzantine (Orthodox) churches and Latin (Roman Catholic) cathedrals existing side-by-side. Personal rights were respected, and certain provisions would be reinforced by Frederick II in 1231.

Ever the curious intellectual, Roger supported numerous scholarly projects, including al Idrisi's *Book of Roger,* one of the greatest geographical achievements of the Middle Ages (see the next chapter). Foreign men of letters were always welcome at court. Like Sicily's multicultural society, Roger's administration was unique for its time. Norman administration coexisted with older Arab institutions, and official documents were published in Greek, Latin, Arabic and, occasionally, Hebrew and Norman French. Inroads into Byzantine territories in the Balkans and Arab lands in northern Africa further extended his dominion.

King Roger died on 26 February 1154, shortly before the birth of his last child, Constance (mother of Frederick II), who lived until 1198, and is entombed in Palermo Cathedral. He fathered numerous children — legitimate and otherwise — to be succeeded by his son, William I, crowned as *rex filius* (legally co-monarch) in 1150. This was a common Norman practice, followed by Henry II of England twenty years later, to ensure uncontested succession.

It would happen that the Hauteville legacy was inherited by the daughter born following Roger's death, by her son, Frederick.

Elvira of Castile

There was never, strictly speaking, a reigning "Queen of Sicily" who ruled in her own right. Each of Sicily's queens was legally a "queen consort" whose status, function and role was based on her marriage to the reigning monarch.

That said, several were regents until their young sons (future kings) reached the age of majority. That was the case, for example, of Margaret of Navarre, widow of William I (Elvira's son) and mother of William II, and Constance de Hauteville (Roger's daughter by his third wife, Beatrice), widow of Emperor Henry VI and mother of Frederick II. Whatever their official duties, apart from producing as many male heirs as possible, some of Sicily's early queens were indeed very strong women. This was certainly true of Elvira of Castile, Sicily's first queen, wife of Roger II, the island's first king.

Elvira was born in Toledo around 1100 to King Alfonso VI of Castile by his fourth wife, Isabella. It is thought that Isabella may have been the Zaida, initially Alfonso's Muslim concubine, who was baptised as Isabel.

Alfonso's reign was marked by a certain degree of internal dissent and chaos, and of course warring with the Moors. Yet following his death a series of equally violent wars erupted among Spain's various Christian kingdoms. His realm, like Roger's, was a multicultural, polyglot society of Christians, Muslims and Jews, but characterized by less accord and cooperation than what was then known in Sicily. Nevertheless, the environment into which Elvira was born was not too different from Sicily's.

Elvira's birth coincided with the end of the colorful era of El Cid (Rodrigo Díaz de Vivar), who had served her father in his struggle against the Moors. This hero's exploits are much romanticized. A sober reading of history reveals that the motives of the Cid (from the Arabic *sayyid* meaning "lord") were occasionally mercenary, and he sometimes fought alongside Muslims against Christians. Like Sicily's Hautevilles, he is frequently mentioned by historians as one of the most adventuresome figures of western Europe in the eleventh century. The point is that Elvira's background prepared her for what she was to encounter in Sicily.

The young princess wed Roger II in 1117, when the aspiring monarch was twenty-two and she was about seventeen. However, she rarely saw him in the years immediately following. Roger spent much of his time in military exploits, often against his own rebellious barons in mainland Italy. Like his father (Roger I), he was Great Count of Sicily, but fellow Normans were reluctant to recognize the superior authority of somebody whose immediate ancestors were little more than their knightly peers.

Roger had "illegitimate" children — most notably Simon of Taranto born around 1122 — during his marriage to Elvira.

It was when Roger was crowned as Sicily's first king in 1130 that Elvira became Queen. Her authority increased, but she seems to have exercised her power at court only rarely. She bore Roger a number of children, most of whom predeceased their father, including Henry (who died in infancy), Roger (died 1148), Tancred (died 1138) and Alfonso (died 1144). William succeeded Roger II as King William I. Adelisa wed Joscelin, count of Loreto; she died after 1169, and was the best-known of the daughters of Roger and Elvira.

Elvira died early in February of 1135, following eighteen years of marriage, and Roger went into reclusion out of profound mourning, for so long that rumors spread that he was dead. He did remarry (to Sibyl of Burgundy) much later, in 1149, but Elvira was the wife of whom he was fondest. Constance, who wed Emperor Henry VI and bore Frederick II, was the daughter of Roger's third wife, Beatrice of Rethel.

Roger's children were not always at peace with each other. William I, who earned from his subjects the unflattering nickname "the Bad," disdained his illegitimate half-brother, Simon, and divested him of the lucrative County of Taranto, a wealthy port city in Apulia. As retribution, Simon plotted with Matthew Bonellus, the lord of Caccamo (a fortified town near the Madonie Mountains), to overthrow William during a revolt in Palermo in 1161. One of William's young sons was killed in the chaos.

Elvira, Beatrice and Elvira's uncrowned sons (Henry, Roger, Tancred and Alfonso) were buried at the twelfth-century Church of Saint Mary Magdalen, a Norman-Arab structure now within the courtyard of the Carabinieri barracks along Piazza Vittoria near Porta Nuova in central Palermo. Although the church has been restored to its original condition, the graves' markers disappeared long ago.

CHAPTER 15

Abdullah al Idrisi

Abu Abd Allah Abdullah Mohammed ibn Mohammed ibn Ash Sharif al Idrisi (or Edrisi) was born in Sabtah, now Ceuta, Morocco, around 1100, descended through a long line of distinguished and aristocratic personages from the Muslim prophet, Mohammed. It is possible that his family was traditionally associated, perhaps through commerce, with Sicily's northwestern emirate, with its capital of Bal'harm (Palermo), and Idrisi certainly had kin in Sicily. His immediate ancestors were the Hammudids of the caliphate of Spain and north Africa, a branch of Morocco's Idrisids, and it was at Cordoba and Marrakesh that Idrisi received his earliest education. He eventually visited the Holy Land and Asia Minor, as well as parts of France and possibly England.

Before Idrisi, an account of life in Sicily was written by Mohammed al-Qasim ibn Hawqal, who visited in 972. Mohammed al Makdisi, who died in 991, also wrote about Sicily.

According to the contemporary Arab traveller bin Jubayr (1145-1217), Idrisi's Hammudi family was influential among Sicily's Muslims, and Idrisi's fame as a man of letters was known before his invitation to the court of King Roger II. He arrived in Sicily around 1145, and may have first visited as early as 1139.

Idrisi produced a number of works based on astute scholarly research, and it has been observed by modern Arabic scholars that he was an exceptional poet and writer of Arabic prose.

His famous planisphere, a large global map made of precious metal (mostly silver), did not survive the twelfth century, but it is known to have been a noteworthy work of geography — probably the most accurate map of Europe, north Africa and western Asia to have been created during the Middle Ages. An atlas produced during this period survived, and has been published in Germany and Iraq. A multilingual "Book of Simple Drugs" is also known to us. A minor geographical treatise written during the reign of Roger's successor, William I, has been lost to time.

His greatest surviving work is, without doubt, his "Pleasure Excursion of One Eager to Traverse the World's Regions," better known as the *Book of Roger*. Much of the information is secondhand. He describes England's dreary weather, for example, but we know not whether Idrisi ever set foot in that country. It is quite possible, however, as England, like Sicily, was a Norman realm, and there was much contact between the two kingdoms.

Closer to home, the book provides much information about Norman Sicily's economy. In a casual observation, Idrisi mentions the making of spaghetti in Trabia. It is to Idrisi that we owe much of our knowledge of the entire Mediterranean. Some of the book's statements were unorthodox for their time, things like "the earth is round like a sphere." Today, the *Book of Roger* is considered one of the most important scientific works of the Middle Ages.

That was not always the case among Europeans. Effusively praised by Sicily's Muslims, Jews and Eastern Christians, the work was not immediately appreciated by the medieval Popes or the Roman Catholic clergy, and for that reason its knowledge was sometimes suppressed in western Europe. Like

Marco Polo, Idrisi was a traveler who wrote about what he saw, but his work was much more scientific, and generally more objective, than Polo's. More importantly, it survives in its original, autographic manuscript.

Eurocentric historians who long considered medieval times to have been Europe's "Dark Ages" overlook the developments of the Arab and Byzantine worlds that touched Norman Sicily, where scholarship and the arts flourished in a manner then unknown in most of northern and central Europe. In such a world, Palermo assumed its place as a center of learning and expression alongside Cordoba, Byzantium, Alexandria and Baghdad. Idrisi's accomplishments were part of this trend.

The *Book of Roger* was completed early in 1154, shortly before the death of the king for whom it was named. We know little of Idrisi's life afterward. The court geographer must have been disappointed to learn of the theft of his planisphere during looting by some rogue Norman nobles in 1161. The revolt bore the marks of "European" Sicily's embryonic anti-Arab sentiments. Abdullah al Idrisi died around 1166, either in Sicily or in his native Morocco.

CHAPTER 16

The Norman Palace and Genoard

It looks medieval, with a generous dose of the Baroque added over the centuries, but the legacy of Palermo's Norman Palace, with the Palatine Chapel as its centerpiece, was built — quite literally — on ancient foundations. In times past an extensive park and hunting ground was located to its immediate south.

Origins

If Palermo lacks a Romulus and Remus, it can nevertheless claim an antiquity equal to Rome's. Neither city was built in a day. The site where the Norman Palace now stands was fortified with heavy stone walls by the Phoenicians, who founded the city as a trading colony, an event coinciding with the Greeks' colonization of eastern Sicily. The Phoenicians' descendants, the Carthaginians, returned three centuries later to develop and fortify their city of Zis into what later became known successively as Panormos, Panormus, Bal'harm and finally Palermo.

To the Greeks the port city was an irritating reminder of Carthaginian power in western Sicily and a springboard for Punic attacks on Greek cities like Himera to the east. Zis, of course, was not the only such annoyance; there were also Motya (Mozia) and Kfra (Solus or Soluntum), the latter of which fell to Greek power in 396 BC. Following the fall of

Greek Sicily to Rome, the rulers of the emerging Empire simply couldn't tolerate a competing power in the central and western Mediterranean. And so the Punic Wars, with Palermo as one of their main battlegrounds, unfolded as a series of major campaigns. The Romans had, in a sense, inherited the Greeks' complex power struggle against the Carthaginians.

Carthage fell, and in time it was followed by Rome. The Vandals and Goths discovered Panormus but didn't stay long. For the Byzantine Greeks, Palermo, and the high ground around what is now the Norman Palace, never warranted so much attention as Syracuse on the Ionian coast. In the meantime the shoreline receded and the population dwindled, to be augmented by the Arabs in the ninth century. They built the emir's large citadel, *al Kasr,* over the walls of the Carthaginians' crumbling fortress overlooking the Kemonia River nearby, and expanded their new metropolis in every direction, erecting administrative buildings in the district claimed from the sea, *al Khalesa* (today's Kalsa). Until the unification of Italy, the street near the palace, now called "Via Vittorio Emanuele," was known simply as the "Càssaro." The Càssaro district, like the Kalsa, had come to be known by the latinized version of its Arabic name.

By 910, Sicily's Aghlabid emirs ruled by authority of the Fatimids, their suzerains for the next few decades. Under the Aghlabids' successors, the local Kalbids, the unified Emirate of Sicily, such as it was, split several times, though Bal'harm remained the island's nominal capital and its most important city. Al Kasr became the fortress of Sicily's rulers. Under the Normans it was restructured around four large towers: the Pisan, Greek, Kirimbi and Joaria.

View from the Palace

Almost everybody who visits the Norman Palace comes to see the Palatine Chapel, but there's much more to discover.

Apart from the Palatine Chapel, the structure's main attractions are the Punic archeological site, the "crypt chapel" with the donjon passages nearby, Roger's Salon, the astronomical observatory and various Baroque rooms throughout the palace.

Overlooking the visitors' entrance, the battlements have been preserved, but these pointed merlons are relatively recent modifications. Most of its medieval walls, both inside and out, are now obscured by the less attractive additions of subsequent times, but the exterior of the Pisan Tower looks much as it did nine centuries ago.

If its exterior is less than impressive, the palace's interior still evokes much of its former grandeur.

The Royal Palace now houses the Sicilian Regional Assembly, the parliament of Italy's largest semi-autonomous "regional" government. Roger II ordered the palace's enlargement sometime before 1132, though the existing structure already included the simple Byzantine chapel (now the "crypt") near ground level. The structure was actually a castle in the most traditional sense, complete with a garrison (the royal bodyguard), victual stores and armory — though featuring a lavishness of design rare in western Europe in the twelfth century.

The Palatine Chapel

The Romanesque floor plan is rectangular with a rudimentary transept. Resplendent with traditional Orthodox iconography and a painted Arabic *muquarnas* ceiling (made partly from the timber of local Nebrodi Fir, now rare) bearing numerous figures of beasts and people, the Palatine Chapel is a Monreale in miniature, though it antedates that church by decades. Of particular note are the fine icons of Saint Peter and Saint Paul, to whom the chapel is dedicated. The large central mosaic

icons in the apse and cupola (dome) represent Christ Pantocrator (Ruler of All), one of several such medieval Byzantine
images in western Sicily.

Recently restored, the ceiling has some interesting images,
and even Arabic script. Lions and eagles are prominent. One
of the more remarkable images shows chess being played —
an indication of the intellectual pursuits of the medieval Paler-
mitans. Dancing is also depicted. Islamic practice generally discouraged the artistic representation of humans in portraiture,
but these paintings in tempera, part of what is widely considered the largest single Fatimid painting of its day, seem to reflect the relaxed norms of a tolerant society.

Though the architectural construction of the chapel was
probably completed by 1140, the artistic phase certainly required several more years. The ceiling is the work of local and
Tunisian artists. The mosaics — many representing Biblical
scenes — were created by Orthodox monks from Sicily, mainland Italy and Greece (and as far away as Constantinople), the
same artists who worked on the Martorana. The stone inlay
of the floor and lower walls is also a very demanding craft re-
quiring much skill and effort.

The Old Testament scenes of the nave walls offered the
advantage of appealing to Christian, Jew and Muslim alike, but
there are also New Testament images representing events in
the lives of Jesus, Peter and Paul.

On the wall behind the royal dais is the coat of arms of
Aragon added some time after the Sicilian Vespers war of 1282
when that dynasty began its reign in Sicily. The mosaics outside
the chapel are modern additions.

Roger's Salon

The "Sala di Ruggero" is one of several rooms in the palace
which exist in something close to their original condition. This

one has mosaics, some of which doubtless representing animals in the Genoard park to the south (described below), while others are clearly symbolic. The pairing of animals, sometimes as mirror images, is typical of Byzantine iconography, even if none of these images are explicitly religious. This part of the royal apartments probably was a place for dining or entertaining. Despite what one may occasionally read, Roger II and his grandson, Frederick II, did not keep harems in a formal way; officially there were beautiful, young, single women resident in the palace whose principal occupation was weaving and who were not part of the court.

It has been hypothesized that there was a fountain at the entrance of the room in the middle of the open tower. With or without the fountain at its entrance, "Roger's Salon" represented Paradise as described in the Koran. The room was an *iwan* and retains its square shape with an open side facing towards the atrium (and possibly the fountain) as an *iwan* should.

Astronomical Observatory

This modern addition to the Pisan tower is now essentially a museum of nineteenth-century telescopes and other scientific instruments. The first large asteroid, the dwarf planet Ceres, was discovered through observations here in 1801.

Crypt Chapel and Donjon

The original "palatine chapel" was this one, located in a quiet and secure area just below ground level, constructed late in the eleventh century. (This is not actually a crypt.) It predates the construction of the upper levels of the castle's superstructure and towers. A mosaic in fresco has been preserved from this early period. Parts of the surrounding corridors and rooms (the donjon) date from before the arrival of the Normans. This is the oldest surviving part of al Kasr readily visible to us today, other walls having been destroyed, extended upward or incorporated into more recent rooms.

Punic Wall

While it's not nearly so extensive as the Punic walls at Erice or Mozia, this site is one of the oldest of its kind preserved in Palermo. It cannot be dated precisely, being either Phoenician or Carthaginian. Precisely cut and constructed, it is similar to other Phoenician structures around the Mediterranean. The archway exists in its original condition.

The Genoard

Splendid as the palace is, one of its greatest attractions was the park and zoo to its immediate south, just beyond the city walls.

It was praised by al Idrisi and bin Jubayr, who had seen many wonders of the Arab world. *Gennàt al-àrd,* pronounced *Genoard* by the Normans, meant "Paradise on Earth" in Arabic. This was the name of the extensive park and hunting ground that the first kings of Sicily had Arab architects create for them. Extending southward across the capital's vast fluvial valley and beyond Monreale, Baida, Molara and Altofonte to the rugged mountains encircling the city, it was a marvel of Europe. Although its lakes and rivers are gone, along with most of its woods, a few of its palaces and pavilions survive.

To trace a path through what was a broad, central swathe of the Genoard and the royal hunting grounds beyond, one need only follow what is now Corso Calatafimi from Piazza Indipendenza toward Monreale. The park extended to an area near what is now the Viale Regione Siciliana motorway. This is where the hunting grounds began. (The Genoard map at the beginning of this book shows the park, kanats and the former courses of the rivers; streets are indicated for reference.)

Long before the park existed, the countryside in the Valley of Palermo, surrounded by its natural amphitheatre made up of hills and mountains, was a miracle of flora and fauna, thanks to its fertile soil, rivers and springs. Beginning in the ninth century, long before the Norman conquest, the Arabs introduced new irrigational and agricultural techniques here, where they planted citrus groves, earning the valley its nickname *Conca d'Oro,* meaning "Golden Conch."

The valley was so well irrigated that it was even possible to grow rice. Though rice has not been cultivated in Sicily for many centuries, this culinary tradition survives in *arancine,* or rice balls.

While the precise extent of the Genoard park is unknown today, we do know that it embraced a series of streams and *kanats* (canals) linked to the palaces built in the valley for both emirs and kings, extending from the base of the mountain crowned by Monreale. It should be remembered that Monreale during the twelfth and thirteenth centuries was little more than a small hamlet built around an abbey.

Though the oldest of the Fatimid palaces was several miles east of the Genoard, it is worth mentioning because it was the inspiration for palaces constructed later. The *Favara,* also known as Maredolce in what is now the Brancaccio district of Palermo, was built by Ja'far, the Emir of Bal'harm, at the end of the tenth century. The name derives from the two freshwater springs (*fawwàra* in Arabic) that supplied water to the area, flowing down from nearby Mount Grifone into the Oreto River. These natural springs facilitated the creation of a small lake. This residence was surrounded by a lush park. Unfortunately, only a few walls of the *Favara* remain.

Apart from a few Punic necropoli that dot the area, the oldest structure in the Genoard proper was the *Scibene* palace, probably contemporary to the *Favara* and predating the arrival of the Normans in Sicily. Located off Viale Regione Siciliana, it survives only as a fragment.

Both the *Cuba* and the *Zisa* castles were erected by William I "the Bad" or his son William II "the Good."

Located along what is now Corso Calatafimi, near Via Cuba, the *Cuba*, a square building — "cubic" as its name suggests — was used as a pavilion during concerts and perhaps even jousts. It was surrounded by shallow reflecting pools and included a number of smaller, square, domed buildings similar to the tiny *Cubola* in what is now Villa Napoli less than a mile away. It is thought that there were as many as twenty of these smaller structures in the Genoard.

On the western edge of the park, the *Zisa* castle (located near what is now the end of Via Dante) was a more complex building used as a summer residence by the last Norman kings and possibly as Joan Plantagenet's residence immediately prior to her wedding to William II. This castle, built by Arab architects, had its own air conditioning system, including a fountain hall (an *iwan* with a fountain) where one may still admire some mosaics from the Norman period, at least six separate apartments (two per floor), each fully equipped with its own latrine and running water, an atrium on the upper floor for collecting rainwater with a cistern and, next to the building, a private chapel which still stands, as well as a *hammam* (a traditional Arab-style bathhouse and sauna). Though vaguely inspired by the gardens of the Genoard, today's Zisa gardens are a modern construction.

To paraphrase bin Jubayr, these Arab-style palaces were "jewels about the neck of a stunning lady" which was the Genoard park. Surrounded by lakes, artificial streamlets and fountains, all were equipped with complex cooling systems and internal water ducts like those of the Zisa. Indeed, they were built on the model of the typical Arab *àgdal* outside a city, with a fountain representing the spring of Paradise set in a small lake surrounded by gardens. Another contemporary chronicler who made reference to the Genoard and its delights was the monk Peter of Eboli.

The Genoard had an incredible variety of flora and fauna. There were both common and exotic plants, bushes, and trees such as palms, plane trees (sycamores), citrus (oranges, mandarins, lemons, citrons), almond, pistachio, chestnuts and walnuts, wild olive and fig trees, medlar trees, myrtle and laurel. There was also papyrus and sugarcane growing along the streams and the two rivers — the *Kemonia* and the suitably-named *Papyrus* or *Papireto*. The scent of jasmine and other blossoms was everywhere.

The fauna in the Genoard zoo included exotic birds such as parrots and peacocks, migratory birds like herons, flamingos and the purple swamp hen, but also turtle doves and pigeons. There were reptiles, including Nile crocodiles, and among the mammals exotic ones such as monkeys and giraffes, leopards and lions — some introduced by Frederick II.

A vast hunting reserve and scattered woodlands lay beyond the Genoard, beginning, as we've said, around what is now the Viale Regione Siciliana motorway. Here were deer, hare, rabbits, pheasants, grouse, partridge and black francolin as well as a few small wild cats and hedgehogs. Foxes, wolves and wild boar also thrived here. The woods were comprised of ashes, oaks, birches, and some conifers — perhaps even the rare Nebrodi Fir. The woods overlooking Altofonte, across the valley to the southeast of Monreale, offer us an idea of what the higher parts of the reserve were like into the thirteenth century when Frederick II hunted here. Frederick loved falconry and wrote a lengthy treatise on this avian sport of kings.

Two landmarks dating from this period should be mentioned. Castellaccio is a fortress crowning the mountain above the town of Monreale. Across the valley, in the town of Altofonte, is the Normans' Chapel of Saint Michael. A small Norman castle that served as a hunting lodge once stood on the site of what is now that town's main church.

The first major modifications to the park were undertaken on the orders of Henry VI around 1195. This resulted in a slight reduction of the Genoard itself, with parts of the extensive hunting reserve nearer the city turned over to farming. Over the next few decades, during the reign of Frederick II, several residential hamlets encroached upon the park and hunting grounds. The largest of these is now the town of Altofonte, which until the twentieth century was called *Parco* (park). By 1300, the city was growing southward beyond its Norman walls and into the abandoned park.

As we have said, an artistic record can still be seen in the upper apartments of the Norman Palace. "Roger's Salon" is a fine example of an Arab *iwan* inserted in a *riyàd,* an artificial rendering of a Koranic paradise within an enclosed and built-up space in a city, and it gives us a vivid artistic impression — in timeless golden mosaic — of some of the creatures and plants in the nearby Genoard.

Another part of the Norman Palace seems to allude to the Genoard's delights. On the ceiling of the Palatine Chapel, various animals are depicted. Were there camels in the Genoard? Quite possibly.

The Genoard, with its palaces, pavilions, lakes, streams, bathhouses and the bordering hunting grounds, was truly an earthly paradise.

CHAPTER 17

Margaret of Navarre

For a few years she was the most powerful woman of Europe and the Mediterranean. But she was not unique. During the Middle Ages, a number of women, at one time or another, found themselves ruling kingdoms or other dominions in lieu of their husbands or sons for what was usually just several years — typically as regents because they were widowed and their sons had not yet come of age.

This was the case with Margaret of Navarre (1138-1183), Queen Consort and then Regent of the Kingdom of Sicily toward the end of the twelfth century, who would pilot the Kingdom through a series of intrigues and vicissitudes.

Margaret was the daughter of King Garcìa Ramìrez of Navarre, called "the Restorer" for having restored the independence of the Navarrese crown from the Kingdom of Aragon, and of his first wife Marguerite de l'Aigle, daughter of Gilbert de l'Aigle and Juliana du Perche.

When she was still very young, Margaret married William of Sicily, the fourth son of King Roger II. Although eyewitnesses at the Norman court of Sicily described her a woman of extreme beauty, William, eventually nicknamed "the Bad," who was said, like his father, to have kept a harem of concubines (officially silk weavers) in his palace, appeared to take little interest in his wife after his coronation. Notwithstanding this, he fathered four sons with her, namely Roger, who was killed at the age of nine during a rebellion brought on by Matthew Bonellus (who we shall meet) and some royal conspirators; Robert, who also predeceased his father; William II, the future King of Sicily, later known as William the Good; and Henry, Prince of Capua.

Margaret had a very strong personality, and on several occasions she was the driving force behind the king finally taking action in important matters, as he was normally slow and passive in taking decisions. But she was rarely alone in this decision-making: Maio of Bari, William's Governor, was the man who was truly running the kingdom at the time. The dictatorial Maio was disliked by nobles and populace alike, but the Queen used him as an instrument against her husband's opponents. Indeed, Maio, who King William trusted implicitly, was the root of much unrest in the kingdom.

One of the reasons for this ill-feeling was that during William's reign Sicily lost her possessions in Northern Africa, where rebellion against the Sicilian King's men began in 1156 and ended in early 1160 with the surrender of Mahdia, the Sicilian Normans' last North African stronghold. During the rule of Roger II such an outcome would have been highly unlikely considering the Crown's vast military and naval resources managed by a competent Governor, George of Antioch.

Such a devastating outcome as the total loss of these territories was certainly a blow not only to King William's image, but to that of Maio of Bari, who henceforth could not even compare to the kingdom's previous governor.

This was the scenario that led to a conspiracy to kill Maio of Bari. Incredibly, this plot had as one of its main conspirators Matthew Bonellus, a wealthy Norman nobleman as lord of Caccamo, who was Maio's intended son-in-law, having asked for the hand of the Governor's daughter. During his time on the mainland, Matthew fell to the pressures of conspirators headed by Countess Clementia of Catanzaro, who is described as breathtakingly beautiful, and who apparently had an influence on Bonellus that went beyond politics.

The plot succeeded in eliminating the much-hated Governor. In November of 1160, Maio of Bari was killed by Matthew Bonellus in the city of Palermo. At first, considering Bonellus' popularity among the aristocracy, King William was compelled to grant him a pardon for having killed his Governor. But soon afterward, William became irritated with Matthew's arrogance, and with the Queen's encouragement he eventually moved against the insolent baron just in time, for Matthew had fallen under the conspirators' pressure to plan killing the king.

In this attempted regicide, Bonellus conspired with two close relatives of the king himself — his half-brother Simon (an illegitimate son of Roger II), who had been removed by King William as Prince of Taranto, and his nephew, Tancred, count of Lecce, who had been thrown into the palace dungeons for a few years after having begun a revolt against his sovereign.

Following much planning, Matthew and his accomplices bribed their way into the Norman Palace for a *coup d'état*. This seemed easy enough with the support of Simon and Tancred, who knew the palace well. At this point, though, Queen Margaret herself and two of her sons were made prisoners in her private apartments, while the rebels started plundering the palace and killing helpless servants, including the king's concubines, who were violated and slaughtered in the palace harem. The massacre extended out into the streets, and it led to the killing of people of different ethnic backgrounds, including Arab merchants, coin-minters and silk-weavers, and this brought on an angry response among the citizens of Palermo who sided with the king, who had always been respectful and fair with all his subjects.

Within just a few days, the king and his men were able to put an end to the rebellion, but not before William lost his son and heir, little nine year-old Roger, who had been struck by a stray arrow. A few months later, Bonellus was arrested, mutilated and thrown into the dungeons where he died soon afterward.

Now William put his kingdom into the hands of three men, each having different roots, who formed a kind of triumvirate: the Englishman Richard Palmer, a layman at the time, who would later become Bishop of Syracuse; a certain "Qaid" Peter, a Christian Arab who became Great Chamberlain of the Palace; and Matthew Ajello, a notary of the Lombard bourgeoisie.

The king at this point went back to living his previous life of leisure and pleasure, without having to worry any longer about governing his kingdom, but he had only a short time to enjoy it all. In 1166 he died of dysentery at the age of forty-six.

In the long run, William was not remembered as a good king, for he had lacked confidence in his own power and capabilities to rule the kingdom. It must have come as a surprise to his people when, as Queen Regent, Margaret started making decisions immediately after the king's death, despite the triumvirate's doubts about a woman effectively ruling in place of her twelve year-old son, the future William II.

The first thing Margaret did, right after her young son was crowned, was to declare a general amnesty and to abolish the collection of "redemption money" which was supposed to have been paid by rebellious towns of the Kingdom of Sicily, which at that time extended northward into the Italian peninsula to a point just south of Rome. She harbored serious doubts about the ruling triumvirate, and she felt it important that she and her son not be too closely associated with them in the public mind as they represented the previous rule of her unpopular husband.

In the beginning, she gave full power to but a single member of the triumvirate, Qaid Peter, who of the three was the one furthest from the local aristocracy. At first, it seemed like a good choice, but soon the kingdom started to fall out of control, and Peter fled to Tunisia where he was said to have converted back to Islam. Out in the streets, people spoke against Margaret and began to call her "the Spanish woman," regretting the loss of King William, who, though never particularly popular, had not seemed so foreign to them.

After such a blow, the Queen had an even more difficult choice to make, but in the end she replaced the triumvirate, not with the most likely candidates chosen from the local aristocracy, nor from men of the Church who hovered around the court, and not with her half-brother Rodrigo who had recently arrived in Palermo, or her cousin Gilbert who she could not trust, but with a young cousin of hers, Stephen du Perche.

Upon arriving in Palermo, Stephen did not seem to harbor any ambitions of running the kingdom. He had just finished preparing to leave for the Holy Land and had with him a retinue of thirty-seven French soldiers. Before leaving on Crusade, together with his men he decided to come visit his cousin Margaret after being invited by another of the Queen's cousins, Rothrud, the Archbishop of Rouen.

After a short while, Margaret was able to persuade him into staying, and she appointed him chancellor in November of 1166. This decision did not fare well with the local nobility. It seemed to them that the court was becoming more and more foreign, especially because, besides his original French entourage, a number of Frenchmen were invited by Stephen to move to Sicily and they were granted fiefs on the island. Now that he had decided to stay, Stephen wanted to surround himself with people he felt he could trust, so unrest was bound to occur among the local nobles.

At least in the beginning, Queen Margaret probably believed she had made a wise choice with the new chancellor. Stephen showed himself to be something of an idealist and the first thing he did was to introduce new reforms, which would have been impossible for a Sicilian less neutral and detached than an outsider. But although the people liked him, this was obviously something that started to render Stephen extremely unpopular among the local nobility.

As if the problems in her realm were not enough to render her life complicated, a potential intruder started to move in closer: the Emperor Frederick Barbarossa. Frederick had opposed the election of the new Pope, Alexander III, and had given his full support to the anti-pope, Victor IV. In the meantime, when he was still alive, King William had always been the most faithful ally of Pope Alexander, and had continuously made his support felt, not only politically, but also by sending the Pope money and gold up until his final days. This meant that the Queen had a valued confederate after the death of her husband. She kept up a continuous correspondence with the Pope and with one of his faithful English followers, Thomas Becket, who trusted her enough to send some of his kinsmen to her court when they were exiled from England during Becket's troubles with King Henry II. It seems that the Archbishop of Canterbury's close friend Richard de Laigle was a relative of Margaret's mother Marguerite de l'Aigle.

Fortunately for the Sicilians, Emperor Fredrick's army was forced to stop its advance into the Norman Kingdom by a plague that hit it during the hot month of August 1167, and the Holy Roman Emperor had to make his way back home over the Alps.

In the meantime, Margaret chose Stephen as the new Archbishop of Palermo and had him anointed just a few days after he had been ordained a priest, although Stephen seemed not to ever have had a calling for the Church. Now as both chancellor and archbishop, he found not only the local aristocracy but the clergy against him. Even Matthew Ajello made no secret of despising him, and Stephen suspected everybody except his French entourage of continuously plotting against him.

Rodrigo, the Queen's half-brother, who now called himself "Henry" (or Enrico) in order to seem less a foreigner, returned to Palermo in the hopes of regaining some power, only to find Stephen in his previous position. Thanks to his natural charm, Stephen won him over, and soon his cousin Henry was one of his strongest supporters. But as time went by, Stephen's enemies convinced Henry that his sister was having an incestuous affair with handsome young Stephen, and that it should have been Henry, the Queen's brother, heading the government, and not du Perche.

In an extreme attempt to protect his power and the kingdom from all the conspirators, whose ranks included not only Henry but also a large number of Spaniards and locals, Stephen moved the court to Messina in early Winter of 1167 with the excuse that he was preparing to take young King William to the mainland the following year. Here Stephen was able to unmask Henry and the others, and to arrest them.

The scheming against him, though, was not yet at an end. Shortly before the court returned to Palermo, Matthew Ajello was preparing to kill Stephen. Fortunately the chancellor was informed of this plot just before his arrival, and so he arrested Matthew and the others as soon as he set foot in the city. But Stephen's administration was not meant to continue. The Sicilians' distrust of the French had grown deeper. Rumors about incest between Stephen and the Queen persisted, becoming more widespread.

Although Matthew was locked up in prison, he continued to conspire against Stephen, who fortunately had spies that warned him before this new plot could succeed. Unrest continued in the city, with both Christians and Muslims alike hoping for the chance to rid themselves of the French chancellor. Finally violence erupted.

Stephen had a group of friends and guards to defend him, but they would not stand a chance against the angry crowds that rose up against him outside the palace. Even the young king, who was still an adolescent at the time, tried to speak to the crowds and get them on the chancellor's side. In the end, Matthew Ajello and his people decided to give the chancellor and his French followers a chance to escape. The terms were set and signed, and du Perche, who by now had no choice, agreed. They were to leave immediately for the Holy Land, never to set foot in the Kingdom of Sicily again. Mob rule had won the day.

Margaret was downcast. Her cousin Stephen, the only person who she felt she could have trusted completely with governing the kingdom, was gone, forbidden to ever return. Her son still had a few more years to go before he could ascend the Throne. She was discouraged to make any decisions as regent regarding the government, as none of the nobles, the clergy or the palace officials wanted her or her relatives involved in Sicilian affairs. A council was constituted without her say, and it included all three of these factions — aristocrats such as Richard of Molise, bishops such as Richard Palmer of Syracuse and Walter "Offamilias" who was soon to take the place of Stephen as Archbishop of Palermo, and of course Matthew Ajello.

Margaret hoped that one day her dear cousin Stephen would be able to come back and take up his old government positions again, but all her letter-writing to Pope Alexander and to Thomas Becket was done in vain. Stephen himself arrived safely in the Holy Land with his small group of followers, but we know from the historian William of Tyre that he would expire just a few years later after falling seriously ill.

After the election of Walter as the new archbishop, Margaret realized that she could no longer hope to command the government ever again. In 1171, her son William II came of age and was finally able to rule his kingdom. A few years later, in 1177, he married the young Joan of England, daughter of King Henry II "Plantagenet."

Margaret of Navarre lived for another six years. During this time she built a monastery in eastern Sicily next to the eleventh-century Church of Santa Maria of Maniace, north of Mount Etna. In 1183, she passed away at the age of fifty-five, and today she rests in the transept of the glorious Cathedral of Monreale that her son built, amidst the splendor of golden and colorful mosaics.

CHAPTER 18

Bin Jubayr

Some of the most important descriptions of Norman Sicily come to us from Arab and Muslim sources. These are especially important in their objectivity because, unlike visitors from northern, Christian Europe, those from prosperous Muslim regions brought to their observations a somewhat more sophisticated point of reference. They weren't easily impressed by the more superficial aspects of a wealthy kingdom. Idrisi is the best known of the Arab geographers to have visited Sicily, but another is equally distinguished.

Abu Hussain Mohammed bin Ahmad bin Jubayr (or Jubair) al-Kenani was born around 1145 in Valencia, then a thriving region of "Moorish" Spain, and by 1182 he was high secretary for the Emir of Granada. The following year Jubayr left for a Hajj (pilgrimage) to Mecca. His travels took him across the Mediterranean, reaching Alexandria in the Spring of 1183. On his way back to Spain, in early December 1184, he reached Sicily, where he was shipwrecked at Messina but given hospitality by an Arabic-speaking monarch, William II. His Sicilian travels took him westward by ship, with stops at Cefalù, Termini, Solunto and finally Palermo. Following a week in the capital, he departed by land for Trapani, passing Alcamo along the way. Among many other features, he describes several castles which no longer exist.

Here is how he described the volcanic Aeolian Islands:

"At the close of night a red flame appeared, throwing up tongues into the air. It was the celebrated volcano (Stromboli). We were told that a fiery blast of great violence bursts out from holes in the two mountains and makes the fire. Often a great stone is cast up and thrown into the air by the force of the blast and prevented thereby from falling and settling at the bottom. This is one of the most remarkable of stories, and it is true. As for the great mountain in the island, known as the Jabal al-Nar (Mountain of Fire), it also presents a singular feature in that some years a fire pours from it in the manner of the 'bursting of the dam.' It passes nothing it does not burn until, coming to the sea, it rides out on its surface and then subsides beneath it. Let us praise the Author of All Things for His marvelous creations."

His description of Palermo is an equally vivid one:

"It is the metropolis of these islands, combining the benefits of wealth and splendor, and having all that one could wish of beauty, real or apparent, and all the needs of subsistence, mature and fresh. It is an ancient and elegant city, magnificent and gracious, and seductive to look upon. Proudly set between its open spaces and fields filled with gardens, with broad roads and streets, it dazzles the eyes with its perfection. It is a wonderful place, built in the Cordoba style, entirely from cut stone known as kadhan (limestone). A river splits the town, and four springs gush in its suburbs. The Christian women of this city follow the fashion of Muslim women, are fluent of speech, wrap their cloaks about them, and are veiled."

He also described the Martorana church, and specifically its bell tower (higher then than now). He observed that the city of Messina was predominantly Greek Orthodox, with a dwindling Muslim community. Some of his comments are cryptic. He mentions a tax on Muslims, without making clear whether this tax was also levied upon Christians and Jews.

Jubayr recorded the story of the words of King William II to his subjects following an earthquake in 1169: "Let each of you pray to the God he adores; he who has faith in his God will feel peace in his heart."

It is clear from his writings (expressed here through Ronald Broadhurst's masterful translation) that Jubayr was devout in his Sunni faith, even something of a dogmatist. But the winds of religious intolerance were gathering force, and perhaps that is what he inferred from what he saw in Sicily, where he might have hoped to see more Muslims.

Jubayr's record is useful in establishing the continuity of the Palermitan cultural atmosphere over the centuries. It is, in effect, a link in a chain. Mohammed ibn Hawqal, a merchant from Baghdad with a penchant for geography, described an Arab-Byzantine Sicily in the time long before Idrisi and Jubayr, and a capital just as prosperous as in the time of Jubayr.

Jubayr also visited Jerusalem and other places, and wrote about these. He died in Alexandria in 1217.

CHAPTER 19

Joan Plantagenet

She remains a footnote to Sicilian history, her role perhaps close to that of the typically sheltered, if not passive, medieval European noblewoman, bound by a sense of duty all but abandoned in our modern world. Nothing like the bold image of her mother, the crusading Eleanor of Aquitaine, or the strong-willed Constance of Aragon, wife of Frederick II.

That Joan of England never produced a surviving heir to the Sicilian throne is historically significant because it heralded the effective end of the Hauteville dynasty. Yet she is an interesting figure, and part of a wider Anglo-Norman influence in twelfth-century Sicily — and a witness to great historic events that shaped the destiny of Sicily, England and France. Her quiet courage despite a lifetime of difficulty is, in itself, a lesson in the virtue of steadfast strength in the face of overwhelming adversity.

Born at Angers Castle (Angers, Anjou) in France in October 1165, blond-haired Joan was the seventh and youngest surviving child of King Henry II of England and his Queen Consort, Eleanor of Aquitaine. (Henry fathered illegitimate children as well.) As one of their three surviving daughters, Joan (or Joanna) passed her earliest years in England but mostly in France, where her mother lived in Poitou, effectively separated from her father. Joan was attractive and, according to what few accounts exist, rather intelligent even as a child. Her brother, the future Richard I "Lionheart," was the only one of her siblings known with certainty to have visited her in Sicily. As a young girl at the Abbey of Fontevrault, Joan learned Saxon English, Norman French, and at least the rudiments of Latin, in addition to a range of skills deemed appropriate to the mistress of an aristocratic household. Like Joan, her sisters were betrothed to European monarchs: Matilda wed the Duke of Saxony in 1168 and Eleanor married the King of Castile in 1177. In the case of Joan's marriage to William, however, there was a very special Norman link.

A great-grandson of William I "the Conqueror," the French-born Henry was Norman to the core, often occupied with his dominions in France, some of which he ruled by virtue of his marriage to Eleanor, an heiress. So busy was he with foreign matters that in thirty-four years as King of England, Henry spent a mere fourteen in that nation. Eleanor was the divorced consort of King Louis VII of France (and kin to both husbands), who later fought a brief war against Henry. Such were the complexities of medieval court life, shadowed by equally complicated political alliances in which inter-dynastic marriages were thought to cement loyalties. (Officially, Eleanor's marriage to Louis was annulled for close consanguinity, but in reality the French monarch seems to have been more worried about his wife's propensity for producing daughters than with any canonical formality.)

Henry II is noted for his legal and administrative reforms, leading to the development of fundamental English institutions such as common law and trial by jury. His Constitutions of Clarendon (1164) re-established royal prerogatives not unlike those embodied in the "Apostolic Legateship" of the kings of Sicily. A coincidence, perhaps, but contact between the Norman courts of London and Palermo were remarkably close considering the geographical distance between them. In view of the increasing power of the Crown and its juridical institutions, a legal dispute with the Church was inevitable. This fostered ill feeling with the Archbishop of Canterbury, Henry's onetime friend and chancellor Thomas Becket, leading to Thomas' exile from 1164 to 1170. The archbishop's close relatives were likewise exiled, and some found refuge in Sicily.

Joan's relationship with her father probably left something to be desired, and this may partly account for her later devotion to Saint Thomas Becket, the archbishop her father's nobles murdered. True, Henry did public penance for this act at Canterbury in 1174, but this could not attenuate the impact of such dramatic events on an impressionable girl raised in a society where respect for religious institutions was part of daily life. The mosaic icon of Saint Thomas Becket in Monreale Abbey is the earliest public image of the saint known to survive, and several twelfth-century churches in Sicily are dedicated to the archbishop soon venerated across western Europe.

In 1173, coincidentally the year Becket was canonized, Joan's mother, the strong-willed Queen Eleanor, led a revolt against King Henry, supported by their three surviving sons (Henry's illegitimate sons supported their father). Following the failed rebellion, Eleanor, at the age of fifty, was imprisoned (placed under "house arrest" in a castle) for what was to stretch into a fifteen year incarceration, and Joan was living with her at Winchester in early 1176 when a Sicilian delegation arrived to confirm, among other things, the exceptional beauty of the ten year-old princess, before formally requesting her hand from Henry. William himself was reasonably attractive, of average height with reddish hair. His father was William I, his grandfather Roger II.

As a young girl, Joan had been formally betrothed to William II on the basis of a prior agreement (in 1168) and provided with a feudal dowry in Italy. In the event, the Sicilian

Hautevilles were not haunted by the money problems that plagued the English "Plantagenets." In the 1170s, the royal tax revenue of Palermo, a prosperous and cosmopolitan capital of some 200,000 citizens, exceeded those of all England.

William II ascended the Sicilian throne upon the death of his father (William I) in 1166, though he lived for several years under his mother's regency.

Led by Bishop John of Norwich, the embassy of King Henry II arrived in Palermo in mid-1176 in advance of Joan's party, which stayed behind in England. The Bishop of Winchester handled details for Joan's voyage, and Henry met William's delegation in August.

Joan's voyage to Sicily, accompanied by a large suite of ladies-in-waiting, knights, clergy and various retainers (everything from cooks and seamstresses to grooms and blacksmiths), was typical of the travels of royalty and the highest nobility in the Middle Ages. What distinguished it was the exceptional youth of its protagonist. Following a feast, Joan bid farewell to her mother and father. The trip began with the short stretch from Winchester to Southampton, escorted by the archbishops of Canterbury and Rouen, the Bishop of Evreux and Joan's uncle Hamelane, natural brother of King Henry. Then Prince Henry, her oldest brother, the twenty year-old heir apparent, accompanied her across the Channel and into France to Poitiers. There she was met by her brother Richard, who escorted her through the Duchy of Aquitaine (nominally his), across the allied County of Toulouse to Saint Gilles Port, where Bishop Richard Palmer welcomed her in the name of the King of Sicily.

Twenty-five Sicilian ships awaited the young princess. It was mid-November, and the gales had already decimated the fleet of Bishop John of Norwich, returning from Messina with King William's gifts for his future father-in-law. (It seems typical of what King Henry believed to be his own poor luck that most of the royal treasure destined for him was lost.) Some six weeks later, Joan's suite, following the coast, finally arrived at Naples, then the fourth-largest city of William's kingdom (which encompassed almost half the Italian peninsula). She fell ill — probably with seasickness — and the remainder of the journey, with the exception of the crossing of the Strait of Messina, was completed overland in early January through Campania into Calabria.

She crossed into Sicily and reached Cefalù in the last days of that month. The journey of a prince with a small escort of knights would have been quicker, but more time was required when travelling with a large group of "civilians" including numerous ladies, of whom Joan was probably the youngest. More than half of Joan's journey, and nearly the entire overland segment, traversed the domains of her father and her future husband (see the map section for territories under Norman control in 1180).

The evening of 2 February 1177, William greeted Joan. The future Queen was riding a docile palfrey, and met William at one of the city gates — probably in the Kasr district not far from the palace. The city was splendidly illuminated, and William accompanied his fiancée and her suite to their temporary quarters — for the ladies possibly the Zisa, Cuba or one of the other palaces in the vast Genoard royal park.

The child bride married William II "the Good" at Palermo Cathedral on 13 February 1177 (Monreale Abbey was not yet complete) and was then anointed and crowned Queen of Sicily by Walter Offamilias, Archbishop of Palermo, in the Palatine Chapel. She was just eleven, her husband now twenty-three.

Despite a few surprising similarities, Palermo and Sicily were very different from London and England, and this must have made an impact on Joan and her suite of ladies-in-waiting, accustomed to the lifestyle — and even the flora and fauna — of England and northwestern France. Sicily's sunshine seemed as endless as England's clouds, and the cuisine (featuring many delights unknown in northern Europe) was especially varied.

Sicily's Anglo-Norman bishops included Richard Palmer, who we have already met, and Hubert of Middlesex, with canons bearing names like John of Lincoln and Richard of Hereford, as well as dozens of others unknown to us.

One chronicler mentions that Joan bore a son, called Bohemond, in 1182, but that the child died in early infancy. She may also have had miscarriages during this period. Her father, Henry II, died in July 1189. In November of the same year, Joan was widowed when William died, following an illness, in Palermo, at the age of thirty-six. Though he was in many ways a sovereign typical of his era, William's expansionist Mediterranean politics and unenlightened local government have led historians to regard him as a mediocre monarch. He was also an heirless one.

The only potential legitimate heir was William's aunt, Constance, a posthumous daughter of King Roger II now wed to the Emperor Henry VI of Germany (by whom she eventually bore a son, Frederick II). The Sicilian Crown was contested, claimed by Tancred, an illegitimate grandson of Roger II who for a few years managed to impress the advantages of his leadership upon the unruly Norman barons of southern Italy. Knowing Joan to support the dynastic claim of Constance of Hauteville, and probably fearing her influence among the Sicilians, Tancred marginalized her (restricting her movement around the Kingdom), depriving the Queen of her feudal revenue from the County of Mount Sant'Angelo she had received at marriage.

These facts did not set well with her brother, Richard, at thirty-three now King of England and making his way to the Holy Land on Crusade. From Salerno, Richard made it known that he wanted his sister freed and her revenues restored immediately. Furthermore, he wanted her to be provided with the golden throne which he believed to be her right as a Norman queen. His threats were not idle ones; his army of Crusaders probably could have defeated Tancred's Norman barons, and Lionheart may have had his own designs on Sicily. Richard indicated that he would not leave Sicily until his demands were met. Arriving at Messina in September 1190 to meet King Philip II of France, Richard ordered his troops to construct a fort of timbers on a hill overlooking the city where he would be staying for several months.

Tancred complied, though in the end he kept Mount Sant'Angelo and compensated Joan for its loss, and Joan soon arrived at Messina. Richard took her to an abbey founded by Roger I a century earlier near Bagnara, in Calabria across the Strait of Messina, and left her under the protection of a strong garrison.

Returning to Messina, Richard's army occupied an Orthodox monastery for lodging. This was only the most recent in a series of English outrages that offended the citizens of the predominantly Orthodox city, who were already annoyed at things like the English knights' overtly lustful treatment of the local women. A popular revolt ensued. In response, the English (and some of the French) sacked the city. Tancred, in nearby Catania, could do nothing to stop the violent riots, though Richard finally restored order.

Meeting *en famille* at Catania a few days later, Tancred and Richard made peace. Tancred's dynastic position was tenuous, and an alliance with the English king might prove effective in curbing the ambitions of Constance and her German husband, keenly watching Sicilian events from afar. In April, Eleanor, who Richard had freed following his father's death, arrived at Messina with Berengaria of Navarre, Richard's future wife, to visit her son and daughter; Eleanor had called on King Roger II at Palermo forty-four years earlier while returning from a pilgrimage (actually a crusade) to the Holy Land. Now sixty-nine, Eleanor visited Sicily briefly before returning to England. Joan left with Berengaria to visit Palestine, followed by Richard.

In the Holy Land, Richard proposed that his sister marry Saladin's brother, an idea which was soon cast aside. However, the incident does lend credibility to the thesis that Richard "liberated" his sister from Tancred not out of fraternal affection but as a pretext for a dispute which might justify his own full-scale invasion and conquest of Sicily. In December 1192, returning from Palestine, Joan and Berengaria (now Queen of England) visited Palermo to be received *en fête* with a properly royal reception from Tancred and his wife, Sibylla. Past acrimonies, if indeed they were ever very serious, had been set aside. The two young queens then set off to France and England.

Joan preferred France, where she spent much time among the cloistered nuns at Fontevrault. In October 1196 she wed, as his fourth wife, Raymond VI, Count of Toulouse, a cousin (through her mother), by whom she bore three children, namely Raymond (VII) in 1197 who died in 1249, Wilhelmina in 1198, and Richard in 1199 (died in infancy). Joan died in childbirth in September 1199, still a young woman. She is buried at Fontevrault Abbey (Fontevraud, Berri) with her mother, Eleanor, who died in 1204, her father Henry, and brother Richard. Count Raymond VII of Toulouse named his daughter, Joan (1220-1271), for the mother he barely knew.

Joan is commemorated in Elizabeth Fries Ellet's fictional *Scenes in the Life of Joanna of Sicily,* published in 1840.

CHAPTER 20

Benjamin of Tudela

As his name implies, Benjamin was born in the town of Tudela in Navarre, probably about 1130. Around 1165 he set out on a journey across the Mediterranean to the Holy Land. This pilgrimage took him through Spain and France, through Italy to Brindisi, and then from Greece into Asia Minor. From Jerusalem and Damascus he made his way to Baghdad and the Persian lands, then into the Arabian peninsula, northeast to the port of Basra, then southward around the peninsula to Egypt, then crossing the Mediterranean to Palermo before sailing back to Spain.

We don't know the reasons for his voyage, which took at least ten years. Pilgrimage was a motive, certainly, but he probably wanted to visit the various Jewish communities or even pursue commerce. Benjamin, first and foremost, was a rabbi. His book is a work of geography comparable in scope and tone to Idrisi's, but with an emphasis on the Jewish communities rather than the Muslim ones. He is one of the first westerners of his time to mention China by name but, unlike Marco Polo a century later, he never went that far east.

Written in Hebrew, *The Voyages of Benjamin* was noteworthy for what historians have deemed its reliability regarding medieval life. It was subsequently translated into Latin and other languages, making its appearance in English in the nineteenth century. Benjamin's descriptions of Rome and Baghdad were particularly detailed. Urban centers are the focus of his account, and he visited around three hundred localities.

He arrived at Palermo toward the end of his voyage, along the return route toward his homeland, which he finally reached in 1172. His description of the Sicilian city is detailed, picturesque and consistent with that of Abdullah al Idrisi.

Benjamin seems to have been received at the court of the young King William II, whose mother, Margaret, the Queen Regent, was of the royal house of Navarre. Like her, many at court were from Benjamin's homeland.

Tudela provides an informal "census" of Sicily's Jews, mentioning, for example, that there were only around two hundred Jewish families in Messina in the 1170s. His account is the primary historical and statistical record of the Jews of the Diaspora in the twelfth century.

Palermo's Jewish community thrived until the forced conversions or voluntary deportations of 1493. The first Jews of Sicily were living at Siracusa (Syracuse) toward the end of the Greek era. In the sixth century they had a large synagogue at Palermo but this was eventually claimed by the Christians. Around 831, with the arrival of the Arabs, their lot improved somewhat, but it was the Normans, arriving in 1071, who instituted full religious equality.

The death of Emperor Frederick II in 1250 marked a sad turning point, as by then most Muslims, as well as Orthodox Christians, had converted to Catholicism, leaving the Jews the only significant religious minority. There are, however, accounts of isolated Jewish communities converting before 1250.

Benjamin died in Castile in 1173.

Wherever he went, Tudela's accounts of intellectual life, always precise, reflect his own intellect and learning, exceptional for a twelfth-century traveller. Our knowledge of medieval Judaism would be the lesser without him.

CHAPTER 21

Monreale Abbey

Monreale's cathedral and abbey are good reminders that the beauty of a particularly splendid church transcends that of any single work of art. Overlooking Palermo, the town of Monreale, from the Latin *Mons Regalis* ("Royal Mountain"), straddles a slope of Mount Caputo about eight kilometers south of Palermo's cathedral. At around three hundred meters above sea level, the town overlooks the *Conca d'Oro,* as the valley beyond Palermo is known. The cathedral and its cloister represent the largest concentration of Norman, Arab and Byzantine art in one place. True, Palermo's cathedral is larger, but Monreale's interior exists in something far closer to its original state. This wondrous place is much more than "just another church." If one's impression of the overused word *multicultural* is anything less than favorable, the effect of Monreale Abbey will prompt a conversion to another way of thinking.

East meets West

The focal point of the town is its cathedral, an amalgamation of Arab, Byzantine and Norman artistic styles framed by traditional Romanesque architecture, representing the best of twelfth-century culture. The mosaics covering the cathedral walls are one of the world's most extensive displays of this art, surpassed only by Istanbul's Basilica of Saint Sofia, once an Orthodox church. In Italy, only the older mosaics of Ravenna rival those of Monreale.

The mosaics of "Santa Maria la Nuova" (New Saint Mary's), the official name of Monreale Cathedral, are far more extensive than those of the cathedral of Cefalù, and while the mosaics of the Palatine Chapel in Palermo's Norman Palace are of equally exquisite craftsmanship, they leave one with the impression of a complex work of art in a restrictive space.

It is tempting to identify each element of the abbey complex with a specific culture and tradition, but in truth these overlap considerably. The mosaics are a Byzantine element, while certain structural details, such as the geometric inlay of the apse exteriors, are of Islamic inspiration. The cloister, on the other hand, reflects a fusion of influences.

Attached to the cathedral, the Benedictine cloister court-yard is framed by over two hundred columns (paired, with four at each corner), some decorated with Byzantine mosaic inlay, each supporting an ornately carved capital. The capitals themselves depict scenes in Sicily's Norman history, complete with knights and kings, as well as Biblical events. They strongly reflect the Provençal styles of the twelfth century, and at least three of what are thought to have been five or six master sculptors were probably from that region.

Royal Origins

Building Monreale Abbey was the idea of King William II "the Good," grandson of Roger II. On or near the site of Monreale — possibly at the base of the mountain — had stood a small Arab hamlet named *Ba'lat* (or Bahlara) where local farmers would gather each morning to cart their produce to the souks of Bal'harm (Palermo), whose only remaining street market from this era, Ballarò, probably takes its Sicilian name from this farming community. It appears that an Arab watch tower or other fortification stood in the vicinity of the cathedral site.

In Norman times the area around Ba'lat formed part of the royal hunting ground beyond the *Genoard* park.

Walter Offamilias, the Bishop of Palermo, was the head of a faction of nobles that sought to influence and persuade the young king into granting them more power. This faction also hoped to attenuate the power of the Muslim ministers and functionaries of William's court. William was just thirteen years old when his father, William I, died in 1166, and until he reached his majority in 1171 he was subject to the regency of his mother, the steadfast Margaret of Navarre.

Upon reaching the age of majority, King William's first objective was to establish himself firmly as sovereign. When the young monarch wished to demonstrate his independence through the erection of a grand cathedral, the Benedictines, already present in Sicily, readily obliged. Construction began in 1174. The massive superstructure took just a few years to erect. Work on the mosaics and cloister was completed by the time of the young king's death in 1189. Visitors are sometimes surprised to learn that the large church was erected so quickly; presuming uninterrupted work by a crew of equal number, a Romanesque cathedral like Monreale could usually be constructed far more rapidly than a Gothic structure.

Apart from demonstrating his true power to the Sicilian nobility, it is possible that William wanted the cathedral to impress his subjects in an equal measure. Here he succeeded.

Some Muslims from Palermo had fled to the hill country surrounding the capital after a rebellion against William's father in 1161, and others already lived in towns in the hinterland. Led by Matthew Bonellus, a vocal element of the Norman nobility had begun to support an anti-Muslim policy, leaving some of the "Saracens" to establish themselves in easily-fortified towns of the interior, though they were nominally loyal to William. The new cathedral, built in the manner of a fortress — complete with towers, battlements and loopholes — was strategically important for guarding the passes that served as the gateway to these communities. Castellaccio Castle, overlooking Monreale, supported this military scope.

Though little of the monastery survives except the cloister courtyard, it originally boasted a dozen embattled towers and thick walls. A few of the massive towers are still visible. The Arabs did eventually rebel, after King William's death, in reaction to the mistreatment and excessive taxation imposed upon them by the Abbot of Monreale, under whose feudal authority they had been placed by William and the Pope. The cathedral itself was attacked by the Muslims on several occasions, the worst incident occurring in 1216 during the reign of Frederick II. However, the "rebellions" were never a serious threat to royal rule. In 1246, Frederick II dispatched troops from Palermo to rein in what resistance remained, taking firm control of Corleone and San Giuseppe Jato.

Another reason for William's construction of the cathedral was his desire to establish the Roman Catholic Church, known as the "Latin" Church in those days, as the official Christian denomination of Sicily. There were still many Orthodox Christians in twelfth-century Sicily. Thus, despite the mosaic icons which give it the appearance of an Orthodox basilica (there was once an icon screen), Monreale played its small part in the "Latinizing" of Sicily.

Pope Alexander III granted the abbot of the Benedictine monastery episcopal privileges in 1174, and elevated Theobald to the rank of archbishop in 1183. Placing a bishop in Monreale who owed his position only to pontiff and sovereign and who, as an outsider, had no stake in local politics, neatly accomplished the political purposes of both Church and Crown.

Building a Dream

As we've mentioned, work on the cathedral was begun in 1174. In 1177, at twenty-four, William wed Joan, daughter of King Henry II of England. The marriage made William brother-in-law to Richard I "Lionheart" and John "Lackland," Henry's sons and England's future monarchs. In 1170, William's father-in-law had instigated the murder of Thomas Becket, then Archbishop of Canterbury. Canonized in 1173, Saint Thomas "of Canterbury" is depicted in a mosaic icon of the cathedral's main apse near the altar (as one faces the apse it is the second icon to the right of the central niche). This is believed to be the first public work of art venerating the English saint.

Though William sought to make his realm a more European one, he engaged in certain practices atypical of medieval Christian monarchs. Not only did he have many Muslim ministers, astrologers and doctors at his court, William is said to have kept a "harem" in his palace (officially young women employed as weavers), and to have spoken, read and written Arabic. That work on the cathedral was completed before William's death — aged just thirty-six — in 1189 was indeed a fortunate thing, for the period of quasi-anarchy which ensued as rival claimants sought to ascend the Throne did not bode well for costly construction projects.

Externally, most of Monreale Cathedral is not particularly striking. Its front façade faces west, looking onto Piazza Guglielmo. Two massive square bell towers flank the main church entrance. The porticos are not original components of the structure but the lateral one is medieval. The sides of the cathedral are over a hundred meters long. From Via Arcivescovado, the street behind the cathedral, can be seen the complex geometric inlay of the apse — a symmetry that reflects Muslim spirituality.

Framed by a typical medieval arch, the Romanesque bronze doors under the main (front) portico were manufactured in the workshops of Bonanno of Pisa in 1186. Constructed in the same year, the side doors were designed by Barisano of Trani, set within a squared frame decorated in Arab mosaic. Each door features panels on which are depicted various religious figures amidst floral and symbolic motifs.

The floor plan of the cathedral combines elements of both a traditional Western (Latin) basilica and an Eastern (Orthodox) one. This combination of Greek and Latin elements is a distinctive feature of Norman architecture in Italy.

The cathedral has a wide central nave between two smaller aisles. Monolithic columns, each crowned by a Corinthian capital, support the arches on each side of the central aisle. Each capital is sculpted with a different motif featuring religious figures and symbols. Carved and painted in great detail, the present wooden ceiling replaces the original Fatimid roof destroyed by fire in 1811.

Mosaic Art and Icons

The splendid mosaics in the interior of Monreale cathedral are its principal artistic attraction, covering most of the surface of the walls. The style is essentially "Komnenian," the movement taking its name from the Byzantine dynasty of the time.

All of the cathedral's mosaic figures (most are icons) are placed upon a background of gold mosaic *tesserae* (tiles). The interior of the church is about a hundred meters long by forty meters wide. There are over a hundred individual mosaic scenes inspired by Biblical and other religious events. The Old Testament is depicted on the walls of the central nave, starting from the Creation and ending with Jacob's Flight. The mosaics on the side aisles illustrate the major events in the life of Jesus, from birth to crucifixion, and include a cycle depicting the miracles worked. Many of the mosaics are accompanied by in-scriptions in Latin or Greek.

Dominating everything is the imposing mosaic of Christ Pantocrator (Ruler of All) located in the central apse over the main altar. Beneath the stupendous portrait of Jesus is a mo-saic of the *Theotokos* (Mother of God) enthroned with the Christ child on her lap. This depiction is flanked by mosaics of the angels and various saints and apostles. There are icons of numerous other saints and scenes from the Gospels all about the transept area, including the icon of Saint Thomas Becket already mentioned. Two noteworthy mosaics are lo-cated on the sides of the presbytery, over the royal and epis-copal thrones. The one above the royal throne shows Christ crowning William II. It is patterned on the icon in the Mar-torana (in Palermo) showing Roger II crowned directly by Christ. The mosaic over the episcopal throne shows William II offering this cathedral to the Virgin Mary, its patron. In the West it was rather rare for living monarchs to be represented in a Heavenly setting in this manner.

Monreale Cathedral also houses several royal tombs. That of William II "the Good" is a white marble work dating from the sixteenth century. William's father, King William I "the Bad," rests in the red porphyry tomb dating from the twelfth century. William II's mother, Margaret of Navarre, is also in-terred at Monreale. Curiously, so is the heart (and liver) of King Louis IX of France (Saint Louis). The royal cortege stopped here for a funeral *en route* to France following Louis' death dur-ing the Tunisian Crusade (in 1270) when his less-saintly younger brother, Charles of Anjou, ruled Naples and Sicily.

The Cloister

Apart from the cathedral itself, the cloister court proper, already mentioned above, is the largest part of the monastery preserved in its original condition (the adjacent dormitories are now an art museum and exhibit area). Its plan is a perfect square enclosing a covered walkway. Carved into the capitals of the columns are all manner of Biblical figures, mythological scenes, Arab warriors and Norman knights, as well as floral motifs and fauna.

The absence of identifying insignia on the shields of the knight figures implies that armorial heraldry had not yet been introduced in Sicily when the cloister was built.

The crowning glory of the cloister is the Arab fountain in the southwest corner. (A copy stands in Palazzo Falson in the Maltese city of Mdina.) The fountain is enclosed within its own four-sided colonnade, a tiny "cloister within the cloister." Longstanding tradition says that William, who had a small palace behind the cathedral, often washed his face in the fountain's pool.

The garden terrace, or "belvedere," is also worth visiting. Affording a panoramic view of Palermo, it is reached through a courtyard near the cloister, in a corner of the square.

Crypt, Museum, Roof

While the small crypt is usually closed to the public, the cathedral's Treasury Museum houses some interesting relics and various ecclesiastical items. The stairs and passages to the roof encircle the church, offering exceptional views of the cloister, the inside of the taller tower, and of course the valleys around Monreale.

CHAPTER 22

Thomas Becket and Sicily

He is the only personage profiled in these pages who never set foot in Sicily, but Thomas Becket's influence was felt on the island, and this connection exemplifies the close bonds between the Norman kingdoms of Sicily and England.

Thomas Becket was born in 1120 into a predominantly Norman, but non-aristocratic, family of London. His father Gilbert was a prosperous merchant who sent his son to various schools in England and also to a school in Paris, which was a common practice at the time for English boys trying to move up the social ladder.

A few years after his schooling, Thomas began working as a clerk for Theobald, the Archbishop of Canterbury. According to most biographies, it seems that in the beginning young Thomas felt no call to the clergy. Appreciating his clerk's potential and good will, and having in mind his promotion, Archbishop Theobald sent Thomas first to Bologna and then to Auxerre so that he could study law. By this time, the young man had finally found his calling for the Church, though this was not immediately obvious.

Thanks to his acquaintance with Archbishop Theobald, Thomas entered into the graces of King Henry II, eventually becoming the royal chancellor and one of his closest friends. This friendship though was destined to render Becket's life difficult.

After having worked at Henry's court for a number of years, in 1162 Thomas was appointed Archbishop of Canterbury, the highest See of England, by the king, who in doing so believed that he would have a steadfast ally within the Church. Until now, Thomas had always supported the King's decisions, but as archbishop of such an important diocese, he felt that his loyalties no longer lay with his sovereign, but with God and the Church.

The love affair between Sicily and Thomas Becket began a few years later when the Archbishop of Canterbury was forced to flee to France in self-imposed exile after having refused to accept the provision of Henry's Constitutions of Clarendon whereby the sovereign placed his royal authority over that of the Church in England — as judge not only of laymen but also of bishops and other clergy accused of high crimes. In practice, this was not too different from a principle that already existed (albeit in a different form) in Sicily, whose monarchs frequently found themselves at odds with the Papacy in jurisdictional matters of this kind.

Becket's exile to France in 1164 was not his alone. Some of his friends and kinsmen also had to flee England, and they found refuge at the Sicilian court with young King William II of Sicily and his mother Margaret of Navarre; there exists a letter of Becket thanking them for this hospitality. Support also came from some of Becket's Anglo-Norman friends in Sicily, particularly Archbishop Richard Palmer.

Even abroad, Becket was a thorn in Henry's side, but the situation did not sour relations with the Sicilians. Around 1168, King Henry II of England sought to betroth his youngest daughter Joan, who was only a toddler at the time, to William II of Sicily, who had not yet reached the age of majority.

The King of England hoped in this way to strengthen the ties between the two Norman houses. A few English Normans living in Sicily, including Archbishop Palmer, were already negotiating with Pope Alexander III to smooth the path for a Plantagenet marriage in Sicily, but before the marriage contract was approved, a terrible scandal broke out in England. Thomas, who had just returned to the country in the hope of a reconciliation with Henry, was murdered in Canterbury Cathedral on 29 December 1170. Four of Henry's knights were responsible for Becket's death, although when questioned they claimed that they were only following the king's desire to be rid of a "meddlesome priest."

At this point — probably due to Papal intervention — the marriage was called off, but a few years later Henry performed public penance on the tomb of Becket, who was canonized in 1173. Negotiations resumed and in 1177 Joan and William were finally married.

Almost immediately after the canonization of Saint Thomas Becket, two important works were started in Sicily in honor of this much beloved saint.

The mosaic icon of Becket in the main apse of Monreale Abbey is the earliest artistic representation of the saint in a public setting. The inscription reads simply "Saint Thomas of Canterbury."

The Cathedral of Marsala, in western Sicily, is still dedicated to the saint despite having been restructured several times. A smaller church in the city of Palermo was likewise dedicated to him.

Some contemporary reliquaries bearing the saint's likeness have been preserved. In 1538 Henry VIII of England destroyed Thomas Becket's tomb and dispersed his remains. Later, a few relics of the saint were sent back to England from different places in Italy, including Sicily. Some are preserved at the small Catholic church dedicated to Thomas in Canterbury itself. In death, Becket thus shared a similarity with Saint Louis, whose heart and liver are preserved in Monreale while only a finger remains at Saint Denis, where the royal tombs were despoiled by revolutionaries.

Sicily's links to England were many. Richard Palmer, Archbishop of Siracusa, has already been mentioned. Hubert of Middlesex was Archbishop of Conza near Naples. Thomas Brown, known to Sicily's Arabs as "Qaid al Brun," was first a clerk to the King of Sicily and later treasurer to the King of England. It was probably Brown who introduced Hindu-Arabic numerals, and perhaps even certain principles of Maliki law, in England.

It should not be forgotten that Odo of Bayeux, half-brother of William the Conqueror, died in Palermo in 1097 during a visit with Roger I *en route* to the First Crusade. Richard Lionheart passed through Sicily about a century later on his way to a subsequent Crusade.

CHAPTER 23

The Swabians

If the Normans brought Sicily back into the European orbit following centuries of Byzantine and Arab rule, the Swabians made it one of the most important regions of Europe. Swabia is a region of southwestern Germany which in the twelfth century encompassed part of Bavaria and eastern Switzerland. It takes its name from a Germanic people, the Suebi, who settled there in antiquity near their neighbors, the Alemanni, another Germanic tribe.

The reference to the "Swabians" in Sicilian history is something of a misnomer, or perhaps even a euphemism for "German," as their number included a great many persons from German-speaking parts of the Holy Roman Empire well beyond tiny Swabia's borders. Indeed, the ethnonym *German,* like *Arab,* was based at least as much on the language and culture of this population as on the territory they controlled.

The Swabian Staufer (Hohenstaufen) family emerged as a powerful dynasty before 1100. Their name comes from Stauf Castle, built near Göppingen in the Jura Mountains by Count Frederick (died 1105). Their early history was not too different from those of other central European nobles emerging in the high medieval era, but the Dukes of Swabia became Kings of the Germans during the rule of the distinguished Frederick I "Barbarossa" ("Redbeard"). Until 1254, the Hohenstaufen ruled as emperors of the loose feudal confederation known as the Holy Roman Empire.

The sovereign state of Swabia itself was dissolved after 1268, its lands seized by lesser families, but in the 1190s it was the focal point of a kind of vaguely-defined German unity.

Voltaire may have been correct in asserting that it was neither holy, nor Roman, nor an empire, but the confederation founded by Charlemagne was medieval Europe's most powerful monarchy.

In early 1184, Constance Hauteville, the youngest child of King Roger II of Sicily, was betrothed to Henry VI, second son of Frederick Barbarossa. By some accounts beautiful and shy, she was the wealthiest heiress in Europe. This marriage, celebrated at Milan's Saint Ambrose two years later, was seen as a way of sealing the Normans' rapport with the dynasty that controlled not only the Alpine regions but most of Italy north of Bologna.

By virtue of the birthright of his consort, Henry claimed the Sicilian crown in 1194 following the brief and ineffectual reign of Tancred, Constance's illegitimate nephew through her eldest brother, Roger of Apulia (died 1149). Sicily's importance was on the wane, but now the Hohenstaufens restored some of the kingdom's lustre.

When Henry VI was crowned in Palermo, he found himself in control of the island of Sicily and all of mainland Italy except for a central region (the Papal State) controlled by the Papacy, a situation the Pope and other sovereigns found disturbing — indeed overtly threatening.

Rarely contested in the German lands, the Emperor's power in Italy was not absolute. Eventually, a rivalry between factions developed, with the *Guelphs* (Welfs) opposing the *Ghibellines* (Hohenstaufen supporters who took their Italianized name from the Staufen fortress of Waiblingen). In time, the Guelphs supported the Pope (and the Angevins) against the Swabians.

This undercurrent shaped Imperial politics in northern Italy for decades, and one day it would seal the fate of Sicily.

His wife may have been a Norman princess, but the Sicilians did not welcome Henry and his suite of German knights and retainers very warmly. The new king installed several commanderies of the nascent Teutonic Order of knights in Sicily, appropriating for them Palermo's Magione church and constructing for them the Church of Saint Mary of the Germans in Messina, the earliest Sicilian example of Romanesque-Gothic ecclesiastical architecture. Constance gave birth to Frederick II who, like his grandfather Roger II, was one of Europe's most enlightened rulers.

Henry VI died in 1197. As regent, his widow raised their young son in Sicily, only to see many of the island's unruly barons renege on their feudal obligations. Upon reaching the age of majority, Frederick sought to remedy this. His realm eventually included regions from Saxony to Palestine, effectively ruled from Italy; he traveled almost continually.

The kingdoms of Sicily and Jerusalem were not part of the Holy Roman Empire; they were separate realms which just happened to be ruled by the same monarch. Furthermore, the kingship over the Germans was one thing, the emperorship something more.

Most historians regard the Swabian period as a continuation of the Norman rule of Sicily. However, Sicily changed greatly under the Swabians.

Despite Frederick's quarrels with the Papacy, leading to excommunication, the Church in Sicily became almost completely Latinized during his long reign. By 1250, there were no Byzantine dioceses in Sicily — only a few Orthodox monasteries remained. Following a series of revolts, a few thousand Muslim Arabs were deported to Lucera in Apulia, while thousands more converted to Catholicism. By 1250, mosques were a rare sight.

When Frederick was born, Sicily was a multicultural kingdom; by the end of the Swabian era a half-century later it was an essentially "European" piece of Christendom. This was true of customs, language (Sicilian) and law. All bore the mark of Arab and Byzantine influences but were now almost "Italian."

It was during the Swabian period that the Sicilian language later recognized by Dante and then Boccaccio truly evolved. The sonnet is thought to have been born at the court of Frederick II. Ciullo of Alcamo was one of the greatest exponents of the new language.

Architecture gradually lost its Byzantine and Arab features. An Italianate Romanesque Gothic emerged. Though present in many Norman-era castles and churches, most of the arched two-light windows visible around Sicily date from the Swabian period or the century following it. Frederick built a number of imposing castles, such as the fortress at Catania.

The people themselves did not immediately change. Sicily was still the heart of an important realm. In the countryside, feudalism flowered.

German garrisons loyal to Frederick were installed in several towns, the native Norman nobles being considered fickle and potentially disloyal. Initially, Frederick also had Saracen (Arab) troops. Constance of Aragon, Frederick's wife, brought an Iberian influence to the Sicilian court.

While Frederick was a brilliant man, it appears that he was not generally liked by the Sicilians. Indeed, Swabian rule appears not to have been appreciated either by the nobility or the other classes. Despite this, a stronger national identity was being forged among the Sicilians, continuing what had begun in Norman times. At Frederick's death, in 1250, Pope Innocent IV tightened his grip on the island. The strong Papal influence, which eventually led to Angevin rule and consequently, in 1282, the War of the Vespers, was not at all progressive. For comparison, we may consider that England's *Magna Carta,* issued in 1215, set forth royal and baronial rights and duties for centuries to come. In Sicily, despite numerous "parliaments" and declarations over the years, nothing comparable ever emerged, even though there were efficacious laws, such as the remarkable Assizes of Ariano of Roger II, and of course Frederick's Constitutions of Melfi.

Following the death of Frederick in 1250, three of his descendants claimed the Throne in succession, but the antipathy of the Guelphs and the Papacy had not abated. Frederick's son Conrad IV died in 1254. An illegitimate son, Manfred, was killed at the Battle of Benevento in 1266 when his army was defeated by an Angevin force commanded by Charles of Anjou, the Papal choice to succeed as King of Sicily. Frederick's grandson, Conradin (Conrad's son), was executed in 1268 at the age of sixteen. With the end of the Hohenstaufen dynasty, southern Italy passed into the hands of the House of Anjou, which ruled Sicily from Naples until the House of Aragon, and the Sicilians themselves, challenged French authority in 1282.

The end of Hohenstaufen rule was a turning point in history because henceforth Sicily would only occasionally be ruled by resident kings. Instead, it was usually administered by delegates and (later) by viceroys. Moreover, the island nation was deprived of her importance in world affairs. There is also a cultural factor to be considered. Had the thirteenth-century pontiffs (and their Guelphic allies) not had their way, Italy might have evolved into a state with a society in some ways more Germanic than Latin.

We do not know how many Germans and Lombards remained in Sicily following the Swabian period. Those who received feudal lands certainly stayed, and in several towns certain surnames — and even some commonly used words — bear the mark of Germanic influences. The Teutonic Knights maintained several Sicilian commanderies into the fifteenth century. The most important of these, housed in a monastic complex built during the Norman period, was the Magione, and it is the only one that still exists in something like its original state.

The history of the Teutonic Order, officially the Order of Saint Mary of Jerusalem, merits a few words. Founded on the model of the Hospitallers in 1190 during the Third Crusade, it was recognized by Pope Celestine in 1192. The knights abandoned Palestine in 1291. Like the Templars and Hospitallers, they eventually garnered for themselves extensive holdings in Europe, establishing their grand magistracy in Prussia in 1309. But their zealous military exploits against the Slavs — the infamous Baltic Crusades — rarely earned them any sympathy from the common man. A major defeat by Polish and Lithuanian forces in 1410 spelled the end for the Teutonic Order's military and economic power.

The Magione began its life around the same time as the Teutonic Order. The Basilica of the Holy Trinity (its official name) was built on a site not far from the citadel erected by Khalid ibn Ishaq, Governor of Sicily (and acting Emir), in 937. Under the sponsorship of Matthew Ajello, the controversial chancellor of Tancred de Hauteville, Sicily's last Norman monarch, the church, which included a cloister and dormitories, was given to the Cistercians. It was probably Matthew's son, Richard, who oversaw the erection of the Magione in a lush area near the Termini Gate of the city walls. The French architectural style is pronounced, but the exterior of the Magione's apse reflects the same Arab influences as those of the cathedrals of Monreale and Palermo.

By 1197 the Magione was in the possession of the Teutonic Order. The knights built dormitories, an armory and stables, surrounded by thick walls, some of which — along with knights' tombs, arched two-light windows and recent excavations — can be seen in what is now a small local museum on the side of the cloister opposite the church. There was even a deep well present in the center of the cloister courtyard. Resembling a small castle, the premises were fairly large; indeed, the name *Magione* comes from the Norman French *maisoné,* a large house.

Further expansion was undertaken in 1458 on the orders of the vice preceptor, Leonard von Mederstorsen, but by then, toward the end of the Middle Ages, the days of the Teutonic Order in Sicily were numbered. In 1492, at the request of Pope Innocent VIII, the Crown "resigned" the knights from Sicily.

While it vaguely evokes an image of the fields and gardens that existed when the Magione was built, the unkempt lawn behind the church was the site of homes from around 1500 until 1943, when it sustained extensive bomb damage during the Second World War, following which the area was cleared of buildings.

CHAPTER 24

Frederick II

He was perhaps the most intellectually accomplished ruler of the Middle Ages, earning the nickname *Stupor Mundi,* "wonder of the world." It could be argued that Frederick had good genes. His father's father was Frederick Barbarossa, his mother's father none other than the remarkable Roger II of Sicily.

We met the Swabian Hohenstaufens in the last chapter. How did these Germans end up ruling the Kingdom of Sicily?

At his death in 1154, Roger II was succeeded by his son, William I, whose policies often met with opposition from the entrenched Norman vassals. In 1166, William I "the Bad" died and was succeeded by his young son William II, known to posterity as "the Good." In 1189, at thirty-six, this sovereign died and was succeeded by his aunt, Constance, the last, posthumous child of Roger II. Constance was married to the Holy Roman Emperor Henry VI, who claimed the Sicilian throne by right of his wife.

This pretension did not go uncontested, but it eventually prevailed over the rival claim of Tancred, a bastard grandson of Roger II. Henry was crowned King of Sicily in Palermo Cathedral on Christmas in 1194. The following day, at Jesi, near Ancona, the previously childless Constance gave birth, at forty-one, to a red-haired son christened Frederick Roger. Henry could not be present, but numerous witnesses were, making

Constance's delivery one of the most crowded in history.

Henry was not liked in Sicily, but the Imperial couple had managed to defeat their enemies and secure the support of a few nobles and the Pope. Henry established his authority over the unruly but still very wealthy Kingdom of Sicily, which encompassed most of Italy south of Rome. In addition to this, the Holy Roman Empire included most of northern Italy and central Europe. Henry's life and reign in Sicily were brief, however, and upon his death in 1197 young Frederick succeeded his father, with Constance as Queen Regent. He was crowned in 1198 and his mother died later that year. With Pope Innocent III as his guardian and protector, Frederick's future seemed secure.

Stories are told of his childhood in Palermo, then a city of stupendous gardens and beautiful Norman-Arab architecture. He learned social survival but also respect for various peoples and religions, acquiring a working knowledge of Arabic, Greek, Latin, German, French and a new vernacular, Sicilian, influenced by all these languages. In Palermo, the stories tell us, Frederick could listen and learn from returning sailors and merchants of exotic foreign lands and customs to the south and east. Frederick absorbed much knowledge from scholars, philosophers, historians, artisans, chroniclers and sundry scientists. The names of a few are known to us. Michael Scot, the court astronomer, mathematician and science advisor, translated important works from Arabic and was a mentor to the young Leonardo Pisano Bigollo, or Fibonacci, the mathematician who introduced Hindu-Arabic numerals in northern Italy and other parts of Christian Europe. (These were already used in Sicily, and Spain's *Codex Vigilanus,* compiled in 881, features Hindu-Arabic numerals.)

Among his recreational interests, Frederick cultivated a passion for falconry, about which he wrote an illustrated guide. In Europe at this time falconry was the sport of kings and aristocrats.

In 1209, at the age of fourteen, he married Constance of Aragon, who was many years his senior. In fact, she often served as his regent, a kind of "viceroy," during his frequent absences from Sicily.

Frederick's long reign took him into the heart of Germany to tame his rebellious vassals, and to the Holy Land on crusade. The details of the international intrigue and conflicts that engulfed Europe and Frederick II in the early decades of the thirteenth century could fill many volumes. We shall keep to generalities about administration and society under the Emperor, who needed a firm and reliable base of operations in the perpetual power games of the era.

A scientific thinker, Frederick enjoyed the company of scholars of the natural sciences. His curiosity about philosophy and religion led to an active interest in law.

He enlisted some of the greatest juridical minds of the era to collect and interpret the previous Norman, Arab and Byzantine laws in order to establish firm and orderly legal procedures. The town of Melfi was host to this endeavor, the so-called Constitutions of Melfi (described in the next chapter). Eventually, royally-appointed judges (justiciars) replaced the cronies of local aristocrats in the exercise of justice. Agriculture, currency and a new professional army were also organized to suit the needs of an efficient kingdom. Annual taxes were levied on certain activities and raw materials, while the Crown assumed sole control of production of others such as iron, silk and, above all, salt.

Shrewd accountants and bookkeepers from Genoa were invited to administer the king's tax income. Under Frederick, feudalism in Sicily existed as a sophisticated institution which, if not exactly enlightened, reflected an improvement over earlier models. It was during this period that heraldry was belatedly introduced in Sicily.

But Frederick did not forget his mainland realm. In 1221 he established a great secular (non-clerical) seat of learning in Naples which to this day functions as the university that bears his name. As we've mentioned, he also found time to trek through northern Italy into Germany, the heart of his Holy Roman Empire, to remind his vassals of their feudal fealty and obligations; most had never met their young Emperor. Frederick also ruled Burgundy. With his realm firmly in his grasp, he could confront the other powers of the era steadfastly, with determination and skill.

Constance died in 1222 and Frederick married his second wife, young Yolanda of Brienne (Isabella II of Jerusalem), in 1225. She bore him a son, Conrad, but died giving birth to him at the age of sixteen in 1228.

The Popes wanted Frederick to lead a crusade against the Muslims in the Near East, to occupy Jerusalem and re-establish Christian rule on the eastern shores of the Mediterranean. For a time, Frederick adroitly avoided this Papal imposition, but by 1227 he could no longer postpone this mission.

He arrived in Palestine in 1229, securing control of the Holy Land not through military prowess and bloodshed but by skillful persuasion and delicate diplomacy, negotiating with the Muslims in Arabic, the language of the Koran. Frederick was crowned King of Jerusalem, by right of his second wife, in the Church of the Holy Sepulchre as the only Holy Roman Emperor to be so honored. The island of Cyprus also came under Frederick's control, though only briefly. Now Frederick's expansive realms (see the map section) extended from Saxony to Sicily, with wealthy outposts in the eastern Mediterranean. He was clearly the most powerful European ruler. Indeed, the Sixth Crusade could be considered the very zenith of Frederick's political life. However, his pacific methods did not please everybody in Rome.

In Frederick the Papacy found a worthy adversary unwilling

to bend to every pontifical conceit. If anything, his courage and determination in the face of Papal opposition to his policies bolstered his prestige among fellow monarchs.

But Frederick von Hohenstaufen's life was much more than a series of military escapades. He fostered an interest in poetry and literature; the Sicilian language flourished at his court, where the sonnet is said to have been born. Falconry, ecology and efficient government were just a few of his obsessions. A king with an intellectual passion was as rare in the thirteenth century as it was in the twentieth.

Some of Frederick's exploits still elicit curiosity. His zoo, for example, included camels, elephants, panthers and what was probably the first giraffe ever brought to Europe — all gifts of the Sultan of Egypt, Malik al Kamil, with whom Frederick had negotiated his treaty in Jerusalem. He paraded these animals, to public amazement, during a visit to Ravenna in 1231.

In 1235 Frederick wed Elizabeth Plantagenet, daughter of King John of England (and sister of Henry III). She died in 1241 and was buried next to Yolanda in Andria Cathedral in Apulia, not far from Frederick's favorite fortress, the distinctive Castel del Monte. Each of these women was around twenty years younger than Frederick, and he apparently kept them largely secluded from public life. Like many monarchs of his era, he had a coterie of concubines, but his was similar to a harem.

Composing a profile of Frederick's personal character has proven elusive. He rarely displayed hubris. On the other hand, he fathered numerous children outside his marriages, and his treatment of his later wives left something to be desired, even by the standards of the times. His personal religious beliefs were ambiguous at best. He was certainly a freethinker, and not especially devout. He may have been what today would be called a deist.

The fiercest modern criticisms of Frederick's personality reflect a conventional view of him as taciturn, obstinate, even sardonic — inferences drawn from just a few contemporary accounts.

After years of conflict, frenetic activity and constant travels, Frederick II was struck down with fever in December 1250 in Apulia. He died just before his fifty-sixth birthday and was interred in the cathedral of his favorite city, Palermo, where he rests today next to his mother, father and wife.

Frederick's death signalled the beginning of the end of Sicily's great multicultural experiment, a decline that within fifty years would culminate in a Sicilian "monoculture."

Petty dynastic power struggles and a brief war of independence (the Sicilian Vespers) followed, but never again would Sicily achieve the glory, prosperity and true independence she enjoyed under this most singular of sovereigns.

Frederick was succeeded by Conrad, his son by Yolanda of Brienne. In 1246 Conrad had married Elizabeth Wittelsbach of Bavaria, who bore him a son, Conradin, in 1252 (about whom more below).

Amidst Papal intrigues and challenges to his royal authority, Conrad died of malaria in Basilicata in 1254. He was succeeded by his half-brother Manfred, a natural son of Frederick born in 1232 of Bianca Lancia of Agliano, a Piedmontese noblewoman. Legally, Manfred was regent for young Conradin, but he had himself crowned at Palermo in 1258 based on unfounded rumors that the boy had died.

Manfred was killed by Angevin forces at the Battle of Benevento in 1266. (His daughter, Constance, wed Peter III of Aragon in 1262.)

Young Conradin Hohenstaufen attempted to enforce his birthright, but following a military defeat by the Angevins at the Battle of Tagliacozzo he was beheaded in October of 1268. This effectively ended the Hohenstaufen rule of Sicily. However, supporters regarded Constance, the daughter of Manfred, as the heir of the Hohenstaufen kings.

CHAPTER 25

Law: Melfi and Maliki

Is it possible that certain personal rights were protected in Sicily in 1231 that didn't even exist on the island seven centuries later? Yes, and divorce is one of them. Here we shall introduce a few principles of law enforced in Sicily into the thirteenth century. The *Constitutions of Melfi* promulgated by Frederick II in 1231 are the better known; this was civil (statutory) law based on a legal code. Next we will consider early common law as it existed in Sicily; this was introduced by the Muslims' *Maliki School* and may have been one of the inspirations for English common law.

Sadly, neither survived the Middle Ages as "living law" in Sicily or anyplace in Italy. A lengthy summary and analysis is beyond the scope of this chapter, and these are not intended as detailed treatises, but let's outline a few characteristics of both developments.

The Constitutions of Melfi

The Constitutions of Melfi (also called the *Liber Augustalis* for Frederick's Imperial title) were intended as a general legal code in the tradition of the Assizes of Ariano promulgated by Frederick's grandfather, Roger II, in 1140, and Frederick's own Assizes of Capua of 1220.

Truth be told, these legal codes were not very different from many issued in England and elsewhere during the same period. Like his Sicilian counterparts, Henry II of England was in frequent conflict with the Popes, and of course with Thomas Becket closer to home, and some of his legislation reflected this political struggle, as did Roger's and Frederick's.

Frederick's laws clearly had to take into account the cultural diversity of his southern Italian realm, which even in 1231 still had sizeable Muslim, Jewish and Byzantine (Greek Orthodox) populations. The Constitutions also considered certain differences between the Frankish Law of the Normans and the Longobardic Law of the Lombards (and some Germans), important factors in feudal matters such as land inheritance and the designation of heirs.

Not only did the new legal code reinforce royal authority over the nobility and the use of natural resources, its references to heresy and to Roman canon law effectively formed the groundwork for the Kingdom of Sicily evolving into a predominantly Roman Catholic country within a few decades. By the War of the Vespers in 1282, just three decades after Frederick's death, most Muslims and Orthodox had converted to Catholicism, even if a few isolated pockets of Byzantine influence remained for some time afterward in places like the Nebrodi Mountains.

A few laws stand out.

Like England's *Magna Carta,* the Constitutions of Melfi made a speedy judgment the right of civil litigants and even criminal defendants.

Juridical procedures are clearly established, while practices such as trial by combat (knights duelling to win a legal dispute) are essentially abolished.

The idea that justiciars (district judges) could not hear cases in lands where they held feudal estates was a prescient idea, similar to modern statutes proscribing conflicts of interest which might require a judge's recusal from a case.

Jews, but not Christians, could practice usury, though Judaic law formally discourages this.

A man of the kingdom could divorce his wife if adultery were proven; the same practice among Muslims presumably already existed and may have been an influence here.

The law on divorce, though clearly weighted in favor of the husband, was innovative for its era. In fact, divorce had existed, in one form or another, among Christians since the faith's earliest days. It was only later that the Catholic hierarchy attempted to suppress the practice. Italy was one of the last major European nations to legalize divorce, in 1970, with a referendum ratifying the law four years later.

The sale of toxic foods and potions was outlawed, and the burning or disposal of certain toxic substances was prohibited — flax and hemp couldn't be soaked in water near towns and yew (which can emit toxins) could not be disposed of in rivers.

Theft, trade and even the comportment of physicians are considered at length. So is cattle rustling, coin shaving and the forgery of documents, for which the punishment is severe.

Extensive legislation is devoted to women's rights, and to those of children. The statute defining penalties for mothers who prostitute their daughters implies that this occurred, but there are equally severe penalties for rape, and violence against prostitutes.

In a precedent which paralleled developments elsewhere, daughters were allowed to succeed to feudal property and titles of nobility in the absence of male heirs — a practice which survived into the nineteenth century. This is the origin of the so-called "Sicilian Succession."

A few laws seem less enlightened. Adultery itself is a crime, but a husband might not be punished if he kills his adulterous wife and her lover immediately upon catching them in the sexual act *in flagrante delicto*. A peasant who strikes a knight or noble might have the offending hand chopped off unless he can prove that he acted in self defense.

Capital punishment existed and is mentioned, but some scholars contend that the term as used in the Constitutions sometimes refers to loss of citizenship rather than loss of one's life. Translation of several Latin words is debated; the term *serf* may be more accurate than *slave* in certain statutes, actual slavery being all but unknown in the Kingdom of Sicily by 1231.

It is in the Constitutions that Frederick establishes that only the son of a knight or noble may become a knight unless, in the case of a man of common birth, royal assent to the investiture is granted. In practice, such assent was probably obtained quite often, yet the law is a clear attempt to restrict entry into the aristocratic class.

A curious section — to the modern mind — is the proscription on the use of paper for legal documents, with requirement of the use of parchment or vellum for this purpose. Parchment was, of course, more durable, less susceptible than paper to damage from moisture, folding or even ink. The Kingdom of Sicily was ahead of most of Europe in the use of paper, introduced in the Emirate during the ninth century, a development described at greater length in Chapter 9.

There are also attempts to regulate local government and the construction of towers and castles, probably to discourage the development in southern Italy of communities similar to the northern Italian city-states which challenged Frederick's authority as Holy Roman Emperor.

Throughout the Constitutions it is abundantly clear that Frederick exercised an absolute authority in the Kingdom of Sicily that he did not enjoy in the German and northern Italian regions under his control.

No legal code is perfect, but Frederick's was significantly evolved for its time. It has been suggested that perhaps Frederick was a deist or freethinker who looked to "natural law" for some of his inspiration. This we can never know, but the Constitutions speak eloquently enough for themselves.

The Maliki School and Common Law

Could certain principles of early English common law be rooted in Islamic ideas introduced through contact between the Norman kingdoms of England and Sicily? That is the thesis advanced over the last decade by several legal scholars in Britain, the United States and a few other nations. While there exists no absolute proof of a causal connection, circumstantial evidence strongly supports, at the very least, the possibility of a broad exchange of legal ideas during the twelfth century.

Before encapsulating these, we should define "common" and "civil" law, and consider the social environment of Sicily and England in the twelfth century

In the beginning there was *civil*, or statutory, law — legal codes with the Ten Commandments as their archetype. The Romans, in particular, developed highly sophisticated legal codes which were inherited at the fall of the Western Empire by the Byzantine Greeks, influencing law in the early Church. Indeed, Europeans sometimes refer to civil (statutory) law as "Roman Law." (Legal terms vary according to time and place. In some quarters "civil law" came to denote laws outside the Church, and Americans refer to "civil law" as opposed to "criminal law.")

The origins of *common* law, or "case law," are largely obscured by the mists of time, but here it seems that the tribal law of the Romans' Germanic adversaries, the Goths and Vandals, who we met in Chapter 5, was influential to a great degree. In simplest terms, civil law, of which the Code of Justinian is a prime example, was established by legislation, while common law evolved from accepted social practice. Unlike civil law, common law is uncodified.

Among the Germanic peoples described by Tacitus, a local council of elders would meet to adjudicate cases, and the norm, or at least the chief objective, was compensation rather than punishment. An example often cited concerns larceny. Let's say that a man in a certain village had stolen another villager's horse and somehow the stallion had been lost or killed. The first task of Roman civil (or statutory) law might be to imprison the convicted thief, while Germanic common (or "tribal") law would be more likely to force the thief to compensate the horse's owner for loss resulting from the theft. For the most part, the Germanic tribes had rudimentary legal norms but no written language, making oral tradition very important. The elders or judges had to *memorize* the cases. Uniformity in treatment was desired to promote *equal* justice, so the decision rendered in an earlier but similar case by fellow elders might be taken into account, perhaps establishing a *precedent* to be respected in all future cases.

Farther afield, many social customs of the various Nordic, Celtic and Slavic communities were essentially similar to those of Germanic society so far as we know, though there were distinct localized differences, such as Brehon Law in Ireland.

How did Germanic law in its unadulterated form come to an end?

Christianization brought with it legal practices rooted in the civil (statutory) law of the Romans, though this was usually localized. Canon law was established around the time of the Council of Nicea in 325, giving an impetus to the diffusion of the Christian faith. In time, oral Germanic law readily gave way to written Roman law, colored by Biblical influences — Mosaic Law was "statutory law" *par excellence.*

Over the next few centuries, as region after region embraced Christianity, civil law of one form or another became the norm. To cite just a few examples, the Visigothic "Code of Euric" was written in Latin in 471, followed by the *Lex Romana Visigothorum* in 506. Traces of a few common law practices survived this ideological onslaught in the mixed legal system the Romans called the *leges barbarorum,* or "barbarians' laws." The voluminous Code of Justinian was formulated by 534, and then its *Epitome Juliani* manuscripts were distributed.

When the Goths and Vandals occupied Sicily, they left the legal system and government of the moribund Roman Empire intact.

Which traditions of the Germanic tribal cultures flourished into the Christian era?

Antiquated rites of betrothal, such as the original form of handfasting, find their roots in Germanic practices, and so do some of our modern nuptial customs, which the early Christians of the dissipating Roman Empire disparaged as "pagan." Customs concerning land ownership and military service spawned the earliest forms of what we now call feudalism (more about that below).

To cast a glance over Norman law of the eleventh century is to envision scenes typical of the medieval life depicted in literature and cinema, particularly jousts and torture.

Well into the era of their conquests of England and Sicily, which began in the 1060s, the Normans still employed "trial by ordeal" in criminal cases. This holdover from their Norse forebears subjected a suspected criminal to a physical test, his survival of (for example) attempted drowning by full immersion in water thus "proving" a favorable decision by God.

For personal disputes, "trial by combat" pitted one man against another in a mortal struggle to decide personal claims over property — be it land, a horse or even a pretty maiden.

In such circumstances, from which the legal term "trial" comes to us, only the physically strong, martially able or extremely fortunate could hope to attain justice.

By the twelfth century, however, combat was for the most

part a legal remedy reserved to knights. Where there was a dispute over property, be it land or cattle, possession was sometimes the primary or exclusive basis for claiming ownership.

A better system was needed, and simply adapting the Church's legal codes to those of wider society seemed inadequate.

King Henry II of England (ruled 1154-1189), generally viewed as a reformer, stood at the juridical vanguard. What were his ideas?

One of the fundamental principles involved land ownership. Laws addressed property disputes by placing an emphasis on written agreements rather than simple physical possession of property. True, early manorial deeds and *Domesday Book* already defined such rights through the written word, but those laws applied to feudal property held by aristocrats. The new laws considered the rights of the ordinary person as well. The assize of *novel disseisin* (literally "recent dispossession") established in 1166 is thought to derive from Islamic law.

How could this be?

The most likely explanation is that several Islamic legal ideas found their way to England through the Plantagenets' contact with Sicily. Henry's son, Richard Lionheart, passed through Messina *en route* to Palestine during the Crusades, and his daughter, Joan, wed King William II of Sicily in 1177. During their exile from England, several of Thomas Becket's kin received hospitality in Sicily, where Marsala Cathedral is dedicated to "Saint Thomas of Canterbury."

Such connections were nothing new; a few of the knights who fought at the Battle of Messina in 1061 also fought at the Battle of Hastings five years later. But during the twelfth century, with Plantagenet territories extending from England into southern France (Aquitaine was the dowry of Henry's wife Eleanor), and the Siculo-Norman kingdom extending almost as far north as Rome, contacts were more frequent than ever.

It was an Englishman, Robert Selby, who served for some years as King Roger's effective viceroy in mainland Italy, in places like Salerno. A number of English-born clerics were prominent in Norman Sicily. Richard Palmer, to cite just one of many examples, was Bishop of Syracuse and then archbishop of Agrigento. While we usually think of such clerics leaving England for sunny Sicily, Simon of Apulia, a friend of Henry II, went from Sicily to England, where he became dean of York and then Bishop of Exeter.

Most relevant here is the man known to Sicily's Arabs as "Qaid al Brun" (born Thomas le Brun in England and known to later historians simply as "Thomas Brown"), who was the chief treasurer to King Roger II of Sicily. Following the Sicilian monarch's death in 1154, Brown returned to England right around the time that Henry ascended the Throne, and was retained by the newly-crowned English king to reform the royal exchequer. There he introduced Hindu-Arabic numerals, but this numeration system was not readily embraced at the English court except by Brown himself.

On an artistic note, Brown's return to England coincided with the inception of armorial heraldry, the hereditary insignia known as *coats of arms*. Here an interesting development was the adoption of the gold lion passant guardant as the heraldic symbol of the Plantagenet kings. It survives as the ubiquitous "English Lion." This emblem can be seen in Sicily's Norman Palace, where it graces a wall of Roger's Salon as well as the wall behind the throne dais in the Palatine Chapel (see Chapter 16). It is quite possible that Brown — or perhaps one of his contemporaries who migrated from Sicily to England during the same period — suggested this symbol to Henry, whose sons Richard and John made use of it later.

In the event, Thomas Brown is one of the most likely persons to have influenced Henry intellectually in matters of administration. If a single candidate were to be advanced as the person who prevailed upon Henry to accept a few principles of Muslim law, it would be Thomas Brown.

For context, we should remember that the Sicilian and English kings of the twelfth century were perpetually contesting Papal power in their realms. Henry's conflicts with Becket were but a single example of this. The English king's Sicilian counterparts, as "apostolic legates," could actually nominate bishops. The fact that Henry might seek a system of law somewhat different from the one espoused by the Church is hardly surprising.

The Maliki School of law, or *Maliki Madhab,* was popular in northern Africa, its fundamental precepts formulated by Malik ibn Anas ibn Malik ibn Abi (or simply "Imam Malik"), who was born around 711 in Medina where he died in 795. He was the greatest Islamic scholar of his age, and his ideas were popularized among the Sunni populations of the expanding Muslim world.

Were Imam Malik's ideas inspired by Arab tribal customs similar to those of the tribal Germans? Are councils of elders common to most tribal peoples?

Although the roots of Maliki law were Sunni, by the twelfth century most Muslims in the Kingdom of Sicily were Shiites of the Kalbid-Fatimid tradition. This may seem paradoxical until we consider that the Aghlabids who conquered the island were for most of their history Sunnis whose legal practices and institutions in Sicily were inherited by their successors the Fatimids and Kalbids (who were Shiites). This phenomenon is not unlike Christianity "inheriting" certain tenets of Judaic law.

In Sicily the principal legal code (civil law) in Henry's time was what is now known as the Assizes of Ariano, promulgated by Roger II in 1140. Sophisticated for its era, it derived its precepts not only from Norman, but also from Muslim and Byzantine (especially Justinian) legal ideas. The Assizes governed virtually every aspect of life. Over in cloudy England,

Henry's Constitutions of Clarendon, promulgated in 1164, may have been influenced by the Assizes of Ariano, but in great measure they concerned the power of the Crown in its relations with the Roman Church.

Common law is another matter. Before considering it further, however, let's digress briefly to think about *why* certain legal principles, including some Islamic ones, did not survive in Sicily beyond the latter decades of the thirteenth century.

Shortly after they conquered Palermo in early 1072, the Normans established that Muslim, Jew and Christian ("Greek") would each be judged by his own law, and this policy continued for a few decades until the Assizes of Ariano. For the Arabs this meant the Maliki School of law of Tunisia, where a jury of several men could sometimes substitute for the personal testimony of a few witnesses. But the eventual disappearance of the island's Muslim-Arabs as an identifiable population spelled the end of the historical continuity of their legal traditions in Sicily, once part of the Fatimids' vast empire.

As early as 1161, some Norman barons openly rebelled against what they viewed as excessive indulgence of certain courtiers and subjects, and the revolt bore the crude mark of bigotry toward Arabs and "Greeks." At the death of Frederick II in 1250, there were few Muslims left on the island; most had converted while some had emigrated or been deported.

Let us return to England, where what emerged was actually a *mixed* legal system drawing from both common law and civil law. The concept of feudal tenure, for instance, did not change significantly with the introduction of common law.

Some principles believed to emanate from the Maliki School are the right not to testify to incriminate oneself, proscription of the use of hearsay as evidence in trials, the accused's right to trial by jury, the weight of a contract as right to possession or transfer of property (rather than actual physical possession as sole proof of title), and the importance of judges' decisions in establishing legal precedent.

In 1215, the *Magna Carta* declared specific individual liberties, particularly for nobles, establishing that a free man could not be imprisoned, tried or sentenced except by a jury of his peers. Clearly the concept of trial by jury had become known in England.

Among the English institutions thought to have been influenced by Islamic law are the Inns of Court and perpetual endowment. As early as 1955, Henry Cattan noted the striking similarity between the perpetual endowment of a trust and the Muslim principle of *waqf*. More recently, a thesis along these lines has been advanced by John Makdisi in the United States and Omar Faruk in the United Kingdom.

In contract law we find some remarkable similarities, such as *force majeure* and recission. Another important example is that a contract — as for the sale of goods — becomes effective immediately upon acceptance of an offer. This is expressed in Ranulf de Glanville's definition of a valid contract based on agreement and consideration.

No country's legal system is based exclusively on common law. The few nations where common law exists, such as the United Kingdom and the United States, also have penal, commercial and financial codes. The authority of the "uncodified" British constitution is established partly by common law (by the judiciary) and partly by legislative law (by parliament).

Common law principles are also found in the legal systems of Ireland, Canada, India, Australia, New Zealand and Pakistan. Italian constitutional and statutory law are the fruit of baroque legal codes to which have been added some socialist elements.

Much that has been outlined here elicits lively debate from historians and jurists alike, but despite their contentions most would probably agree, at the very least, that Maliki Law and the Constitutions of Melfi represented a considerable improvement over trial by ordeal.

CHAPTER 26

Ciullo of Alcamo

Ciullo, or "Cielo," of Alcamo was one of the best known poets of the "Sicilian School" that found the epitome of its expression at the court of Frederick II. Here the sonnet was born, possibly developed by Giacomo of Lentini. It is possible that, had Frederick's dynasty — and Sicily's political importance — survived the thirteenth century, the modern Italian language we know today might be based on Sicilian rather than Tuscan.

Little of it has been preserved in documented form, but the earliest known prose written in the Italic (Romance) language of Sicily was composed only during the twelfth century. Until then, the language spoken in most of peninsular Italy — though less in Calabria and around Bari — was the Latin Vulgate, not widely known among Sicilians.

Under Norman influence, Sicily's linguistic landscape was becoming Latinized thanks to the introduction of the Roman Church (with its Latin) and, to a lesser degree, the Norman French tongue. The principal "Sicilian" vernacular languages encountered by the first Normans to settle the island in the eleventh century were Siculo Arabic and Byzantine Greek, with enough use of the Latin Vulgate as a second or third language in some communities — and perhaps a primary language in a handful of isolated localities — for strangers outside these cultures to communicate with each other. Sometimes this

Vulgate was a mixed language rather similar to an early form of what is now known as "Mediterranean Lingua Franca," spoken by merchants, diplomats, crusaders and pirates. Siculo Arabic survives in a modern form as Maltese.

Many Sicilians — though we cannot know how many — were bilingual. In 1100 it would not be unusual to encounter a Sicilian fluent in both Arabic and Greek. But at that date there was no "native" Sicilian language as we understand such a definition today.

In the Roman and Byzantine periods the island's literate element read (and wrote) both Greek and Latin, and the former was actually the more popular spoken language even in the days of Cicero. That was true in the more eastern regions of the Empire well into Christian times. Greek, considered the language of the educated classes, was spoken as a second language by many Roman patricians in the West.

It is clear that by the early years of the thirteenth century Latin influences were gaining ground in the Kingdom of Sicily. (However, rabid Sicilianists who claim that a distinctively "Sicilian" tongue had existed since the ninth or tenth century can cite no written examples to support their thesis.)

Which modern languages sound most like Sicilian and Calabrian?

To the ear, Catalan is strikingly similar to Modern Sicilian. Beginning in 1282, Sicily was closely associated with Catalonia until the second decade of the fifteenth century, and thereafter Spanish rule would last until the eighteenth century.

Ciullo of Alcamo, about whom little is known, appears to have resided, or held land, in the Sicilian town of Alcamo, an Arab locality mentioned by the court geographer Idrisi. Ciullo's given name seems to derive from *Cielo* or *Micele* (a medieval form of *Michele* for Michael). His only complete surviving work is the *Dialogue,* variously known as *Rosa Fresca Aulentissima,* for its first phrase, or *Il Contrasto.* This romantic poetry, probably composed before the death of Frederick II, reflects the true beginning of the Age of Chivalry in Sicily.

It has been suggested that the authors of the Sicilian School were notaries or scribes rather than full-time court poets. Differing from the majority of Sicily's chroniclers (who were clerics), they took their inspiration from the wandering troubadours. Though essentially Italic, the language bore the marks of Arabic and Greek.

Ciullo and his poem are commended by Dante in his *De Vulgari Eloquentia* ("On Eloquence in the Vernacular") written early in the 1300s. By then, the prominence of the Sicilian language had vanished along with the polyglot kingdom that gave birth to it.

What many scholars regard as the most important work in Sicilian was a near-contemporary history of the War of the Vespers. *The Rebellion of Sicily against King Charles* was written anonymously around 1290. Its Sicilian title is *Cronica di lu Rebellamentu di Sichilia contra Re Carlu.*

The Sicilian of today, though distinctive, is but a shadow of this medieval tongue, and only rarely has it seen print; the Bible, the world's most popular work, has never been published in Sicilian. This brings us to an important point that some Sicilians might prefer to overlook. Whereas the Medieval Sicilian of Ciullo of Alcamo and Giacomo of Lentini was a *literary* language, Modern Sicilian has only recently made its way into print, having long been considered the vulgar "dialect" of the common (and often illiterate) people.

This is not the place for a treatise on Modern Sicilian. Succinctly, we shall note that it is a rather guttural tongue lacking a true future tense or standard orthography. The long "u" is often used in words similar to Italian ones which use the long "o." We find *picciottu* instead of *giovanotto* (young man), *chiddu* for *esso* (it), *chistu* for *questo* (this), and so forth. Its verb forms make Sicilian as distinct from Italian as it is from Spanish. Certain nouns and adjectives are rather peculiar: *parrinu* instead of *prete* (priest), *beddu* for *bello* (beautiful), *iddu* for *egli* (he) and *idda* for *ella* (she).

The Sicilian word *tascio,* which means "tacky," falsely sophisticated or lacking in good taste, is understandably offensive in fashion-conscious Italy, though to refer to somebody as *vastaso,* "uncouth," is far more insulting. Certain Sicilian phrases seem appropriate sometimes. *Ammunì* sounds much more persuasive than the Italian *Andiamo* ("Let's go").

Some words come directly from Arabic: *babbaluci* (also the Greek *boubalàkion*) for *lumache* (snails), *fatùk* for pistachio, *saia* (from *saqiya*) for "canal," *gébbia* for "reservoir" (the Arabs introduced sophisticated irrigation systems), and *azzizata* ("beautified") from a*ziz.* Other words rooted in Arabic: *favara* (a well), *mischinu* (an unfortunate person), *zagara* (orange blossom), *zammù* (anise), *balata* (stone), *cafisu* (a liquid measure, from *qafiz*), *tarì* (a coin minted until 1860).

A number of Sicilian words derive from Norman French: *buatta* (jar, from *boîte*), *custureri* (tailor, from *coustrier*), *largasia* (largesse), *racìna* (grape), *vuccèri* (butcher, from *boucher*), *accattari* (to buy, from *acater,* modern *acheter*).

And from Medieval Greek: *carusu* (boy, from *kouros*), *cona* (icon, from *eikona*), *crastu* (ram, from *krastos*), *pistiari* (to eat, from *apestiein*), *naca* (cradle, from *nakè*), *bucali* (pitcher, from *baukalion*), *grasta* (a terracotta vase, from the classical *gastra*).

Among words from Middle High German we find: *arbitrari* (to work, from *arbeit*), *vardari* (to wait or watch, from *warten*), *sparagnari* (to save money, from *sparen*), *guastari* and *vastari* (to waste, from *wastjan*).

Provençal has made a few contributions, notably: *lascu* (thin or sparse, from *lasc*), *addumari* (to light, from *allumar*), *aggrifari* (to kidnap, from *grifar*).

There are, of course, many words from Latin and Catalan. On a more hypothetical note, the Indo-European etymologies of a few Sicilian words may be connected to the language of the Sikels who already populated the island's eastern region when the Greeks arrived. Two oft-cited examples are: *dudda* (various red berries, akin to the Welsh *rhudd* meaning "pink" and the Romanian *dudà*), *scrozzu* ("short" or "undeveloped," similar to Germanic *scurz* and Lithuanian *su-skurdes*).

Sicilian is a bit more guttural than other modern Italic languages. Contrary to a common notion, it is not a "dialect" of Italian, and recent years have seen a renewed interest in Italy's regional languages.

But would medieval writers like Ciullo and Giacomo recognize Modern Sicilian?

More importantly, although Francis of Assisi wrote his *Canticle* in a form of vernacular Italian a decade or two earlier, most philologists consider Ciullo's *Dialogue* the earliest true "Italian" poetry of the Middle Ages. To describe it as a bridge between the Vulgate and Tuscan might be an exaggeration, but it did represent an important step in linguistic development.

Rarely has the language of love been so eloquent.

CHAPTER 27

The Angevins

Anjou is a region of west-central France closely associated with the French ruling family. The term *Angevin* refers to both the "Plantagenet" dynasty of England from 1154 to 1399 (descendants of Geoffrey, Count of Anjou, and Matilda, daughter of Henry I) and the French dynasty that ruled southern Italy from Naples beginning in the thirteenth century. The term can be misleading; in Sicily the people generically referred to as "Angevins" were from various parts of France, not only the Anjou region, but they arrived during the reign of Charles I Anjou of Naples.

Chosen by the Papacy to become King of Sicily, Charles was the less saintly younger brother of Saint Louis. Canonized in 1297, the devout Louis IX of France is widely venerated in Sicily, where his heart is kept in Monreale Abbey.

The vicissitudes that resulted in the extinction of the Hohenstaufen dynasty were described in the chapter on Frederick II.

Charles of Anjou was crowned King of Sicily in 1266 by authority of Pope Clement IV, a Frenchman. Following a series of battles, the last Hohenstaufen heir, the young Conradin (a grandson of Frederick II), was executed in 1268. From this death was Italy's Angevin period born, in a dynastic transition representing the ultimate form of Papal hegemony.

This anticlimax came as no surprise. Following the death of Frederick II in 1250, it was clear that no Pope would be content to share the Italian peninsula with so formidable a force as a Holy Roman Emperor who also ruled southern Italy.

The Angevin era marked the beginning of the decline of Sicily, and particularly Palermo, as a center of political and economic power. Charles ruled from Naples, which previously had been a prosperous but politically less important city than Palermo, Bari or Salerno.

In Sicily, the changes were immediate. Thousands of French troops arrived, and taxes were increased. For the first time in centuries, Sicily was the dominion of a ruler who saw no reason to visit the island except on the rarest of occasions. This fact of rule from a distance is often cited as the underlying cause for a great many complaints by the Sicilian barons.

Now Sicily became almost entirely Latinized. Except for a few monasteries in the Nebrodi and Peloritan regions, the Christians were Catholic. The new regime openly resented the Arabs of Lucera (in Apulia) and Sicily, who it coerced into conversion. Mosques were gradually abandoned — some forcibly — and many were converted to churches. Jews were tolerated, though their communities became fewer outside the major cities.

From the beginning, the Sicilian nobility viewed the Angevin French in a negative light, initially as something of a nuisance and then as a repressive instrument of royal power. Charles of Anjou was anything but an enlightened ruler. His son, Charles "the Lame," was regarded by all, including his father, as weak and incompetent.

The expansionist policies of Charles were ambitious indeed. Apart from influence in northern Italy, he claimed the Crown of Jerusalem borne by Frederick II. After Louis IX died on crusade in Tunisia in 1270, his son, Philip (who ruled France as Philip III), fell under the spell of his conniving

Uncle Charles.

By 1282, Charles ruled Sicily and southern Italy, Albania, a few pieces of France and (if only nominally) Jerusalem. He was preparing an invasion of Constantinople that would have finally brought the Byzantine world — and its Orthodox Church — under Latin control.

Manfred Hohenstaufen, an illegitimate son of Frederick II (but putative heir to the thrones of Sicily and Germany) killed by Charles' Angevin forces at the Battle of Benevento in 1266, had betrothed his daughter, Constance, to Peter of Aragon. On this tenuous basis, a number of Sicilian nobles exiled from Charles' court for over a decade sought the alliance of Peter, whose realm ruled from Barcelona, in Catalonia, constituted a small empire.

Clearly, the rivalry between *Guelphs* (supporters of the Papacy and now the Angevins) and *Ghibellines* (supporters of the Holy Roman Emperor and Swabians) had not abated, but what followed was completely unexpected.

On Easter Monday, 30 March 1282, a popular revolt broke out beyond Palermo's city walls (near the Cistercians' Holy Spirit Church). According to a popular but apocryphal story, the spark that ignited the revolt was an Angevin soldier's improper search of a Sicilian woman while checking for concealed arms. Was this event a catalyst for revolution, or was it a pretext for war?

Whatever its cause, this localized riot immediately provoked wider unrest in northwestern Sicily, leading to the deaths of hundreds of French, including numerous civilians of both genders. The populace had tasted blood, and the uprising spread across the island in a matter of days. The result was nothing less than terrorizing.

This "War of the Vespers" was the first revolt of its kind to garner such astounding success. Almost simultaneously, the French castellans and garrisons of Sicily's fortified cities were isolated and killed in Palermo, Trapani, Sciacca, Marsala, Caccamo, Vicari, Girgenti (Agrigento), Milazzo, Castrogiovanni (Enna), Taormina, Catania and elsewhere. So were a great number of innocent people, including women and children. Those Angevin troops that could flee made their way to Messina, where they embarked for Calabria across the Strait.

King Charles was incredulous. Pope Martin IV, a Frenchman who supported Charles, was equally stupefied. The reports arriving from Sicily were shocking, inexplicable. Charles was about to launch a large scale invasion of Constantinople which would have changed the course of history — placing the Orthodox Church under Rome and fortifying the region against Muslim expansion. Instead, he had to divert troops to Sicily.

In September, Peter was formally elected King of Sicily by the island's nobles. That, however, was not the end of the war.

In a series of battles at sea and skirmishes on land, the Angevin forces were defeated by Aragonese-Sicilian ones. In one of the war's comical episodes, Charles and Peter were to meet for a duel to decide the fate of Sicily, each accompanied by a hundred fighting knights. This was to take place in June 1283 at Bordeaux, capital of the neutral French territories of Edward, King of England. Each warring king agreed to appear with his suite but it was tacitly understood that each would arrive at a different time. Then each sovereign claimed that the other was a coward. In another incident, King Charles' incompetent son, Charles "the Lame" (the future Charles II), was taken prisoner at a sea battle in June 1284 and held in the citadel of Cefalù.

By the time King Charles died, Angevin power in Sicily had vanished. The new king of Naples, Charles II, was still a prisoner, and the Papacy at first refused to recognize him as the late monarch's heir. In the event, Pope Martin himself died a few months after King Charles. In a gesture of alliance with his Angevin cousins, Philip III of France attacked Aragon, but his army was quickly defeated — as much by malaria as by force of arms. The key players all died in 1285: Charles of Naples, Philip of France, Peter of Aragon, Pope Martin (born Simon de Brion).

The ineffectual Charles the Lame went on to reign in Naples as Charles II, but by most accounts he lacked his father's mettle. Despite his retaining a few lands in the Balkans, his world, like that of future Catholic monarchs of the Middle Ages, was to be confined to the West. The age of Crusades and Conquests in the eastern Mediterranean was well and truly dead.

James, the second son of Peter of Aragon, became King of Sicily. He was nineteen years old when he was crowned at Palermo in February 1286. But James eventually left Sicily to ascend the Aragonese throne.

A series of intrigues continued until 1302, ending with an Angevin-Aragonese treaty known as the "Peace of Caltabellotta."

Considering its effects on Mediterranean history, particularly the aborted invasion of the Byzantine Empire, the resonance of the Vespers is justified. The revolt was certainly atypical of its era, yet very unlike the modern revolutions to which it is often compared. Verdi's opera, *I Vespri Siciliani,* is much romanticized.

In retrospect, nothing can exculpate the Sicilians' massacre of French civilians during the earliest phase of the Vespers, for such an act of mass violence can never be completely expiated. But it would be inaccurate to portray the uprising either as the result of a sophisticated conspiracy or, on the other hand, a wholly improvised revolt. It bore the elements of both.

The Sicilians seem to have met surprisingly little resistance from the Angevins. In what has become a popular anecdote, captured soldiers suspected of being French were made to say the word *cìciri,* Sicilian for *ceci* (chickpeas or garbanzos), and anybody who pronounced it with a French accent was killed. According to another story, Sicilian women pregnant by French men were ripped open.

At this distance of time, the veracity of such accounts cannot be established conclusively, but certain aspects of the revolt are curious indeed. That Peter's fleet arrived with uncommon alacrity suggests early notice. Except for high officials, notably the kindly Jean de Saint-Remy, the Angevins' justiciar for Palermo, most of the French brought to Sicily from 1268 to 1282 were soldiers. They were not enfeoffed knights. This meant that very few of the Sicilian barons were themselves French, so their sympathies did not lay with the Angevins. Failure to seed the local population with his own people was just one of the errors for which Charles would become infamous.

In considering the military strategy and tactics, let us remember that each baron was a man-at-arms who could count on the assistance of at least two or three mounted knights and perhaps a few archers. In this way, even three or four bannerets could muster enough force to overthrow the token garrison guarding a small, isolated castle, and this is what happened at Vicari and other fortresses across the island. Caltanissetta Castle, for example, fell to a handful of men without resistance, and its cowardly castellan lived to complain about it to the new king. The Angevin castellans' undermanning of fortresses goes a long way to explain how Sicily fell to local knights so quickly. Contrary to popular belief, the success of the revolt owed little to the violence of riotous crowds except in Palermo and a few other key cities.

Under the Angevins, Sicily's was a subject population, something resented by many Sicilians. Whether or not the revolt itself was actually instigated as part of a conspiracy by the island's disgruntled Norman-Swabian nobility, the barons certainly wasted no time lending their support once it had begun.

Was the War of the Vespers nothing more than part of a grand conspiracy to divert Charles' invasion away from Constantinople, or was that merely an unintended consequence? Here certainty lies beyond our grasp, but the known facts suggest a plot as a distinct possibility, with John of Procida, friend of Frederick II, sowing the seeds of dissent, and the Genoese, occasional allies of the Byzantines, as covert supporters and obvious beneficiaries. In the Middle Ages, machinations of this kind were the rule, not the exception. Much of the planning would have occurred during the pontificate of Pope Nicholas III (1277-1280), a friend of Procida's who, like earlier Popes, probably feared the concentration of Mediterranean power in one man, the wily Charles.

On a wider stage, the swiftness, efficiency and ruthlessness of the Vespers quickly became known to monarchs across Europe, but its clarion call went unheeded, for what was its overt message except that common people in large cities could take up arms? Owing to its political impact, the Vespers War is referred to by a few modern historians as "the world war of the thirteenth century."

Paradoxically, the Vespers would serve as the impetus for centuries of rule from abroad, which was one of the things that the Sicilians ostensibly resented about the ousted French. Thus began Sicily's long "Spanish" period, though Spain itself would not be unified for another two centuries.

The backlash transcended this political question, for the Vespers conflict was a *coda,* the definitive culmination of the island's multicultural experiment.

At all events, the Angevin presence in Sicily was transient at best. To historians, the island's medieval French legacy is essentially a dynastic question, a phase to be marked but not remembered.

CHAPTER 28

The Aragonese and Castilians

Governed from the Catalonian city of Barcelona, the "Crown of Aragon" was an ethnically diverse region, contiguous to the area once ruled by the Visigoths — from whom its nobility claimed descent — with several languages and its own tiny empire. Like *Swabian* and *Angevin,* the term *Aragonese,* as it is used in Sicilian history, is something of a misnomer. Aragon, with its capital at Zaragoza, was just one of several territories ruled by the Aragonese kings of the thirteenth century. The Crown of Aragon included Catalonia, Valencia, Navarre, Roussillon, the Balearic Islands and other regions, encompassing nearly a third of Spain and a piece of France. The cumbersome phrase "Aragonese-Catalan-Valencian" might be more descriptive, but for convenience we'll conform to convention and use *Aragonese.*

The Crown of Aragon emerged as a powerful force in an age when most of the Iberian monarchies were struggling against the Moors, a conflict which was to continue well into the final years of the fifteenth century.

The royal house of Aragon effectively ruled Sicily from the time of the War of the Vespers in 1282, described in the last chapter. The "Peace of Caltabellotta" established a tenuous truce, but for their part the Angevins never forgot the jewel the Aragonese had snatched from their hands.

King Peter of Aragon, whose wife was considered the last heir of the Hohenstaufen dynasty of Swabia, thus became King of Sicily, but he died just three years after the Vespers. He was succeeded in turn by two of his sons.

In theory, the Crowns of Aragon and Sicily were to remain separate, meaning that the same monarch could not simultaneously rule both Aragon and Sicily. In practice, of course, this principle was only rarely applied.

At first, ordinary Sicilians may have rejoiced at the expulsion of the hated French, but it is a French phrase that best sums up the situation prevalent in Sicily by 1300: *Plus ça change, plus c'est la même chose.* It wasn't long before the Sicilians' petulance gave way to disillusion and then indifference.

In the war's immediate aftermath, Aragonese (or Catalonian) rule brought relative peace and prosperity to Sicily. But this was punctuated by periods of unrest, and the nobility never seemed content.

The Aragonese brought a number of nobles to the island, and the ensuing envy by the native "Latin" baronage, represented by leading families such as the Chiaramonte, provoked a destructive feud against the Alagona and other "Catalan" clans, who ostensibly acted in Aragonese interests. The roots of this movement can be traced to certain families seizing fiefs formerly belonging to the defeated Angevin nobility, but simple greed and avarice were the real culprits. Aggravated by the absence of the king and the presence of the Bubonic Plague, the chaos led to much rural destruction for several decades of the fourteenth century.

Despite a few isolated pockets of prosperity, Aragonese Sicily was undistinguished for intellectual, economic or social initiative — though it was during this era that many castles were constructed — and the island was usually exploited to support Aragon's treasury and wars. Entire regions were deforested, and the precious timber of the Nebrodi Fir nearly made the species extinct. (Today it is endangered but protected.)

The Sicilian nobility decayed into a sleepy, unmotivated yet greedy class uninterested in genuine economic development or progress. A true mercantile class failed to develop except among the Genoese merchants who established themselves in Messina and Palermo.

Not that many decried the situation. Few ever paused long enough to ponder it at all. The nobility sought ever greater privileges and grander titles. Whereas formerly the feudal nobles were content to be barons or enfeoffed knights, in 1296 the Chiaramonte sparked a trend by becoming counts, and in successive centuries the ranks of the aristocracy swelled to include dukes, viscounts and marquesses. The titles grew more pompous as the general literacy rate plummeted.

The Catalan Gothic architectural movement influenced the style of a number of Sicilian palaces and churches built in the fifteenth century, particularly in Palermo: Santa Maria della Catena, Palazzo Abatellis, Palazzo Aiutamicristo, Palazzo Alliata, Palazzo Marchese. Taormina's Palazzo Corvaja, though constructed during the Arab period, was later embellished with details reminiscent of the Catalan Gothic. In Barcelona, where the movement originated, a fine example is Palacio Requesens.

A dynastic transition altered little in Sicilian society. The reigning House of Aragon died out in 1410, to be succeeded two years later by the rulers of Castile. Sicily's first university, at Catania, was founded by Alfonso V in 1434, more than two hundred years after Frederick II chartered the University of Naples.

Like earlier rulers, the Castilian kings minted coinage in Sicily, establishing an important mint around 1450 in what is now Palazzo Cefalà in Palermo's Via Alloro, the street's name deriving not from the modern noun for laurel but from the phrase *all'oro,* "of the gold." Another mint was operated at

Messina. (Palermo was home to a mint until 1836.)

Alfonso, who lived and reigned until 1458, was an enlightened monarch, but his immediate successors, John and then Ferdinand "the Catholic," were nothing of the kind, and before long the Sicilians were victims of a repressive dystopia.

The horrors of the Spanish Inquisition nourished the reactionary elements of the prevailing social milieu, discouraging free thought in any form. Only in 1782 was the Inquisition abolished in Sicily. It had encouraged the growth of underground sects like the semilegendary *Beati Paoli* and the kind of widespread suspicion and clannishness for which (unfortunately) the Sicilians have come to be known. The Sicilian social culture we see today is largely the product of this period.

Ferdinand the Catholic was one of the forces who managed to forge Spain into a united nation. This he achieved in 1492, the year Christopher Columbus reached America and the year that Judaism was outlawed in Spain and Sicily.

After 1500, in the wake of the expulsions and conversions of the island's Jews, Sicilian society was overwhelmingly Catholic, essentially Italian with Spanish influences. Compared to what she had been under the Byzantines, Fatimids and Normans, Sicily was now in decline. Illiteracy became endemic, defining the educational level of the great majority of Sicilians — and indeed Italians generally — into the nineteenth century.

Most historians agree that the Middle Ages ended around 1453, the year that saw the fall of Constantinople to the Turks and the end of the Hundred Years' War between England and France. By then, the seeds of the Renaissance were sown, and a new era had dawned.

CHAPTER 29

Inheritance

Not for nothing do we study history. Any doubters should consider the words of Cicero: *"Nescire autem quid ante quam natus sis acciderit, id est semper esse puerum."* Or in plain English: "One who is ignorant of what happened before his birth will always be a child."

By its very nature and definition, learning is based on things experienced, revealed, invented or discovered in the past, be it two days or two millennia ago. The lengthy annals of Sicilian history leave a lot for us to learn.

Cicero, as we said in our Introduction, believed in *impartial* history. The historian must be a humanist but never a manipulator. It is not the role of the historian, much less the journalist, to think *for* the reader, but rather to stimulate free thought *by* the reader.

Intriguing as places may be, it is the *people* who bequeath to us a legacy worth preserving. That is why the ancient Greeks, from whom we have learned much, are more important in the literary, philosophical and scientific spheres than their worthy contemporaries the Etruscans, who also built temples and ruled part of the Italian peninsula.

The tangible traces of much of Sicily's history are easy enough to find. It is in seeking the intangible, the ideas, that we risk losing our way. The preceding pages reflect an effort at mapmaking.

We said at the beginning of this journey that the experiences of Sicily's past are not just about Sicilians. They are a legacy for all humanity. It is perfectly understandable for us to wonder why so little worth preserving from the Sicilians' multicultural society has found its way into our times, either in Sicily or elsewhere.

Definitions can prove elusive, but we could call the society of Sicily circa 1100 *cosmopolitan*. As it consisted of three Western faiths and four or five distinct ethnic cultures, rather than dozens, it might well have prospered for many centuries. Not until the twenty-first century, with the arrival of numerous immigrants from Asia and Africa, would Sicily experience a pluralism even remotely similar to that of the twelfth century.

Sicily's varied history, so cherished by foreigners, is largely ignored by the overwhelming majority of Sicilians. The dearth of good general histories of Sicily authored by Italians is painfully obvious when the best books available in Italian are translations from English works by the likes of Norwich and Abulafia; for comparison, imagine a definitive biography of Henry II of England written by an Italian rather than by an eminent British historian like Richard Barber. Sicily's independent scholars do produce some good monographs and specialist research — albeit almost exclusively in Italian — but extremely few academicians are as originative.

As we have said, the atrophy had already begun by the time of the War of the Vespers in 1282, and the inexorable denouement was complete before 1500. We have also said that general literacy was probably higher in 1061 than in 1861, and that high medieval literacy was partly due to the Arabs' introduction of paper, mentioned in Chapter 9. Matters improved during the twentieth century, but it was reported in 2010 that Italians read fewer books *per capita* than the residents of every other European Union nation except Greece, and that not a single

Italian university was ranked in the world's top hundred.

One of the most astounding examples of the philistinism that prevailed by the middle of the fifteenth century can be seen at Palermo Cathedral, where a column supporting the Gothic portico bears a passage from a sura of the Koran carved in relief. (This is one of at least five similar pillars preserved in Palermo which once supported the entrances of mosques.) Incredibly, the local architects responsible for the portico's construction probably didn't recognize the ornate script as Arabic. We should rejoice in such serendipity. Had the architects recognized the writing, they might have ordered the beautiful column destroyed!

Even the language has undergone radical transformation. To compare today's guttural Sicilian to the poetic tongue of Ciullo of Alcamo is like comparing modern English to the language of Chaucer.

But didn't the diversity of cultures that flourished in the Arab, Norman and Swabian periods meld to form the Sicilian culture of modern times?

All contributed to the mix, and a few traces of each are evident in cuisine, language, religion, the arts and folk traditions, but by the end of the Middle Ages they were overwhelmingly subsumed in the essentially Latin monoculture we see today. An intrinsic shortcoming of a monocultural environment is its endogamy. It is rarely a place where foreign ideas can take root.

How is a culture extinguished? The chapter on religions explained how certain faiths disappeared in Sicily. Assimilation and amalgamation are the norm. Change is usually gradual and subtle, even insidious. Cataclysm is not the rule but the all-too-frequent exception. Ethnic cleansing and genocide are only the most extreme examples of social metamorphosis by force. In 1917, the American entry into the First World War brought about the immediate end of German organizations and publications in the United States, where German toast became French toast and many German surnames were anglicized; across the U-boat-infested Atlantic the British royal family, known as *Saxe-Coburg and Gotha,* became the House of Windsor.

In Sicilian history, events like the Vespers uprising and the expulsion of the Jews excised particular cultures from the fabric of society almost overnight. Historians have even coined a term for it: ethnocide. How often have we seen modern nations repeat such errors?

The historical landscape is strewn with the names of extinct societies and cultures. We have met a few in the preceding chapters.

Culture survives only when perpetuated, rarely thriving on sufferance alone. It requires a nourishing environment and sometimes a certain degree of determination. The sustaining lifeblood of any culture is continuity, its transmission from one generation to the next. The Jewish Diaspora is the quintessential example of the preservation of an ancient culture unto our times despite efforts from outsiders — and perhaps a few insiders — to suppress it. Here a faith, a philosophy, a language and a cuisine have been maintained by a hereditary group for millennia. Indeed, the priestly class, the *Cohanim,* arguably constitutes the world's oldest familial caste, established around 1200 BCE (BC), its kinship network over the ages confirmed through genetic research. Many Jews consider their Judaic heritage, at once ethnic and religious, to be an ancient birthright worth preserving.

Conversely, the classic example of a historical "disconnect" is the Italian who proclaims that "my ancestors built the Colosseum," referring not to a grandfather or even a chain of known antecedents but to remote predecessors, with many centuries of names and proven lineage missing between AD (CE) 72 and the near present. Of course, many things have been transmitted to us from ancient Rome, including the Latin alphabet and Christianity, but a personal, familial tradition is lacking.

Can anybody claim a birthright without knowing of its existence?

Reviving a dormant culture, one removed from the collective memory, is not unlike modern attempts to revive medieval music. To resist the relentless march of time is an exercise in futility. There is a saying that we cannot "unring a bell." What existed in Sicily in 1100 represented more than one culture and it can never be resurrected as something identical to what it was. The mother cultures have moved on. Today the Normans in Normandy and the Arabs in Tunisia are not what they were in the Middle Ages, so it would be impossible to "transplant" their medieval cultures to Sicily as if we were reintroducing a traditional variety of grape. Artificial ethnogenesis rarely meets with lasting success.

But we can try to resuscitate the spirit of the Norman kingdom. Lofty egalitarian principles are greater than any single time or place.

Sicily fell into the orbits of the united Spain in 1492 and then the united Italy in 1861, and neither state was too concerned with the fate of Sicily or other peripheral regions. These developments reflected nothing like a cohesive plan or a grand conspiracy; they were simply the result of general political trends, even creeping momentum.

The foibles and failures of the neocratic Kingdom of Italy culminated in its inglorious demise before the middle of the twentieth century, millions of its citizens having emigrated in their hopes of better lives abroad. It counted among its monarchs no Emir of Emirs, no *Stupor Mundi*.

Learning takes effort. Inscience is always disturbing. Epictetus declared long ago that only the educated are free, and his words still ring true today.

A sober reading of history tells us that the social progress of the united Italy was laggard at best. The infamous "racial laws" of 1938 nearly eradicated the few pockets of Judaism left by that time. Women gained the right to vote only in 1946, and then only on the orders of the Allies occupying the war-torn country. As recently as 1950, in Piedmont, where Turin was the country's most industrialized city, rice was still being planted manually by women called *mondine*. Beginning around that time, when such immigration was resumed — having been interrupted by the Second World War — a multitude of Italians embarked for the United States, Canada, Australia, Argentina and elsewhere, and today hundreds of thousands still leave Italy each year in search of opportunities abroad.

Social developments in Italy between 1861 and 1946 need not concern us here except to recognize that the historiography advocated by both Church and State supported a homogeneous view of a monolithic Italian culture, a monoculture devoid of any mention of the Shiite Muslims, Orthodox Christians and Sephardic Jews who once populated Sicily. Then again, western Europeans of that era were generally reluctant to embrace things Islamic, Byzantine or Judaic.

Only the maps tell us that unpolished, untamed Old Palermo is part of a place called *Europe*. To visit Piazza Ballarò on a Saturday evening in April around eight, just as the stands of the nearby street market close and darkness envelops the labyrinth of surrounding streets, is to step back in time a thousand years to an age when this was a *souk*. The newest residents are African and Asian, the evening crowd seeded with youngish European tourists. As the nightlife commences, the din of a dozen languages — Sicilian among them — can be heard in the asymmetrical square dominated by a medieval tower. Every kind of food and drink is on offer. Every kind of music fills the air. Some places are just more intriguing after dark, and this is one of them. It's exactly the kind of "ordered chaos" that screenwriters and travel pundits love to explore, when they can find it. Londoners seeking a Sicilian St Christopher's Place, along with New Yorkers looking for the Palermitan St Mark's Place, are directed to staid Piazza Olivella, with its pizzas and kebabs, next to the archeology museum ten blocks away. Ballarò, on the other hand, is where the *cognoscenti* come to enjoy spicy, roasted chicken-on-a-stick served with a cold Guinness. A museum might preserve the past, but this place captures its spirit. Were he alive today, this is where a young Frederick II would come for dinner and a drink. And why not? Isn't this his neighborhood? Are these not his people?

As we have said, the story of The World's Island is not only about Sicilians, but by now readers who happen to be descended from Sicilians may have arrived at the realization that the blood in their veins is multicolored.

History and culture touch every one of us. Let us learn more *about* the past so that we may learn more *from* it.

And let a multicolored world learn with us.

APPENDIX 1

Chronology

"The stream of time, irresistible, ever moving, carries off and bears away all things that come to birth, plunging them into utter darkness, both deeds of no account and deeds which are mighty and worthy of commemoration."

— Anna Comnena, *Alexiad* 1148

History, of course, is a function of the slow march of time. For context and comparison, the following timeline also notes a few events outside Sicily. Dates before 840 BC (BCE), and a few thereafter, are approximate.

Prehistory

10,000 BC (BCE) - Neolithic peoples are present across mainland Europe and in Sicily. Pleistocene Epoch ends, followed by Holocene (present epoch).

9000 BC (BCE) - Superstructures of first megalithic temples at Göbekli Tepe, near Urfa, formerly Edessa, in Anatolia (Turkey), were erected around this time. Incised cave drawings at Addaura (outside Palermo) and Levanzo have been dated approximately to this period. The cave paintings on Levanzo are the oldest such art in Italy.

8000 BC (BCE) - Probable introduction of agriculture (initially wheat and other grains) in Sicily by eastern Mediterranean neolithic farmers, likely predecessors of earliest Indo-Europeans identified genetically with M172 (J2) haplogroup that originated in Fertile Crescent.

7000 BC (BCE) - Neolithic jewelry crafted in Sicily.

4000 BC (BCE) - Proto Sicanians inhabit Sicily and Malta. On Malta and Gozo they build Europe's oldest free-standing structures at Zebbug, Gantija, Mnajdra, Hagar Qim and Tarxien, and invent the simple wheel (a stone cylinder fitted to a semicylindrical groove carved into a stone block), leaving behind a large hypogeum and various artworks. Earliest Sicilian religion practiced. Equally advanced Minoan (Cretan and Aegean) civilization flourishes in eastern Mediterranean.

Native History: Sicanians, Elymians, Sikels

2800 BC (BCE) - Stonehenge (in England) and earliest pyramids (in Egypt) erected a thousand years after construction of first Maltese temples.

2200 BC (BCE) - Tarxien Culture (last "Temple Builders") of Malta disappears.

2000 BC (BCE) - Sicanian culture dominant in Sicily. Use of copper tools ("Early Bronze Age"), possibly indicating non-Sicilian influences, was prevalent by 2500 BC. Mycenaean and Late Minoan cultures present in isolated eastern localities.

1800 BC (BCE) - Birth of Abraham according to Hebrew tradition (approximate dating).

1700 BC (BCE) - Hittites in Anatolia; possible connection to Sicily's Elymians.

1500 BC (BCE) - Extensive Mycenaean trade with Sikels of Aeolian (Lipari) Islands and parts of the Ionian coast (at Thapsos) and Sicanians. Ausonians, an Italic people, also trade with Aeolian islanders.

1400 BC (BCE) - Iron Age begins in Greece. Estimated arrival date of Sikels (Sicels), an Italic people, in eastern Sicily.

1330 BC (BCE) - Birth of Moses according to Hebrew tradition.

1303 BC (BCE) - Birth of Ramesses II, Pharaoh of Egypt; references in Book of Exodus may be to another personage. Probable period of introduction of domesticated olive cultivars in Sicily by peoples of Aegean cultures.

1220 BC (BCE) - "Sea Peoples" first attack Egypt; Shikelish tribe is sometimes identified with Sikels.

1200 BC (BCE) - Elymians (probably from Anatolia in Asia Minor), arrive in western Sicily, founding Segesta (their Egesta), Erice (Eryx), Entella (outside Contessa Entellina), Hypana (usually identified with a site near Prizzi), probably Iaitas (near San Giuseppe Jato).

1000 BC (BCE) - Indo-European languages and societies identified to this era based on linguistic similarities.

Phoenicians, Carthaginians and Greeks

840 BC - Foundation of Carthage according to most estimates.

775 BC - Greek trading settlement on Ischia becomes their first in southern Italy. Phoenician port of Motya (Mozia near Marsala) may have been founded around this time.

750 BC - Phoenicians establish Zis (Palermo) and Kfra (Solunto) as trading centers.

735 BC - Naxos founded as first permanent Greek colony in Sicily.

733 BC - Syracuse (Siracusa) founded as Greek colony.

730 BC - Zancle (Messina) settled.

729 BC - Katane (Catania) settled by Chalcidians from Naxos.

705 BC - Greeks assimilate Sikels' city of Enna, with which myth of Persephone becomes identified.

688 BC - Gela founded.

650 BC - Himera (Termini Imerese) founded.

630 BC - Selinus (Selinunte) established. (Its standing temples were reconstructed.)

612 BC - Phoenicia falls to Chaldean (Neo-Babylonian) Empire, leaving Carthage as Phoenicians' major city.

580 BC - Akragas (Agrigento) founded.

504-466 BC - Hippocrates and Gelon (from 478), as Tyrants of Syracuse, rule most of eastern Sicily.

500 BC - By this date Carthaginians have repopulated Phoenician city of Zis (Palermo).

490 BC - Athenians defeat Persians at Battle of Marathon. Persian Wars begin, lasting until 479.

480 BC - Carthaginians (encouraged to fight the Greeks by Xerxes of Persia who has won victories in Greece) are defeated by Gelon of Syracuse at first Battle of Himera. Persians defeated at Battle of Salamis.

474 BC - Syracusans win naval victory over Etruscans at Cumae.

455 BC - Aeschylus dies at Gela.

452 BC - Sikel leader Ducetius (died 440) leads revolt.

431-404 BC - Peloponnesian War.

415-413 BC - Athenians invade eastern Sicily, defeated by Syracusans in 413.

410-405 BC - Carthaginians invade western Sicily, destroying Himera in 409, establish permanent military presence at Zis (Palermo). Wars between Carthaginians and Greeks (and subsequently with Romans) continue.

409 BC - Birth of Dion, later *Tyrant* (leader) of Syracuse.

405-367 BC - Dionysius I rules as Tyrant of Syracuse

398-396 BC - Another war of some Greek cities against Carthaginians.

398 BC - Plato in Syracuse; suggests Sicily as model of utopian society. Syracuse has emerged as Sicily's most important city and will remain so until the 10th century when Arabs and Berbers repopulate Panormos as *Bal'harm* (Palermo).

392 BC - Dionysius I makes peace with Carthaginians.

367-344 BC - Dionysius II is leader of Syracuse. Philip II rules Macedonia 359-336.

346-341 BC - Another Carthaginian war in Sicily. Alexander the Great rules Macedonia 336-323.

339 BC - Timoleon restores democratic law in Syracuse.

330 BC - Alexander the Great conquers Persia.

317-289 BC - Agathocles, native of Himera, Tyrant of Syracuse and then (from 304) king.

311 and 280 BC - Carthaginian invasions of western Sicily.

310 BC - Greeks under Agathocles invade Carthaginian territories of African coast. Treaty signed in 306 establishes Halycos (Platani) river as boundary in Sicily.

288 BC - Mamertines occupy Messina.

278 BC - Pyrrhus of Epirus fights "Sicilian Campaign" against Syracuse supported by Taormina, seeks to unite Sicily's Greeks.

Roman Period

265-215 BC (BCE) - Hieron II king of Syracuse. His death signals beginning of Roman control of Sicily.

264 BC (BCE) - First Punic War (Romans against Carthaginians), ending in 241. Second Punic War in 218, ending in 201.

261 BC (BCE) - Romans take Akragas (Agrigento) from Carthaginians.

254 BC (BCE) - Panormos (Palermo) falls to Romans.

241 BC (BCE) - Lilybaeum (Marsala), Drepanum (Trapani) and Eryx (Erice) fall to Romans.

227 BC (BCE) - Sicily becomes first Roman province but Syracuse resists annexation.

218 BC (BCE) - Carthaginian leader Hannibal invades Italy during Second Punic War.

212 BC (BCE) - Syracuse finally falls to Romans; Archimedes is killed.

208 BC (BCE) - Qin dynasty begins construction of Great Wall in China.

146 BC (BCE) - Romans defeat Carthaginians in Third Punic War, which began three years earlier. Romans rename *Panormos* Latin *Panormus*. Earliest continuous Jewish communities in eastern Sicily.

136-132 BC (BCE) - Slave revolt led by Eunus with base at Enna. Slaves conquer large area before defeat by Roman legions.

104-100 BC (BCE) - Slave revolt led by Salvius (Triphon).

70 BC (BCE) - Cicero prosecutes Verres, corrupt Governor of Sicily.

55 BC (BCE) - First invasions of Britain by Julius Caesar.

29 BC (BCE) - Virgil begins writing Aeneid.

23 BC (BCE) (circa) - Diodorus Siculus, historian, dies.

6 BC (BCE) (circa) - Birth of Jesus.

AD (CE) 14 - Death of Augustus. Established *Pax Romana* lasting until AD (CE) 180. In Augustus' time Romans establish maritime trade with southern India.

AD (CE) 31 - Octavian (Augustus) rules Rome alone following Battle of Actium.

AD (CE) 33 (circa) - Death of Jesus.

AD (CE) 59 (circa) - Paul of Tarsus preaches in Syracuse *en route* to Rome, possibly at site of Saint Marcian's Crypt.

AD (CE) 117 - Under Trajan the Roman Empire reaches its greatest geographic extent around this time.

AD (CE) 122 - Roman Emperor Hadrian orders construction of his wall in what is now Scotland.

AD (CE) 166 - A Roman embassy of Marcus Aurelius said to have reached China.

AD (CE) 251 - Saint Agatha martyred; later venerated as patroness of Catania.

AD (CE) 301 - Armenia makes Christianity its official religion.

AD (CE) 303-306 - Diocletian's persecution of Christians. Saint Lucy (of Syracuse) martyred.

AD (CE) 306 - Constantine the Great rules until 337.

AD (CE) 313 - Constantine's "Edict of Milan" permits open practice of Christianity.

AD (CE) 324 - Imperial city of Constantinople (Byzantium) founded on site of older settlement.

AD (CE) 325 - Council of Nicea defines Christian canon and doctrine, condemns Arianism as heresy. By now Syracuse is Christianized.

AD (CE) 330 - Capital of Roman Empire transferred to Byzantium (Constantinople). *Codex Sinaiticus* written; it is the most complete, earliest surviving copy of the Gospels, as opposed to fragments. *Codex Vaticanus* dates from the same period.

AD (CE) 378 - Roman army defeated at Battle of Adrianople, now Edirne in European Turkey. (Goths had been forced into Roman territory by the invading Huns.)

AD (CE) 380 - Christianity official religion of Roman Empire.

AD (CE) 395 - Following death of Theodosius I, Roman Empire definitively splits into Western ("Latin") and Eastern ("Byzantine") administrations. Sicily begins in West but will vacillate between the two.

AD (CE) 402 - Capital of Western Empire established at Ravenna.

Vandalic-Gothic Period

406 - Vandals, Sueves, Burgundians and other tribes cross the Rhine. "Great Invasion" has begun.

410 - Visigothic sack of Rome (no longer the capital) under Alaric; political fall of Western Roman Empire begins.

429 - Vandals under Genseric (Gaiseric) invade Roman province of Africa, within striking distance of Sicily.

440 - Vandal invasion leads to mass raids in western Sicily. Their advance is halted by Byzantines in 441.

452 - Huns led by Attila invade northern Italy.

455 - Vandals sack Rome.

461 - Vandals return to Sicily in long series of raids.

468 - Complete Vandalic occupation of Sicily, lasts until 491.

476 - Odoacer, probably German, deposes Romulus Augustulus, last (western) Roman Emperor. Beginning of Middle Ages usually dated from this time. Genseric, ruler of Sicily and Tunisia, concludes "perpetual" peace with Constantinople.

491 - Ostrogoths achieve complete control of Sicily, ousting Vandals. Their leader, Theodoric, kills Odoacer in 493.

506 - Alaric II, King of the Visigoths (in Spain), issues *Lex Romana Visigothorum* or *Breviarium* of Roman law.

507 - Franks conquer Visigothic lands in France.

Byzantine Period

527-565 - Rule of Justinian I as Eastern Roman ("Byzantine") Emperor. With *Corpus Juris Civilis* (popularly the "Code of Justinian"), *Epitome Juliani* and other issuances, establishes lasting legal code through gradual implementation in localized forms.

529 - Saint Benedict founds religious order. Code of Justinian (see above).

530-532 - Ostrogoths in central Mediterranean under attack by Byzantines.

533-535 - Byzantines under Belisarius defeat Vandals (in Tunisia) and Ostrogoths (in Sicily) and annex Sicily to Byzantine Empire. Gothic rule of Sicily ends except for brief incursion and occupation of some localities in 550 (see below).

537 - Saint Sophia Basilica built in Constantinople; world's largest church epitomizes Byzantine culture.

540 - Byzantines occupy Ravenna. Persians invade Syria and sack Antioch.

541-543 - Plague of Justinian. Pandemic of bubonic plague decimates population of Byzantine Empire in Balkan provinces and Asia Minor, diminishing Byzantine military capacity for decades.

550 - Totila, Ostrogoth leader, lands in Sicily but Byzantines reclaim control following his defeat at Taginae in 552.

568 - Longobards invade peninsular Italy, contesting Byzantine control of many regions.

570 - Birth of Mohammed, founder of Islam as Prophet.

582 - Avars and Slavs invade Balkans following fall of Sirmium. The stirrup is introduced in Europe, facilitating more efficient mounted warfare.

590 - Gregory the Great becomes Bishop of Rome (Pope).

603 - Byzantines and Lombards reach truce in Italy.

620 - Heraclius becomes Emperor of Byzantine Empire until 641. Re-establishes Greek as official language, repels invading Sassanids of Persia in 627.

622 - Mohammed reaches Medina. Muslim era begins.

632 - Death of Mohammed.

637 - Arab forces defeat Persians.

638 - Jerusalem falls to Arabs.

642 - Arabs conquer Alexandria.

643 - Lombard legal code issued by Rothari.

652 - Small Arab force lands in Sicily but soon departs.

654 - King Recceswinth of the Visigoths issues legal code with *Liber Judiciorum,* largely replacing Alaric's legal principles codified in 506 with new ones patterned more closely on Roman civil (statutory) law.

655 - Jews of Syracuse begin construction of their large mikveh around this date.

660-668 - Constans II rules Byzantine Empire from Syracuse. Launches failed attempt to reconquer peninsular Italy from the Longobards (Lombards).

661 - Umayyad caliphate established in Damascus.

670 - Arabs conquer most of Tunisia and Libya, establishing Islamic province of Ifriqiya.

672 - Lombards Christianized.

698 - Arabs conquer Carthage and environs.

711 - Arabs invade Spain. Island of Pantelleria annexed to Ifriqiya around this time. Arab raids on Sicilian coasts until 734.

726-787 - Iconoclast Controversy.

727-743 - Lombards attack Byzantine territories in peninsular Italy.

732 - Charles Martel defeats Arab force at Tours.

740 - Arabs briefly occupy Syracuse but must return to Tunisia to quell Berber revolt. Byzantines defeat Arabs at Akroinon in Anatolia.

750 - Abbasids seize Tunisia and Libya from Umayyads of Damascus.

752 - Arabs attack Syracuse.

762 - Abbasid caliphate establishes Baghdad as capital.

768 - Local Muhallabids rule Ifriqiya under Abbasids until 793.

771 - Charlemagne becomes King of the Franks.

774 - Charlemagne occupies Lombard lands in northern Italy.

797 - Following rebellions against the Muhallabids, general Ibrahim ibn al-Aghlab restores order in Ifriqiya.

800 - Abbasid Caliph Harun al-Rashid grants Ifriqiya to Ibrahim ibn al-Aghlab as a hereditary emir, establishing Aghlabid dynasty. Aghlabids are Sunnis who introduce principles of Maliki law.

826 - Euphemius, general in Sicily disgruntled with Byzantine Emperor Michael II, offers control of Sicily to Aghlabids in return for political asylum.

Aghlabid Period

827 - First major Arab-Berber incursion (over 10,000 men sailing from Tunisia, including some Persians) arrives in July under Asad ibn al-Furat, general of Aghlabid Emir Ziyadat Allah I ibn Ibrahim of Ifriqiya. Mazara is occupied.

831 - In September Bal'harm (Palermo) is conquered by Aghlabids following a year-long siege. Island administered by governors.

831-838 - Continued rule of much of Sicily by Ziyadat Allah I, who sponsored al-Furat's invasion in 827.

838-841 - Rule of al-Aghlab Abu Affan ibn Ibrahim ("Abu Iqal"), brother of Ziyadat Allah I.

840 - Norsemen (Vikings) found Dublin.

841-856 - Rule of Mohammed I Abul-Abbas ibn al-Aghlab Abi Affan.

851 - Death of Governor (and General) Al-Aghlab Abu Ibrahim, who administered most of Sicily from Bal'harm

856-863 - Rule of Ahmad ibn Mohammed. Occasional Norse landings or raids on Sicilian coasts.

859 - Enna (Kasr'Janni) captured by Abbas ibn Fadhl, Governor of Sicily.

863 - Rule of Ziyadat Allah II ibn Abil-Abbas. During 9th century Arabs introduce mulberries (for silk making), oranges, rice, sugar cane and other crops, and superior irrigation systems.

863-875 - Rule of Mohammed II ibn Ahmad.

875-902 - Rule of Ibrahim II ibn Ahmad.

876 - Byzantines begin series of reconquests of Apulia, Basilicata and Calabria.

878 - Jafar ibn-Mohammed conquers Syracuse, Byzantine capital of Sicily.

881 - *Codex Vigilanus* compiled in Spain, uses Hindu-Arabic numerals.

902 - Taormina falls to Arabs.

902-903 - Rule of Abdullah II ibn Ibrahim. By now Arab Bal'harm (Palermo) has supplanted Byzantine Syracuse as Sicily's most populous and important city and all of Sicily is under Arab administration.

903-909 - Rule of Ziyadat Allah III ibn Abdillah. Aghlabid rule as independent dynasty ends in 909.

909 - Norse leader Rollo granted lands in Normandy by Charles the Simple, founding Duchy of Normandy.

Fatimid Period

910 - Fatimids now rule Sicily and major Berber revolts begin against this dynasty. Cluniacs founded, follow Benedictine Rule.

913 - Emir Ahmed ibn-Kohrob declares independence of Sicily, evicting Fatimid governor from Bal'harm, but troops of Fatimid ruler, Abdul'Allah al-Mahdi Billah (Said ibn Husayn), restore the island to their dominion.

915 - Arab troops defeated at mouth of Garigliano River south of Rome by forces of Pope, Lombards and Byzantines.

934 - Death of Abdul'Allah al-Mahdi Billah (Said ibn Husayn), succeeded by the Governor Khalid bin Ishaq, acting as Emir.

937 - Construction of large mosque, citadel and palaces begins in Palermo's coastal Khalesa district (now the Kalsa).

938 - Last in a series of violent, anti-Fatimid revolts by the Berbers of southwestern Sicily suppressed at Agrigento.

941 - Rus-Byzantine War.

Kalbid Period (under Fatimids)

948 - Fatimids (who decide to move their capital) entrust Sicily to local Kalbids, who, like the Fatimids, are Shiites. Emirate of Sicily founded despite rivalry among Sicily's local emirs.

948-954 - Rule of Emir Hassan al-Kalbi, appointed by Fatimid Caliph Ismail al-Mansur. First *kanats* built under Palermo.

954-969 - Rule of Ahmad ibn al-Hassan al-Muizziyya.

963-965 - Rometta, populated by Byzantines, besieged by Arab forces, capitulates.

967 - Sicilian-born Jawhar al-Siqilli founds Al-Qahira (Cairo) in name of Fatimids.

969-982 - Rule of Abu al-Qasim Ali ibn-Hasan, killed at Battle of Crotone (see below).

972 - Mohammed ibn Hawqal visits Sicily. Observes paper making.

982 - Arab forces defeat an army of Holy Roman Emperor Otto II at Crotone in Calabria but retreat to Sicily. Emir Abu al-Qasim is killed. Byzantines join with Arabs to oust Imperial forces from Apulia.

982-983 - Rule of Jabir ibn Ali al-Kalbi.

983-985 - Rule of Jafar ibn Mohammed al-Kalbi.

985-990 - Rule of Abdallah ibn Mohammed al-Kalbi.

990-998 - Rule of Yusuf al-Kalbi.

998-1019 - Rule of Ja'far al-Kalbi. Construction of Favara palace in Palermo attributed to this Emir.

1000 - Approximate period of Norse landings in North America, possibly with Christianized leader Leif Ericsson. L'Anse aux Meadows in Newfoundland is a Norse settlement and both the *Groenlendinga Saga* (the Greenlanders' Saga) and *Eiriks Saga* (Erik's Story) mention such sea travels. Normans are residual Norse civilisation in northwestern France.

1016 - Norman knights first participate in battles in Italy. First Turkish raids in Armenia.

1019-1037 - Rule of Ahmed al-Akhal.

1037-1040 - Rule by Abdallah Abu Hafs, usurper.

1038-1042 - Byzantine forces of George Maniakes briefly occupy parts of eastern Sicily; army includes Greeks, Normans, Lombards and Norse Varangian Guard under Harald Hardrada.

1040 - Rule of Hasan as-Samsam begins.

1044 - Island divided into four qadits. Rivalry among emirs worsens.

1053 - Following death of Hasan as-Samsam and extinction of Kalbid dynasty, three important emirs divide control of Sicily: Ibn al Hawas at Kasr'Janni (Enna), Ibn at Timnah at Syracuse and Catania, Abdullah ibn Hawqal at Trapani and Mazara.

1054 - Great Schism between eastern and western Christianity. Sicilian Christians initially remain "eastern" (Orthodox).

1056 - Arab poet ibn Hamdis born at Noto; leaves Sicily in 1078.

Norman Period

1060 - Unsuccessful Norman attack in coastal northeastern Sicily.

1061 - Battle of Messina. City and parts of Nebrodi and Peloritan region occupied; permanent Norman presence.

1066 - Battle of Hastings leads to complete Norman conquest of Saxon England. Battle of Messina forms partial pattern of this invasion of an island from a continent; some Norman knights fight at both battles. Norman culture influences English government, law, architecture and language.

1071 - Byzantines lose Battle of Manzikert to Seljuk Turks. Normans attack Palermo; Norman invaders are led by Robert de Hauteville, Arab defenders by Ayub ibn Temim.

1072 - Battle of Palermo ends in early January with Norman occupation under Roger and Robert de Hauteville. Greek Orthodox Bishop Nicodemus removed from authority over Christian community. "Latin" Benedictines soon introduced in Sicily, where previously all monasteries were Orthodox.

1081 - Suppression of revolt led by renegade "emir" Bernavert (Bin al Wardi) at Catania; another of his revolts is suppressed at Syracuse in 1085.

1083 - Roger I appoints Latin (rather than Orthodox) Bishop of Palermo and Gallican Rite is introduced in new churches.

1084 - Bruno founds Carthusian Order in Germany.

1087 - Ibn Hammud, Emir of Kasr'Janni (Enna), last major Arab stronghold, surrenders to Normans in 1087; Noto falls in 1091. Dozens of fortified Arab-founded (or repopulated) towns dot the island: Calascibetta, Caltanissetta, Caltagirone, Mussomeli, Marsala (Mars'Allah), Misilmeri, Cammarata, others.

1095 - Roger II, future King of Sicily, is born.

1096 - First Crusade begins; some Norman knights participate under Bohemond de Hauteville (later Prince of Antioch), brother of Roger I.

1097 - Odo of Bayeux, Earl of Kent, younger brother of William the Conqueror, King of England, dies in Palermo *en route* to the Crusade while visiting Roger I. His nephew, William's son Robert "Curthose," continues on to Palestine.

1098 - Roger I, as Great Count of Sicily, becomes Papal Apostolic Legate, with rights to approve island's Catholic bishops. Cistercians, founded as offshoot of Benedictines, begin to establish monasteries in Sicily.

1099 - Crusaders conquer Jerusalem.

1101 - Roger I dies, succeeded by Simon, his eldest living, legitimate son, who is still a minor. Roger's consort, Adelaide del Vasto of Savona, is regent.

1105 - Roger II succeeds his elder brother Simon (1093-1105) as ruler of Sicily under Adelaide's regency.

1112 - Roger is knighted (this ceremony marks his age of majority and sovereign authority following "regency" under his mother).

1113 - Order of Saint John (Knights Hospitaller) based in Palestine chartered by Pope Paschal II. Establish commanderies in Sicily and later (in 1530) receive Malta from Charles V, King of Sicily and Holy Roman Emperor. (They remain there as Knights of Malta until 1798.)

1119 - Knights Templar founded in Palestine. Preceptories in Sicily confiscated by Frederick II following Sixth Crusade. (Order suppressed definitively by Papacy in 1312.)

1123 - First Lateran Council forbids Roman Catholic clerics wives or concubines; until now Catholic priests were permitted to marry before ordination. Knights of Saint Lazarus founded in Palestine around this time; order aids lepers and eventually operates Saint John of the Lepers, Palermo, as lazar-house.

1130 - Roger crowned first King of Sicily (known henceforth as "Roger II"). On his orders Saint John of the Hermits, an Orthodox monastery in Palermo, is ordered rebuilt in Norman-Arab style as Benedictine abbey, completed in 1148. (Site may have housed a mosque for several decades prior to 1072.) Palatine Chapel rebuilt to present form during this period.

1139 - Second Lateran Council makes celibacy mandatory for Roman Catholic priests, reiterating a canon established in 1123 but not widely enforced.

1140 - Roger promulgates Assizes of Ariano, important legal code asserting royal authority. Gothic architectural movement begins in France but Romanesque style dominates in Sicily.

1143 - Martorana church (Palermo) built in Norman-Arab style for Greek Orthodox community by George of Antioch. In this year Nilos Doxopatrios, an Orthodox cleric of Palermo, authors a theological treatise supporting the Eastern (Orthodox) Church over the Latin (Roman Catholic) influences introduced by the Normans.

1147 - Second Crusade begins but participation by Sicilian knights is very limited.

1154 - *Book of Roger* completed by court geographer Abdullah al Idrisi. Roger dies and reign of King William I "the Bad" begins.

1155 - Frederick Barbarossa crowned Holy Roman Emperor.

1158 - Qaid al Brun (Thomas Brown), treasurer at William's court, returns to England to reform exchequer of Henry II, thus influencing European accounting principles. Brown uses Hindu-Arabic numerals, later popularized in Christian Europe by Leonardo Fibonacci of Pisa (briefly a guest of young Frederick II in Sicily) in 1202.

1161 - Matthew Bonellus of Caccamo leads revolt of Norman barons. He is killed in the same year.

1166 - Reign of young King William II "the Good" begins under his mother's regency. Queen Margaret gives hospitality to exiled kin of Thomas Becket. Gradual Latinization of Sicilian language continues; Roman Catholic influence predominates in Christianity.

1170 - Benjamin of Tudela visits Sicily. Peter Waldo establishes evangelical Waldensian church, precursor of Reform (Protestant) movement.

1171 - Saladin defeats Fatimids in Middle East.

1174 - Work begins on Monreale Abbey in Arab village of Bal'at overlooking Palermo. Style is Norman-Arab on Romanesque plan with Byzantine mosaic icons, including earliest holy image of Thomas Becket (canonized in 1173).

1177 - William II marries Joan, daughter of Henry II of England (sister of Richard Lionheart).

1184 - Bin Jubayr visits Sicily and records his impressions.

1187 - Saladin captures Jerusalem.

1190 - Richard Lionheart, brother of Queen Joan of Sicily, occupies Messina with Philip II of France for several months *en route* to Crusade.

1193 - Death of Saladin.

Swabian Period

1194 - Holy Roman Emperor Henry VI von Hohenstaufen arrives. Teutonic Order of knights, accompanies him, establishing Saint Mary of the Germans (Messina) and obtaining Cistercian properties (the Magione in Palermo).

1198 - Frederick II, son of Henry, is king until 1250, weds Constance of Aragon. Swabian German influences in Sicily. Islam and Greek Orthodoxy permitted but practiced by ever-diminishing minorities. Emergent Sicilian language is Italic with Arabic and Greek influences.

1204 - Crusaders sack Constantinople during Fourth Crusade.

1206 - Mongols unite under Genghis Khan (Temujin), who conquers large parts of Eurasia. Later corresponds with Frederick II.

1210 - Francis of Assisi meets Pope Innocent III; founds Order of Friars Minor (Franciscans). Albigensian Crusades begin.

1212 - Frederick II reaches age of majority.

1215 - *Magna Carta* in England. Dominic of Osma (of Caleruega, Spain) founds Order of Preachers (Dominicans or "Blackfriars"), confirmed by Papacy in 1216. By 1500 this is the leading monastic and teaching order in Sicily, supportive of the Inquisition.

1217 - Cleric, translator and scientist Michael Scot (born 1175) translates *On the Sphere* by the Arab astronomer Al-Bitruji (or Alpetragius, who died circa 1204). Fifth Crusade begins.

1221 - University of Naples founded by Frederick II.

1223 - Following execution of Arab rebel leader Morabit (in 1222), thousands of Arabs from Iato area, who had revolted with their leader Ibn Abbad (or Benaveth), are deported to Lucera in Apulia. Many Muslims have already converted to Catholicism. Jews from occupied Jerba (in Tunisia) invited to Sicily.

1226 - Frederick II summons Imperial Diet of Cremona.

1229 - Frederick II, accompanied by Saracen guards and Sicilian and German knights, goes on Sixth Crusade as King of Jerusalem. Signs peace with Muslims without war.

1230 - Upon his return from Jerusalem Frederick suppresses Templar preceptories in Sicily.

1231 - Constitutions of Melfi become legal code for Kingdom of Sicily under Frederick II.

1233 - Cathars of France persecuted as heretics by first Inquisition.

1240 - Ciullo of Alcamo composes poetry in Sicilian language. First of a series of revolts by Sicilian Arabs, including some Christian converts, but Frederick retains trusted Saracen guards and court officers.

1244 - Fall of Jerusalem to Muslim forces.

1248 - Crusade to Egypt by Louis IX of France.

1250 - Death of Frederick II.

1254 - Death of Conrad IV Hohenstaufen.

1258 - Baghdad falls to Mongols.

Angevin Period

1266 - Charles of Anjou (brother of Louis IX of France) becomes king of Naples and Sicily following defeat of Manfred Hohenstaufen, natural son of Frederick II, at Battle of Benevento. Young Conradin, a (legitimate) grandson of Frederick II and last Swabian claimant, is executed in 1268 following Battle of Tagliacozzo. Hohenstaufen Imperial line now extinct. Angevin period begins. It is thought that by now all of Sicily's remaining Muslims have converted to Catholicism. The multicultural golden age is ending.

1270 - Funeral of Louis IX of France at Monreale, where his heart is preserved; canonized as Saint Louis in 1297.

1273 - Rudolf of Hapsburg becomes king in Germany; his dynasty will succeed Hohenstaufens as Holy Roman Emperors.

Aragonese Period

1282 - Vespers revolt expels Angevin French and makes Peter of Aragon King of Sicily. Neapolitan invasion of Constantinople is aborted as military resources must be diverted to Sicily.

1285 - Deaths of Charles I of Anjou and Peter III of Aragon, succeeded by their sons.

1302 - Peace of Caltabellotta treaty signed between Aragonese and

Angevins. By now, Sicily is essentially monocultural and mostly Roman Catholic. Over the next few generations general literacy diminishes.

1307 - Templars suppressed by King Philip IV "the Fair" of France but the estates of this order had already been confiscated in Sicily by Frederick II, ending its presence on the island.

1309-1377 - Avignon Papacy; Papal court in France. Western Schism follows from 1378 until 1417.

1321 - Dante Aligheri's *Inferno* (part of his *Divine Comedy*) mentions several Popes, Frederick II and Frederick's chancellor Pietro della Vigna (1190-1249).

1337 - Hundred Years' War begins between England and France; English invade France in 1346. (This was actually a series of conflicts rather than a single war.)

1347 - Ships arriving at Messina from eastern Mediterranean bring bubonic plague ("Black Death") to Europe, killing some 20 million Europeans.

1353 - Giovanni Boccaccio's *Decameron* mentions Palermo's Cuba palace and King William II of Sicily.

1361 - A second wave of bubonic plague in Europe.

1377 - Chaos following death of King Frederick "the Simple" until arrival of his dynastic successor King Martin continues until 1392. Chiaramonte, Alagona, Peralta and Ventimiglia families (the "Four Vicars") usurp royal authority, sparking a feudal "civil war." Andrew Chiaramonte is eventually beheaded.

1380 - Tatars defeated at Kulikovo by Russians commanded by Dimitri Donskoy (who completed construction of the Kremlin in 1367).

1397 - Sweden, Denmark and Norway united by Treaty of Kalmar until 1523.

1412 - House of Aragon succeeded by Trastámara dynasty of Castile based on Compromise of Ceuta.

1415 - Battle of Agincourt results in English victory.

1416 - Alfonso V "the Magnanimous" crowned King of Aragon, Sicily, later (1442) Naples, establishing diplomatic relations with burgeoning Ethiopian Empire and becoming important patron of the Renaissance.

1447 - Johannes Gutenberg invents printing press using movable type; prints Bible in 1455. (Rudimentary printing plates were developed earlier in China but this publication marks beginning of mass publication.)

1453 - End of Hundred Years' War. Constantinople falls to Ottomans. Conclusion of Middle Ages usually dated to this year, but sometimes to 1492 or 1500. Renaissance has begun. Sicilian-born painter Antonello da Messina is part of this new movement.

1466 - Francesco Laurana, Renaissance sculptor, establishes workshop in Palermo.

1474 - Massacre of over 300 Jews at Modica who refused to pray in a Catholic church.

Spanish Period

1478 - Spanish Inquisition begins; in Sicily it lasts until 1782.

1492 - Edict against Jews (the "Alhambra Decree") forces widespread conversions and some emigrations in 1493. Albanian refugees arrive following Turkish invasions of Balkans. Spanish rule continues in Sicily until 1700s. Columbus lands in America, initiating European colonization.

1497 - Tribunal of the Inquisition formally instituted in Palermo to try "heretics."

1516 - Holy Roman Emperor Charles V, King of Spain and ruler of much of western Europe, becomes King of Sicily. To guard against pirate raids and Ottoman attacks, he grants administration and governance of Malta and Gozo to the Order of Saint John in 1530 without ceding sovereignty; knights render annual feudal tribute of a falcon until expulsion by the French in 1798. Charles von Hapsburg (1500-1558) is figuratively said by historians to be Europe's last "medieval" monarch.

APPENDIX 2

Reading List

"One glance at a book and you hear the voice of another person, perhaps someone dead for a thousand years. To read is to voyage through time."

— Carl Sagan

This list is recommended to anybody seeking a greater knowledge of Sicily's peoples, history and culture from ancient times into the medieval period. The books by Norwich, Abulafia and Runciman are defining works in this field and are highly recommended. The histories by Matthew, Houben and Fuhrmann are detailed but readable textbooks consulted by Oxbridge scholars. In addition to these, a number of medieval source works have been published, some in English or Italian translation from the original language, for example those of Idrisi, bin Jubayr and Godfrey Malaterra.

General

A History of Sicily. (1986) Moses Finley, Christopher Duggan, Denis Mack Smith. Originally published in two volumes in 1968, this remains one of the better general histories of Sicily to appear in English even if a few of its conclusions have been disproved by subsequent research. The two-volume edition separates the flow of history at 1713.

The Middle Sea: A History of the Mediterranean. (2007) John Julius Norwich. Great context for understanding the role of the island at the center of this Sea.

The Great Sea: A Human History of the Mediterranean. (2011) David Abulafia. With Norwich's book (above), unsurpassed for placing Sicily into its Mediterranean and global context.

Antiquity

Sicily Before History: An Archaeological Survey from the Palaeolithic to the Iron Age. (1999) Robert Leighton. Charts the development of Sicily's early cultures from the Paleolithic onward, concluding with an account of the indigenous society at the time of Greek and Phoenician settlement.

Phoenician Secrets: Exploring the Ancient Mediterranean. (2011) Sanford Holst. A pragmatic introduction to this unique civilization and its extensive influences on many societies, including an early presence in Sicily.

Archaeology of Ancient Sicily. (1991, 2000) R. Ross Holloway. A sober, professorial yet readable guide to complement travel books and general histories.

A History of Ancient Greece in Its Mediterranean Context. (2012) Nancy Demand. A highly informative work for understanding Sicily's role in the wider Greek world of antiquity.

Carthage Must Be Destroyed: The Rise and Fall of an Ancient Civilization. (2010) Richard Miles. For centuries, the Phoenicians and their descendants the Carthaginians ruled half of Sicily, a region contested by Greeks and then Romans. Here is the story of the conflict that changed the course of ancient Mediterranean history.

Syracuse: City of Legends. (2010) Jeremy Dummett. A fine examination of what until the ninth century was Sicily's most important city.

Middle Ages

A History of Islamic Sicily. (1975) Aziz Ahmad. Excellent overview of this topic, complementary to the works of Abulafia and Norwich.

Before the Normans: Southern Italy in the Ninth and Tenth Centuries. (1991) Barbara Kreutz. Its focus is peninsular Italy but information on Arab Sicily is also presented.

The Normans in the South (1967) and The Kingdom in the Sun (1970). John Julius Norwich. Originally published in two volumes, this is the best general history of Norman Sicily and was also published in 1992 as an omnibus edition, *The Normans in Sicily.* A good introduction to the following three books dealing with Norman Sicily.

Frederick II: A Medieval Emperor. (1992) David Abulafia. The definitive biography of Frederick II, King of Sicily, King of the Germans, King of Jerusalem, Holy Roman Emperor.

The Sicilian Vespers: A History of the Mediterranean World in the Later Thirteenth Century. (1958) Steven Runciman. The classic work on this period of Sicilian history and its impact on Europe and the Mediterranean for centuries to come. Runciman also wrote a monograph on the Great Schism (see below).

A Short History of Byzantium. (1998) John Julius Norwich. This is the condensed version of a highly recommended three-volume edition: *The Early Centuries* followed by *The Apogee* and *The Decline and Fall.*

The Eastern Schism: A Study of the Papacy and the Eastern Churches during the XIth and XIIth Centuries. (1955) Steven Runciman. A reasonably impartial introduction by a distinguished scholar who wasn't an apologist for either camp, Roman Catholic or Eastern Orthodox.

Orthodoxy and Catholicity. (1966) John Meyendorff. Offers a very good explanation of the differences between the two churches that resulted from the Great Schism of 1054. Unlike Runciman's book (above), this treatment confronts a few issues of the modern era.

The Arabs. (1976) Peter Mansfield. A fine introduction to the history, culture and society of the Arabs and their world.

Travels of Ibn Jubayr. (1952, 2008) Translated by Ronald Broadhurst. Chronicles the pilgrimage of this traveller across the Mediterranean, with a visit to Sicily.

Muslims and Christians in Norman Sicily: Arabic Speakers and the End of Islam. Alexander Metcalfe. (2011) Insightful study into a specific period, with clues to the Arabic influence on the Sicilian language, by a leading scholar.

Siculo Arabic. (1996) Dionisius Agius. An exhaustive study of the language spoken by Sicily's Arabs. A modern form of this tongue is Maltese.

Arabic Administration in Norman Sicily: The Royal Diwan. (2002) Jeremy Johns. A comprehensive examination of the institutions the Normans inherited and adapted from the Arabs. A fine work of scholarship.

The House of Wisdom: How the Arabs Transformed Western Civilization. (2009) Jonathan Lyons. The information reported is not new, but this is a fine presentation, with many references to Sicily.

The Oxford History of Medieval Europe. (1992) George Holmes. A superlative overview of medieval society, with much that is directly pertinent to Sicily.

The Penguin Historical Atlas of the Medieval World. (2005) Andrew Jotischky and Caroline Hull. In addition to great maps, a wealth of information presented in accessible narrative.

Chivalry. (1984) Maurice Keen. A defining work in the field of feudal knighthood and early feudalism, putting to rest many myths and misconceptions.

Mediaeval Feudalism. (1942) Carl Stephenson. A brief but eminently authoritative introduction to this subject, mentioning Norman Sicily.

The Birth of Nobility: Constructing the Aristocracy in England and France 900-1300. (2005) David Crouch. Complementary to Keen's book (above), offering a good background study for Sicilian feudalism under the Normans and Angevins.

William Marshall: Knighthood, War and Chivalry 1147-1219. (1990, 2002) David Crouch. Nothing comparable exists for any identifiable Sicilian knight, but the exploits of William in Norman England and France provide insight into what such a biography might resemble.

Roger II and the Creation of the Kingdom of Sicily. (2012) Graham Loud. Following its accessible introduction, this scholarly volume translates several medieval works into English and presents part of the rare *Catalogus Baronum*.

Roger II of Sicily: A Ruler between East and West. (2002) Hubert Houben. First published in German in 1997, this is an informative biography and a long glance into Roger's reign.

The Norman Kingdom of Sicily. (1992) Donald Matthew. A superb, scholarly overview of the Normans' multicultural Italian kingdom and its polyglot institutions.

The Two Italies: Economic relations between the Norman Kingdom of Sicily and the Northern Communes. (1977) David Abulafia. A fine study of this subject.

The Normans: Warrior Knights and their Castles. (2006) Christopher Gravett and David Nicolle. A general introduction, richly illustrated, featuring information on the Normans in England, France, Sicily and elsewhere.

Henry Plantagenet. (1964) Richard Barber. An excellent work to consult regarding Henry II of England and his times. His system of common law, his children and his onetime friend Thomas Becket are mentioned in the preceding pages.

Germany in the High Middle Ages 1050-1200. (1986) Horst Fuhrmann. A very good background history for those interested in Frederick II and the Hohenstaufen dynasty.

The Monks of War: The Military Religious Orders. (1995) Desmond Seward. A comprehensive introduction to the orders of knighthood present in Sicily in the Middle Ages: Templars, Hospitallers (Knights of Malta), Teutonic Knights.

Four Queens: The Provençal Sisters Who Ruled Europe. (2008) Nancy Goldstone. Concentrates on the period considered by Runciman's *Sicilian Vespers* (above).

The Former Jews of this Kingdom: Sicilian Converts After the Expulsion 1492-1516. (2003) Nadia Zeldes. The definitive work on the fate of Sicily's Jewish population from the last decades of the Middle Ages into the early years of the sixteenth century.

The Kingdom of Sicily 1100-1250: A Literary History. (2005) Karla Mallette. Excellent survey of the literature of this period, with translations and insightful analysis.

Vanished Kingdoms. (2012) Norman Davies. The chapter on the Aragonese Empire is relevant to Sicily, the one on Byzantium equally so.

Travels with a Medieval Queen. (2001) Mary Taylor Simeti. A fine "contextual" biography tracing the geographical and emotional travels of Constance Hauteville, daughter of Roger II and mother of Frederick II.

Women of Sicily: Saints, Queens and Rebels. (2013) Jacqueline Alio. Profiles of ten women, mostly from the ancient and medieval periods.

Genealogy and Heraldry

Sicilian Genealogy and Heraldry. (2013) Louis Mendola. A detailed guide and reference work covering resources for the family historian. Chapters are dedicated to genealogical records, feudalism, rural life, genetics, Jewish families and other relevant topics.

Heraldry of the Royal Families of Europe. (1988) Jiri Louda and Michael Maclagan. This is the "go to" reference for the coats of arms and, more importantly, the pedigrees of the European reigning families since the Middle Ages. The sections on the kingdoms of Naples, Spain and the Holy Roman Empire are especially relevant to Sicily. The first (1988) edition is much more complete in that regard than the revised one published in 2002.

Cuisine

Pomp and Sustenance: Twenty Five Centuries of Sicilian Food. (1998) Mary Taylor Simeti. Republished in 2009, this is an excellent guide to Sicilian culinary history, with many fine recipes, by an author who has spent most of her adult life in Sicily.

Eat, Pray, Love. (2006) Elizabeth Gilbert. An interesting read, this diary dedicates very little space to Sicilian cuisine as such, with no recipes or background. Chapter 36 deals with the author's few days on the island, consisting of brief forays to Taormina, Siracusa and Palermo, something the film adaptation didn't depict.

APPENDIX 3

Places to Visit

"To have seen Italy without having seen Sicily is to not have seen Italy at all, for Sicily is the key to everything."

— Johann Wolfgang von Goethe, *Italienische Reise* 1816

Typically, a trip to Sicily is something undertaken after an initial Italian visit to Rome, Florence, and of course Venice. Most books and websites dealing generally with Italian culture, art and architecture all but ignore our island, but several good travel guides published since around 2000 are dedicated exclusively to Sicily. In recent decades the island in the sun has become a very popular destination, with frequent calls by cruise ships and direct flights from London and other European cities. Those traversing oceans to arrive may have to travel to Palermo or Catania via connecting flights from Rome (an hour) or Milan (twenty minutes longer).

Goethe, whose trip was more arduous, spent over a month in Sicily. Because few of today's visitors have that much time, it's important to know what each place offers. Here travel books and tourism websites are not always helpful because most are unduly influenced by the interests of tour operators and public travel bureaux, making it difficult to decide which things to see.

On the other hand, the *cognoscenti* realize, for example, that Segesta's archeological site is at least as interesting as Agrigento's, and it's only an hour from Palermo, with a stop at beautiful Erice possible during the same excursion. While hardcore archeology lovers may prefer to visit both Segesta and Agrigento, along with Mozia and Selinunte in the same western region, Segesta will usually suffice if time is limited.

Ancient sites are not the only places to fall prey to slanted tourism promotion; Palermo's medieval Saint Francis of Assisi church welcomes many visitors while the Magione (a few blocks away), a former commandery of the Teutonic Knights boasting a beautiful cloister, is largely ignored. Caccamo's castle seems to get more visitors than the equally salient fortress at Mussomeli.

Schedules are especially important in Sicily, where management of historical sites is haphazard. Morgantina is usually open during specific hours, while Iaitas, an Elymian-Punic site near San Giuseppe Jato, can be visited only with special permission.

Some places of interest to visitors have already been described in the preceding pages. There are sections on Monreale Abbey, the Palatine Chapel, the Magione and the Syracusan Mikveh, with mention (at the end of Chapter 6) of a few Byzantine churches off the beaten path in eastern Sicily. At Rometta there is a Byzantine church as well as Byzantine city walls.

The diversity of Sicily's landmarks reflects the diversity of its peoples. Here, arranged by locality (rather than architectural style) is a perfunctory listing of major historic sites relevant to specific periods. Some of these places have been inhabited continuously for close to three thousand years. Sicily boasts hundreds of significant ancient and medieval sites. Those that follow are prominent attractions open to the general public most of the time.

The majority of these can be identified with *several* civilizations. Most Roman sites, for example, are cities that were built upon earlier Greek or Punic settlements. Sicily is one of the few places in the world where one learns that a castle built in AD 1100 stands on the site of an ancient settlement founded in 1100 BC.

"It's a place of such ancient civilization that it makes Rome look like Dallas," is how Elizabeth Gilbert described Siracusa in *Eat, Pray, Love*.

A few generalities may be helpful. Taormina and Siracusa are Sicily's most popular resort towns, followed (distantly) by Cefalù and Erice. Each place is very different from the other three. Beyond these localities, a growing trend is *agriturismo,* accommodation on a working farm (travel writers have coined the term "guest farm").

While Catania and Messina are usually excluded from historical itineraries, no general visit to Sicily is complete without a day or two spent discovering Palermo's medieval treasures. The most impressive ancient archeological sites are without doubt those of Siracusa, Agrigento and Segesta. Sicily's largest amphitheatres are those at Taormina and Segesta. Open hours vary according to season, so it's important to check these before arriving.

Some towns address "niche" interests in art, literature or cinema. Caltagirone and Santo Stefano di Camastra are known for their artistic majolica, while Vizzini was the setting for Verga's *Cavalleria Rusticana* and *Mastro Don Gesualdo*. There are many religious and folk festivals. The Good Friday passion procession at Erice is the most suggestive event of its kind in Sicily, taking place along stone streets like those of ancient Jerusalem. Piazza Armerina's annual *palio* is an entertaining re-enactment of medieval pageantry.

Here the emphasis is history and culture, but of course Sicily offers beaches for sun worshippers and mountain trails for nature lovers, as well as endless opportunities for sampling the local cuisine.

When is the best time to visit? For those interested chiefly in culture, late Autumn through early Spring is without doubt the ideal time to see Sicily, while the crowded months from June through September are best avoided. July and August are torrid, with throngs of visitors arriving to enjoy the copious sunshine.

Architecture and Archeology

Agrigento: The Norman cathedral evokes little of its medieval past. The large archeological park outside town, with its magnificent standing temples, is what most attracts visitors. There is also a classical garden, the *Kolymbetra*. On the edge of the park, near the small archeology museum, stands medieval Saint Nicholas Church. Agrigento's site rivals those of Segesta and Siracusa for appeal.

Caccamo: The castle south of Termini Imerese is Norman and Swabian, built on a site fortified in ancient times and later developed by the Arabs. This is the quintessential Sicilian feudal fortress, once the stronghold of the disloyal Norman baron Matthew Bonellus, who plotted against King William I.

Catania: There are two Roman theatres in the center of town — the large complex in a main square and the smaller odeum. The castle of Frederick II was built along the sea but the shore was extended by lava flowing down from Etna centuries later. The cathedral's apse and a segment of its transept survive from the original Norman structure. This is Sicily's second largest city. Were it not for volcanic eruptions and earthquakes, there would be much more to see, but the ubiquitous Baroque architecture is interesting. There are two large street markets. Catania may not seem very orderly, but it is less noisy than Palermo.

Cefalà Diana: Built during the tenth century, the impressive baths are the largest purely Arab structure remaining in Sicily, and worth visiting for that reason alone. They are part of a complex that includes a feudal castle erected before 1300. (In contrast to the other attractions listed here, a visit to this one may necessitate advance reservation with the local *pro loco* or mayor's office.)

Cefalù: The main attraction is the Norman cathedral, patterned after Saint Etienne in Caen. Its cloister is reminiscent of Monreale's. The medieval Osteria Magno houses a small museum, and the tiny Church of Saint George, patron of knights, is also worth a visit. Atop the cliffs overlooking the town, reached by a series of steps, is the site of a ruined castle and some external walls. Here the Sicanian temple was largely rebuilt by Greeks. Despite claims by local historians, its Greek portal is not a megalithic *trilithon.* (Megalithic temples built by Sicilians long before this one are located on Malta and Gozo.)

Enna: Not much remains of the castle but the view from the rocky summit, named for Demeter, is spectacular. A valley below is where myth says that Persephone was abducted. In a local garden is a geometric tower from the reign of Frederick II that bears a striking resemblance to those of his Castel del Monte near Bari. This city, and Calascibetta nearby, were held directly by the king to keep an eye on the island's central region.

Erice: This town is located near Trapani on an isolated mountain sometimes covered in clouds even when the rest of western Sicily is sunny. There are Phoenician walls, traces of Elymian civilization and a castle, as well as winding streets of gray stone and a medieval church.

Malta: It's not Sicily, but this is the place to see Europe's oldest megalithic temples, built by Sicily's Proto Sicanians beginning around 4000 BC.

Messina: Like Catania, this city has been razed by earthquakes that have destroyed most of its historical treasures. Only a few original walls of the rebuilt Church of the Annunciation of the Catalans (initially Byzantine) and the Church of Saint Mary of the Germans (Romanesque Gothic) survive. The cathedral is essentially a reconstruction.

Milazzo: Most of the older parts of the seaside castle are Norman and Swabian. The site of ancient Mylae is outside the modern town.

Morgantina: Located outside Aidone (near Piazza Armerina), this is just one of many ancient sites in Sicily but it has a good museum (in town) and is usually open to the public. The Roman Morgantium was home to an important mint, and the museum collection includes ancient silverware made locally. The settlement is actually much older, having been inhabited by Greeks, who built its amphitheatre, and possibly Sikels before them. It was briefly Carthaginian before being conquered by the Romans during the Punic Wars.

Motya and Marsala: Known for its wine, Marsala bears some vestiges of Roman and Arab architecture, but the Phoenician harbor at Motya (Mozia), a coastal island, is the treasure that draws most history buffs. Founded as early as 800 BC, this is Sicily's most extensive Phoenician archeological site. Marsala's archeology museum houses what is probably the best surviving Carthaginian ship with its cargo.

Mussomeli: This castle outside a large town in the Sicanian Mountains is similar to Caccamo's, most of it built on a rocky butte during the fourteenth century upon an earlier Arab structure and a smaller Norman one. This site (like the Sutera monastery nearby) is strikingly similar to that of the Metéora monasteries near Kalambaka in Greece.

Noto: Here one can see the Sicilian Baroque, a style born during Sicily's long Spanish period.

Palermo and Monreale: In Palermo the Norman Palace (the Palatine Chapel and Phoenician site are described in Chapter 16), Cathedral, Martorana, Zisa and Cuba are open to the public. An outdoor Roman site is located in Piazza Vittoria, and there are some Punic necropoli near the Cuba with traces of Carthaginian walls around town. Saint John of the Hermits is usually open. Palazzo Steri, with its painted medieval ceiling, is a must-see for medievalists, and Palazzo Abatellis around the corner houses art treasures from the Middle Ages into the Renaissance. The Church of Saint Francis of Assisi dates from the Swabian era and the Magione Basilica belonged to the Teutonic Knights. The archeology museum in Piazza Olivella houses a good collection, including the Palermo Stone and interesting Punic and Arab objects as well as Greek ones. The street markets are worth a visit, and Ballarò stands on the site of a medieval souk. This singular city is rather chaotic, a diamond in the rough, something of a cross between Naples and Istanbul. In Palermo's unkempt historic district, with its labyrinth of streets, it's best to know precisely what you want to see and where it is located before setting out to find it. At Monreale the cathedral and cloister (Chapter 21) are the main attractions.

Piazza Armerina: The town has a medieval castle much altered over the centuries. The main attraction is the Roman Villa a few kilometers away. Here are the most extensive mosaic pavements to survive from any home built in the Roman Empire.

Ragusa: Like Noto, this city has many churches and palaces in the Sicilian Baroque style.

Segesta: Its Doric temple is one of the best preserved in the Greek world. The hilltop amphitheatre affords visitors a fantastic view and the archeological park is extensive. Ancient Egesta began its life as an Elymian city; Greek culture came later. This site competes with Agrigento for grandeur.

Selinunte: Like Gela (down the coast), an important Greek city, but lacking the complete standing temples of Segesta and Agrigento. Selinunte boasts a pristine, grassy park. Note that the segments of temples at Selinunte are actually reconstructions.

Siracusa: This was the greatest Greek city in Sicily. The vast archeological site outside town has an ancient amphitheatre and much more. The archeology museum is Sicily's best. Nearby, Saint Marcian's Crypt is thought to mark the place where Paul of Tarsus preached. In Ortygia is located the cathedral built around a Greek temple, the world's supreme example of this transitional ecclesiastical architecture and a perfect illustration of how early Christianity took the place of mythology. The mikveh (in the *Giudecca* quarter) and catacombs are worth a special visit. Coastal Maniace Castle is not always open but Arethusa's Spring is historic. Like Taormina, Cefalù and Erice, this is a charming district where many streets are closed to traffic.

Solunto: Founded by the Phoenicians and then annexed by Greeks and Romans, this was an important city guarding the coast, with Palermo visible to the west. The scenic archeological site on a mountain near Bagheria has a small museum.

Taormina: Sicily's most popular resort town sits atop a mountain overlooking the Ionian Sea. Ancient Tauromenion was a thriving Greek community, though the Sikels may have been the first settlers. The amphitheatre offers a stunning (and famous) view of Mount Etna and the coast. Roman and medieval walls enclose the old district. Squarish Palazzo Santo Stefano is just one Norman-era building still standing here. Parts of Palazzo Corvaja date from the Arab period. There are several medieval churches, including the *duomo* and (in the archway beneath the clock tower at the beginning of Corso Umberto) a Byzantine icon of the *Theotokos*. The views from Castelmola, above the main town, are worth the ascent. Near the coast, Naxos (in the Giardini district) was Sicily's first Greek settlement.

Termini Imerese: The Himera archeological site outside town has the foundations of a Greek temple. Parts of this, and other finds, are housed in the Palermo archeology museum. In Termini's civic museum are fragments of Fatimid buildings featuring Arabic script.

Landscapes

The Secret Sicily: Sicily's natural features are highly varied for a territory of its size. Mount Etna stands out (literally) among them. This is western Europe's greatest natural wonder and Sicily's highest mountain. Indeed, to the ancient Greeks it was a *sacred* mountain, and it has the longest recorded history of any volcano. Alcantara Gorge, a small canyon, was formed by one of Etna's streams. Some of Sicily's most beautiful areas were mentioned in Chapter 3. Here it is opportune to suggest two exceptional — and very different — scenic routes, one in the east and the other in the west. Sicily offers many such itineraries but these are pleasantly remote from large towns, suited to the tastes of either wildlife lovers or wine aficionados.

Nebrodi Mountains: The Nebrodi Mountains are the most lushly forested region of Sicily. Situated to the immediate north of Etna, the range has the island's highest peaks after the volcano itself and a few rocky mountains in the Madonie to the west. The unique Nebrodian appeal is its complete departure from any prevailing stereotype of "Mediterranean" landscapes. The visitor realizes that much of Sicily looked this way when the first Phoenicians, Greeks and Normans arrived, when there were fewer people in fewer towns. Our favorite drive is along the SS 289 from Cesarò high in the mountains northward to San Fratello and Sant'Agata Militello. With its high snowfall from late December into the middle of March, this region often looks more Swiss than "Sicilian." At 1,847 meters, Mount Soro is the loftiest summit in the Nebrodi. This region is home to the San Fratello horse and the boarish Nebrodian Black Swine.

Wine Country: Sicily's major grape-growing region covers a large patch of the western part of the island. Marsala is the commercial center of this scenic region. One can sample Sicilian wines at virtually any restaurant in Sicily, but the most suggestive viticultural landscapes are elusive. From Salemi, take the SS 188 to Marsala. Along this route one encounters little traffic but an endless array of gently rolling hills carpeted with vineyards as far as the eye can see. It's a magical place that rivals any viticultural region in the world in its serene dignity. It also boasts a more distinguished history than most. Domesticated grapes were cultivated here long before they were introduced into France or northern Italy. Coming from Palermo, Segesta is a convenient stop near Salemi.

Sources

"As this history is intended for the general reader —if he still exists outside the writer's imagination — such distracting paraphernalia as footnotes have been dispensed with as much as possible. The cult of the footnote, involving, at its apogee, a page crammed with encyclopaedic detail in small type to a solitary line of text, is no doubt a proof of diligence, but it may also be a tedious form of exhibitionism."

— Sir Harold Acton, *The Bourbons of Naples* 1956

A great *corpus* of information has been presented in various books over the last fifty years, and many of the facts reported in this one will be found in those given in the Reading List, where care has been taken to include only the most reliable works. Having already listed those titles, which themselves contain bibliographies full of useful resources, we won't repeat them here.

While such definitions necessarily reflect generalities, the preceding pages feature elements of both *social* and *political* histories, the latter represented in the historical outline and chronology.

Most of the facts in this book are contained in the plenteous histories published since 1800, themselves based on older publications in the public domain or original medieval records (see below). For better or worse, the overwhelming majority of recent histories about the remote past are "derivative" in some way. The dates of major battles and the reigns of monarchs, as well as the content of ancient codices and medieval chronicles, are all part of the vast body of public historical knowledge.

Many of the following medieval sources are available in Latin, Arabic or French, with recent editions published in translation. As we sometimes consulted more than one edition in more than one language, we have chosen to list those works generically rather than by the specific edition.

Some of these books are out of print, though they may have been digitized. In some cases distribution was limited and the publishing houses no longer exist, and this poses obvious problems for publications that are not yet in the public domain, even where the copyright holders are (or were) the authors themselves.

As we mentioned in the Introduction, footnotes were considered superfluous to the needs of most readers and to the *raison d'être* of this book.

However, the Reading List, in combination with these Sources, constitutes a syllabus sufficient for anybody seeking to learn more about medieval Sicily.

Much information presented in this book is readily available from various publications. The facts about Western religions, for example, are generally known, and accepted by most theologians and historians.

The best historical authors indulge the reader's desire for an *interesting* narrative — Nancy Goldstone is a good example — while adhering to the facts and citing sources. Where information is presented for the first time, your authors are adamant proponents of peer reviewed publication whenever possible, preferably in English in the United Kingdom or in the United States.

Classical

So numerous are books dealing with the ancient world of the Greeks and Romans that it would serve little purpose to list many here. For the benefit of classicists, we should note that the works of Diodorus Siculus, Philistus and Thucydides are especially pertinent to Sicily. These Greek historians, like some of their Roman counterparts, sometimes blurred the line between fact and myth. A good compendium of Greek mythology is *The Greek Myths* (published in 1955) by Robert Graves, but some readers may find Edith Hamilton's *Mythology* (1940) more engaging.

A primary contemporary source for the reign of Justinian in Constantinople and the Byzantine victories over the Ostrogoths and Vandals is the account of Procopius of Caesarea.

In recent years some historians have reconsidered the presumed time of arrival of the Phoenicians in Sicily, placing it at a date several decades earlier than previous estimations, but still after 800 BC. One should not overlook ongoing research on the three civilizations present in Sicily *before* the arrival of the Phoenicians and Greeks.

As regards these early peoples, *amphorae* excavated at Azor, in Israel, are similar to Sikelian exemplars found in Sicily, supporting the theory that there was Sikelian trade in the eastern Mediterranean. The Sikels are some-times, and only tentatively, identified with the Shikelish tribe of the "Sea Peoples" who attacked Egypt around 1220 BC, and a Shikelish village may have flourished about forty-five kilometers to the south of Azor at the Tel Zeror site. This is an area of research greatly advanced by the distinguished British archeologist Nancy K. Sandars, but none of the Sea Peoples theo-ries are conclusive or even very convincing.

One of the more persuasive arguments supporting an Anatolian origin for the Elymians is the similar script found on ceramic pottery dated to the same period at sites in both Sicily and Anatolia, which suggests, at the very least, a minimal degree of contact and perhaps trade.

Conversely, there is no such evidence to substantiate the contrarian claim that the pyramids in the Etna region are of ancient or even medieval construction. Most were erected between 1600 and 1800. Fruit of unsci-entific reasoning, ideas like the "Sicilian Pyramid Theory" constitute what is sometimes referred to as *pseudohistory*.

Some conclusions are simply untenable even if the evidence itself is legitimate. A current "Sicilian Dolmen Theory" proposes for certain mega-lithic sites an age of origin that has been questioned by serious archeolo-gists.

Medieval

A number of medieval manuscripts are oft-cited by historians. Some exist in published transcription. Most relevant here are the chronicles of Hugh Falcandus (a pseudonym, according to Evelyn Jamison), Falco of Benevento, Godfrey of Viterbo, Peter of Eboli, Richard of San Germano, Romuald of Salerno, Amatus of Montecassino, Godfrey Malaterra and Alexander of Telese. Falcandas is the only one who seems to have spent much time near the center of power in Palermo, which may explain his writing under a false name.

Such chroniclers were, in effect, the journalists of their day. Opinion-ated they may have been, but their reliability for basic dates and events is usually beyond cavil.

Idrisi's geography has undergone — and survived — numerous trans-lations. A particularly useful edition, including a detailed map of the Sicilian localities the famous geographer describes, is Luigi Santagati's *La Sicilia di al-Idrisi ne Il Libro di Ruggero* (2010).

The works of ibn Abi-Dinar and ibn Al-Athir should also be noted, and that of Mohammed ibn Hawqal must not be overlooked. Ali al Masudi left us much information about the Arab-Byzantine world of the tenth century.

Apropos the Byzantine Empire, the *Alexiad,* by Anna Comnena (1083-1153), is indispensable. It covers, among many other events, the wars with the Normans. Celebrated as the first history written by a woman, it offers a unique, "inside" view from a royal court, thus providing exceptional accuracy. Whereas most medieval histories were recorded by monks or other political figures, this one, with its criticism of the First Crusade, broke new ground. Completed around 1148, the *Alexiad* was translated for publication in English only in 1928 by Elizabeth Dawes.

Though peripheral, the writings of Gerhoh of Reichersberg shed light on the Normans' rapport with Rome. A history was published in 1897 as *Monumenta Germaniae Historica.*

Benjamin of Tudela's *Itinerary* (originally "The Voyages of Benjamin") was first published in English translation in 1840. Ronald Broadhurst's translation of bin Jubayr's most important surviving work as *The Travels of Ibn Jubair* saw the light of day in 1952, and this is the source of the passages quoted in Chapter 18.

The Rebellion of Sicily against King Charles was written anonymously in Sicilian around 1290. Some historians attribute its authorship to Atanasius of Iaci, a monk who lived in Sicily during the Vespers War. See also the authors' original research in this area (cited below) regarding the fall of Caltanissetta Castle to a tiny group of besiegers.

The feudal origins of the Sicilian nobility are considered at length in *Sicilian Genealogy and Heraldry.* Although various records mentioning feudal lands and their vassals have been conserved from Norman and Swabian times, the earliest surviving compendium for Sicily approaching anything like completeness is the "Roll of Muscia" of 1296. The *Catalogus Baronum* compiled around 1150 deals only with the Italian peninsular regions of the Kingdom of Sicily (Basilicata, Molise, Calabria, etc.), not the island of Sicily.

Modern

Michele Amari's *Storia dei Musulmani in Sicilia* (1854) is a good outline of the history of the Arabs in Sicily, and scholars in the Arab world consider it reliable. Written a century earlier, Giovanni Di Giovanni's *L'E-*

braismo di Sicilia was a similar ethnography of the Jews of Sicily, though lacking Amari's objectivity and erudition.

Shlomo Simonsohn's multi-volume history, *The Jews in Sicily* (1997-2010), is an important work reflecting exceptional scholarship. To this should be added several monographs, including Nicolò Bucaria's *Sicilia Judaica* (1996), Aldo Saccaro's *Gli Ebrei di Palermo dalle Origini al 1492* (2008) and Raphael Strauss' *Die Juden im Königreich Sizilien unter Normannen und Staufen* (1910). The work of Nadia Zeldes has already been mentioned.

An early English book about the Sicilian Normans was the aptly-titled monograph by Henry Knight, *The Normans in Sicily* (1838), which affords us a fair degree of insight into the scholarship that blossomed in the shadow of Edward Gibbon. Jean Chalandon's *Historie de la Domination Normande en Italie et en Sicile* (1907) is the major work of its era on the Normans in Italy. Building upon such studies is *Roger of Sicily and the Normans in Lower Italy* by Edmund Curtis (1912).

A number of fine works deal with the Sicilian language. One of the best is Salvatore Giarrizzo's *Dizionario Etimologico Siciliano* (1989).

Here we have concentrated on monographs, but there have been many specialist articles ("papers") published over the decades. Typical of these is David Abulafia's "Economic Activity of the Sicilian Jews around 1300" presented at the *Italia Judaica* conference held in Palermo in 1992. Evelyn Jamison authored numerous scholarly articles of great value. Her transcription and translation of the *Catalogus Baronum* was published in 1972.

On the American side of the ocean, James Powell wrote a good translation and analysis of the Constitutions of Melfi, published by Syracuse University Press in 1971 as *The Liber Augustalis or Constitutions of Melfi*. John Makdisi's paper, "The Islamic Origins of the Common Law," appeared in the *North Carolina Law Review* in June 1999.

A great deal of pseudohistory (though less interesting than the "Sicilian Pyramid Theory") involves the Mafia, a criminal organization that emerged late in the eighteenth century, with more imaginative authors attributing its origins to phenomena such as the Sicilian Vespers or the Beati Paoli. One might be forgiven, however, for suggesting that the clannish, secretive mentality pervasive among Sicilians since the days of the Vespers and the Inquisition, in tandem with other developments, provided fertile soil for certain social practices that eventually evolved into organized crime.

Accuracy of Historical Dates

Historians sometimes date medieval events differently because a contemporary chronicle might refer to (for example) an incident occurring "in Winter," which could be in late December of a given year or during the first months of the next one. The date of the betrothal of Constance of Hauteville to Henry VI is such a case. Another example is the Norman conquest of Palermo, as the battle and subsequent siege began late in 1071, ending early in 1072, hence the differing dates. During Sicily's long Spanish administration, a decree might be issued with effect the following year; the Alhambra Decree of 1492 took effect the next year, in 1493, although this was motivated partly by the desire to levy one last tax on the Sicilian Jews before they left Sicily.

Original Research by J. Alio and L. Mendola

Scholarly research germane to the content of this volume has been published in peer-reviewed academic journals and in *Sicilian Genealogy and Heraldry* (2013). In that book, Appendix 5 ("Jewish Nobles in Late Medieval Sicily") and Appendix 6 ("Palermo's Nobles and Jews in 1492") set forth the basis for the authors' observation about the feudal ennoblement of some of Sicily's landholding Jews during the fifteenth century.

In the same book, Chapter 18 ("The Norman Knight Figures of Monreale") supports the conclusion about the dilatory arrival of armorial heraldry in Sicily, while the early use of the gold lion passant guardant (the heraldic "English Lion" of the Plantagenets) as an emblem ("badge") by Sicily's first Norman kings is considered in Chapter 17 ("The English Lion in Sicily"), the evidence suggesting its use in the Kingdom of Sicily prior to use in the Kingdom of England. Both heraldic theses were originally published in the journal of The Heraldry Society, London, in 1994 during the editorship of John P. Brooke-Little, Norroy and Ulster King of Arms.

Specific research concerns military, and perhaps social, aspects of the War of the Sicilian Vespers in 1282. The raid on Caltanissetta Castle, where the castellan was easily overpowered by a small banneret (mentioned in Chapter 27 of this book), does not appear in histories about the Vespers. It was extracted from *De Rebus Regni Siciliae* under entries DCXXVIII and DCXXIX, two decrees of King Peter issued at Solano in March 1283. These manuscripts are conserved at the Archivo General de la Corona de Aragón in Barcelona. Such incidents as the ready capitulation of this castle suggest that the rapid outcome of the Vespers War resulted partly from the inadequate defense of fortified positions by the Angevins, who were probably overconfident.

Remarks about Germanic law are based on published analyses dating back centuries, but the manuscript of the *Codex Legum Longobardorum,* the oldest surviving Lombard legal code (written in 1004), was also consulted. This is retained at the archive of the monastery of Cava dei Tirreni, where Queen Sibylla, a consort of King Roger II, is buried. This is the monastery that established the Benedictine community at Monreale Abbey.

To this might be added the consultation of nineteenth-century vital statistics records around Italy (the literacy survey mentioned in the Introduction), forming part of the basis of the authors' comparative estimate of literacy levels for 1061 (the Norman invasion) versus 1861 (Italian unification).

That is but one of several conclusions presented in this book to be published here in English for the first time. So far as the authors can determine, certain of these are original, or at least explained here in an original thesis that was not previously advanced in published work. The most revelatory of these is the dating of Sicily's significant decrease in general literacy to a specific period, namely the decades immediately following 1300, coincidental to the emergence of the Sicilian monoculture.

This book's authors have accumulated a great wealth of information in their endless travels around the island, and of course in their extensive research in Sicilian archives. This has placed them in an advantageous position to describe certain phenomena, events, details, buildings and sites sometimes overlooked by other scholars. Indeed, unattributed information given in several well-known travel guidebooks published in English over the last decade owes much to revelations that first appeared in articles by this book's authors on popular websites.

Caveat lector!

Every historian is the product of his or her time. By today's standards, the historical writings of certain modern scholars are obviously partial, overtly influenced by the political *zeitgeist* that spawned them. The work of those historians should be read critically. Benedetto Croce (1866-1952) and Ernst Kantorowicz (1895-1963) have come to be regarded as apologists for their nations' unification movements — Italy's culminating in 1861 and Germany's a decade later. This colored their perspectives about (respectively) the Kingdom of Sicily in *Storia del Regno di Napoli* and Frederick II in *Kaiser Friedrich der Zweite.* Not surprisingly, both flirted with the extremist nationalist movements that arose in Italy and Germany after 1920, but to their credit each abandoned his blind nationalism after a few years.

Replete with aphorisms, most of the "histories" of Italy written by Italians during Croce's lifetime were thinly veiled propaganda that sought to glorify a new unitary state where figures like Frederick II were inconvenient reminders of Sicily's historical sovereignty and prosperity. For that banal reason, Sicilian kings were all but ignored by Italian historians, hence the dearth of Italian biographies dedicated to them until very recently.

Voltaire was correct: "History can be well written only in a free country."

INDEX

The emphasis here is relevancy; it was not practical to list every person mentioned in the text, and except for especially prominent Sicilian figures of antiquity (viz. Archimedes), our focus throughout is the Middle Ages. The reader should note the Arabic transliteration and American spelling.

164-166, 171, 192, 199, 206, 210, 235, 245-246, 275, 292, 302, 306

Joan Plantagenet, 74-75, 220, 231, 237-244, 251, 256-257, 280

bin Jubayr, 70, 75, 149, 163, 209, 218, 220, 233-235

Judaism. See Jews.

Judith of Evreux, 196, 200, 240

Julius Caesar, 61, 106, 123-124, 188

Justinian, 64-65, 111, 131, 137-138, 277, 279, 282

Kairouan (Qayrawan), 66-67, 161

Kalbids, 67, 69, 70, 107, 115, 136, 161-167, 199, 214, 282

al Kamil, Malik, Sultan, 172, 271

Kanats, 47, 69, 152, 166, 219

Kasr'Janni. See Enna.

Khalbids. See Kalbids.

Kokalos, 57

Komnene. See Comnena, Anna.

Koran, 47, 66, 113-117, 140, 160-165, 192, 217, 222, 270, 305

Law and legal codes, 45-47, 49, 57, 65, 68, 73, 74, 76, 86-87, 111, 115-116, 124, 131, 162, 170, 192, 199, 205, 263, 273-284

Lemons. See Citrus fruit.

Lentini, Giacomo of, 285, 287

Literacy, 66, 84-85, 147, 150, 163-164, 171, 192, 301-302

Lombards, 40, 64-66, 71-72, 74, 88-89, 133, 139, 168-169, 174, 182, 187-189, 193, 196, 198, 204, 263, 274

London, 190, 198, 238, 241

Longobards. See Lombards.

Louis IX of France (saint), 75, 78, 253, 291, 292

Madiyah (Tunisia), 115, 161

Madonie Mountains, 91-92, 94-95, 102, 208

Madrid, 49, 80, 87

Maghrebim. See Jews.

Magione church, 71, 183, 261, 264-265

Magna Graecia (Megara Hellas), 54, 56, 192

Mahdia. See Madiyah.

al Makdisi, Mohammed, 209

Malaterra, Godfrey, 20, 333

Maliki Law, 28, 47, 115, 162, 258, 277-284

Malta, 43, 52-53, 56, 69, 91, 106, 150, 154, 170, 196, 312

Mamertines, 58

Maniakes, George, 68, 71, 169, 173-176, 188

Margaret of Navarre, 74, 76, 206, 223-231, 246, 249, 253, 256

Marsala, 44, 47, 55, 59, 68, 93, 98, 100-101, 140, 151, 161, 257, 280, 294

Martorana church, 46, 50, 74, 116, 118-119, 143, 177, 183, 204, 234

Mazara, 47, 67, 71, 146, 151, 161

Melfi, Constitutions of, 76, 263, 269, 273-277, 284

Messina, 57-58, 72, 75, 82, 118, 142-143, 146, 150-151, 162, 165, 169, 190, 229, 233, 235, 240, 246,

283, 292

Turkey. See Anatolia, Constantinople, Ottomans.

Turks. See Ottomans.

Tuscan language, 285, 289

Vandals, 45-46, 52, 62-65, 67, 88, 123-133, 137, 154, 178, 214, 277, 279

Varangian Guard, 71, 174, 187

Vespers War, 48, 80-83, 176, 185-186, 216, 262, 272, 274, 287, 293, 295, 297, 299, 300, 304

Vikings. See Norsemen.

Visigoths. See Goths.

Walter of the Mill. See Offamilias.

Wheat. See Grains.

William I, 205-210, 220, 239, 249, 267

William II, 74, 82, 105, 185, 206, 220, 224, 226, 231, 233, 235, 239-241, 246, 248, 253, 256, 267, 280

Wines, 100-101

Zisa Palace, 9, 48, 220, 241

Ziyadat Allah, 67, 161